Modern Data Strategy

Mike Fleckenstein • Lorraine Fellows

Modern Data Strategy

With contributions from:
Krista Ferrante
Swami Natarajan
Mala Rajamani
Stuart Shapiro
Julie Snyder
Bob Toth
Eliot Wilczek

 Springer

Mike Fleckenstein
MITRE
McLean, VA, USA

Lorraine Fellows
MITRE
McLean, VA, USA

ISBN 978-3-319-88698-5   ISBN 978-3-319-68993-7   (eBook)
https://doi.org/10.1007/978-3-319-68993-7

Printed on acid-free paper

This Springer imprint is published by Springer Nature
The registered company is Springer International Publishing AG
The registered company address is: Gewerbestrasse 11, 6330 Cham, Switzerland

Foreword

The (non)management of data has led to (1) reactive instead of proactive initiatives; (2) data being treated as an afterthought (instead of an asset) in the planning, design, and development of systems; (3) the continuous development of stovepipes (organizationally and technically); and (4) practitioners solving the same problem repeatedly. Most often, functionality and repeatable process are successful at individual levels but miss the advantage of an overall strategy for data that leverages common components, elements, and complementary technical infrastructures.

With new methods for capturing and using different types of data and industry's recognition that society's use of data is less than optimal, the need for comprehensive strategies is more important than ever before. Advances in cybersecurity and information sharing and the use of data in its raw form for decision making all add to the complexity of integrated processes, ownership, stewardship, and sharing.

As we address the evolving complexities of managing data, the need for standards and complicity also becomes more evident. Private industry and federal agencies are obligated to an increasing set of directives and mandates that require various disciplines for capturing, sharing publicly, and reporting transparently on the processing and use of data and information.

Over the past several decades and across a broad client base and multiple federal government agencies, experts in data and information management have championed efforts that support organizational collaboration and technical excellence. The life cycle of data in its entirety spans the infrastructure, system design, development, integration, and implementation of information-enabling solutions. These components are disciplines in and of themselves; the data, as a crosscutting component, requires a cohesive approach and sound strategy to be most effective at all phases of the cycle.

With the current challenges on raising awareness of enterprise needs and furthering the implementation of data management and information sharing within and across government agencies, I am grateful for this compilation of core components and their functions and relationships.

This book is a valuable guide to developing data strategies. It covers the core components of governance, architecture, metadata, privacy, security, quality, business intelligence, and data warehousing.

Thank you to the authors of *Modern Data Strategy* for addressing the concept of data as an asset, considering records management as a strategic component of managing data, and offering the view that data analytics and big data are appropriate extensions to the strategic data management domain.

Annette Pence
Sr. Principal, Department Head
Data Management, Integration & Interoperability
The MITRE Corporation
McLean, VA, USA

Acknowledgments

We would like to express our gratitude to the many people who saw us through this book—to all those who provided support, talked things over, read, wrote, offered comments, allowed us to quote their remarks, and assisted in the editing, proofreading, and design.

We would like to thank Annette Pence for believing in, lobbying for, and reading and re-reading the manuscript. We would like to thank Rob Case and Kerry Buckley for providing early and ongoing financial support. And, we would like to thank those experts and authors in respective fields who contributed entire chapters to this book:

Chapter	Author(s)
11. Data Quality	Mala Rajamani
12. Data Warehousing and Business Intelligence	Swami Natarajan
14. Data Privacy	Julie Snyder and Stuart Shapiro
15. Data Security	Julie Snyder and Stuart Shapiro
17. Records Management	Eliot Wilczek, Krista Ferrante, and Bob Toth

We also appreciate the significant contributions of Haleh Vafaie to the "Data Analytics" chapter and of Julie McEwen to the "Data Privacy" and "Data Security" chapters.

We would also like to thank our editor Margaret Hill, who thoroughly reviewed and gently improved our content; Vipin Swarup and Sushil Jajodia, who facilitated review of the book and helped us find a publisher; Kristin Heckman, Frank Stech, and Jill Egeth, who provided insights of their own publishing process; and, of course, all those who reviewed the manuscript to help create the final product.

We thank our families for their continual support. This book would not have been possible without their ongoing encouragement.

Last but not least, we beg forgiveness of all those who have been with us over the course of the years and whose names we have failed to mention.

Disclaimer

The views, opinions, and/or findings contained in this book are those of the individual authors and should not be construed as representing the views or opinions of the MITRE Corporation or as an official Government position, policy, or decision, unless designated by other documentation.

The MITRE Corporation is an independent, not-for-profit organization that operates research and development centers for the federal government.

Contents

Part I   Data Strategy Considerations

1   Evolution to Modern Data Management 3

2   Big Data and Data Management 7

3   Valuing Data As an Asset 11

4   Physical Asset Management vs. Data Management 15
    4.1   Cost 16
    4.2   Quality Fit for Use 18
    4.3   Stewardship 18
    4.4   Architecture 19
    4.5   Obsolescence 20
    4.6   Additional Considerations 20

Part II   Data Strategy

5   Leading a Data Strategy 25
    5.1   Process, Technology, and Data People 25
    5.2   CIO Role 27
    5.3   Emerging CDO Role 30
    5.4   Alternative Executives to Lead a Data Strategy Effort 33

6   Implementing a Data Strategy 35
    6.1   Business Strategy As a Driver for Data Strategy 40
    6.2   Existing Data Management Infrastructure
           As the Driver of Data Strategy 44
    6.3   Determining the Scope of the Data Strategy Initiative 48
    6.4   Skills Needed for a Data Strategy 52
    6.5   Change Management 54

7   Overview of Data Management Frameworks 55
   7.1   DAMA DMBOK 56
   7.2   CMMI DMM Model 56
   7.3   Additional Frameworks 58

Part III   Data Management Domains

8   Data Governance 63
   8.1   What Is Data Governance? 63
      8.1.1   Vision, Goals, and Priorities 65
      8.1.2   Data Management Principles 66
      8.1.3   Data Policies, Standards, and Guidelines 67
      8.1.4   Data Governance and Assurance 68
      8.1.5   Authoritative Sources and Other Resources for Staff 69
      8.1.6   Communications Infrastructure and Periodic
            Outreach Campaigns 69
   8.2   Who Is Data Governance? 70
      8.2.1   Data Governance Framework 71
      8.2.2   Data Governance Operations 71
      8.2.3   Executive Level 72
      8.2.4   Management Level 72
      8.2.5   Data Stewards Level 73
   8.3   Benefits of Data Governance 74
   8.4   Implementing Data Governance 74
      8.4.1   A Data Governance Framework 74
      8.4.2   Assessments 75
   8.5   Data Governance Tools 76

9   Data Architecture 77
   9.1   What Is Data Architecture? 77
      9.1.1   Business Glossary 77
      9.1.2   Data Asset Inventory 78
      9.1.3   Data Standards 79
      9.1.4   Data Models 80
      9.1.5   Data Lifecycle Diagrams 83
   9.2   Who Is Data Architecture? 86
   9.3   Benefits of Data Architecture 87
   9.4   Data Architecture Framework 88
   9.5   Implementing Data Architecture 88
   9.6   Data Architecture Tools 90

10   Master Data Management 93
   10.1   What Is Master Data Management? 93
   10.2   Who Is Master Data Management? 94
   10.3   Benefits of Master Data Management 95
   10.4   Master Data Management Framework 95

10.5   Implementing Master Data Management.................................   97
10.6   Master Data Management Tools   98

11 Data Quality   101
11.1   What Is Data Quality?...   101
        11.1.1   Data Quality Dimensions..   102
        11.1.2   Trusting Your Data   105
        11.1.3   Data Quality Challenges   107
11.2   Who Is Data Quality?...   109
        11.2.1   Data Quality Controls   111
11.3   Implementing Data Quality..   112
        11.3.1   Defining Data Quality   112
        11.3.2   Deploying Data Quality   112
        11.3.3   Monitoring Data Quality...   113
        11.3.4   Resolving Data Quality Issues.....................................   114
        11.3.5   Measuring Data Quality..   115
        11.3.6   Data Classification   115
        11.3.7   Data Certification...   116
        11.3.8   Data Quality—Trends and Challenges   116
11.4   Data Quality Tools   118

12 Data Warehousing and Business Intelligence   121
12.1   What Are Data Warehousing and Business Intelligence?...........   121
        12.1.1   Data Warehouse Architectural Components   122
12.2   Who Is Data Warehousing and Business Intelligence?...............   126
12.3   Implementing Data Warehousing and Business Intelligence........   127
12.4   Data Warehousing and Business Intelligence Tools   128

13 Data Analytics..   133
13.1   What Is Data Analytics?...   133
13.2   Who Is Data Analytics?   135
13.3   Implementing Data Analytics   137
13.4   Data Analytics Framework..   140
13.5   Data Analytics Tools   142

14 Data Privacy   143
14.1   What Is Data Privacy   143
14.2   Who Is Data Privacy   146
        14.2.1   Privacy Components   148
14.3   Privacy Operations...   152
14.4   Implementing Privacy   155
        14.4.1   Collection..   155
        14.4.2   Creation/Transformation...   158
        14.4.3   Usage/Processing   159
        14.4.4   Disclosure/Dissemination   160

14.4.5   Retention/Storage...   161
14.4.6   Disposition/Destruction   161
14.5   Privacy Tools...   162

15   Data Security   165
15.1   What Is Data Security?   165
15.2   Who Is Data Security   167
15.3   Implementing Data Security   169
15.4   Using the Cybersecurity Framework
to Implement Data Security   170
15.4.1   Using the RMF to Implement Data Security   172
15.4.2   Data System Security Control Standards........................   174
15.4.3   Linkages to Other Processes   175
15.4.4   Piecing Together Data Security Implementation
Considerations   176
15.5   Data Security Tools...   177

16   Metadata   179
16.1   What Are Metadata and Metadata Management?.......................   180
16.1.1   Metadata Management..   181
16.1.2   Metadata vs. Data...   181
16.2   Who Is Metadata Management?   183
16.3   Benefits of Metadata Management   184
16.4   Metadata Frameworks...   186
16.5   Implementing Metadata   187
16.6   Metadata Management Tools   191

17   Records Management   195
17.1   What Is Records Management...   195
17.2   Who Is Records Management..   198
17.3   Benefits of Records Management   199
17.4   Components of Records Management   200
17.4.1   Records Management and Data Management   201
17.4.2   Records Management Frameworks.................................   203
17.4.3   Implementing Records Management Programs.............   204
17.4.4   Records Management and Other Tools...........................   206

Appendices..   209

References   257

Purpose and Introduction

Purpose of This Book

This book is intended for the business user who works with data, who needs to manage one or more aspects of the organization's data, and who wants to foster an integrated approach for how enterprise data is managed. Data strategy is a term that is loosely used and not succinctly defined. This book offers a definition of data strategy. Its sections on how to align with a business strategy, a discussion on valuing data as an asset, the evolution of data management, and who should oversee a data strategy provide the reader with a good understanding of what a data strategy is and its limits. Critical to a data strategy is the incorporation of one or more data management domains.[1] Sections on key data management domains—data governance, data architecture, master data management, analytics, and others—offer the reader a practical approach to data management execution within a data strategy. The intent is to enable the reader to identify how execution on one or more data management domains can help solve business issues. The book also offers some insight into how to integrate multiple data management domains to address pressing business needs. The reader can then turn to the appendices for a more in-depth discussion of industry frameworks, mandates and standards, data management drivers, as well as additional references.

This book was written for industry practitioners in general. However, because the MITRE Corporation works in the public interest, this perspective is emphasized. For example, the chapter on "Data Privacy" is particularly suited to the public sector practitioner. The book denotes this in the relevant sections.

---

[1] Note that data management domains are inconsistently termed. For example, DAMA refers to domains as "knowledge areas"; SEI CMMI refers to them as "categories" and "subcategories," which it terms "process areas"; and EDMC terms domains as "component areas." This book will use the term data management "domains."

How to Navigate This Book

The book's introduction provides the reader with an overview of many of the book's topics and how they are integrated. Its three major sections and appendices are as follows:

- **Part I—Data Strategy Considerations**—offers the reader background considerations that provide context and understanding around a data strategy, its evolution, its practicality—even in the current environment of data proliferation—and its limitations. Part I begins with historical insight on the evolution of data management. A discussion on big data explains how traditional data management practices are still (perhaps even particularly) relevant to big data. "Valuing Data as an Asset" discusses a loosely used term, what it means, and its current limitations.

- **Part II—Data Strategy**—focuses on how a data strategy might be scoped, defined, and put in place. "Leading a Data Strategy" weighs the traditional Chief Information Officer (CIO) approach against the trend to put in place a Chief Data Officer (CDO). It also discusses alternative leadership structures. "Implementing a Data Strategy" discusses how to align a data strategy to a business strategy and what this means. The chapter discusses how a data strategy varies depending on business needs, the data management infrastructure already in place, and the amount of resources an organization is willing to devote. "Overview of Data Management Frameworks" introduces the reader to the importance of data management domains that comprise a data strategy.

- **Part III—Data Management Domains**—details key data management domains to consider for a data strategy. It explains how to dive deeper into key data management domains, how to apply each one, and which people and technologies are involved. Having identified the business problem at hand, the reader can use these chapters as a guide to provide insights into effectively standing up or enhancing specific data management disciplines needed to address those business problems successfully.

- **Appendices** provide additional detail for the interested reader. Throughout the book, there are many pointers to appendices that offer valuable additional material regarding, for instance, data management frameworks and industry drivers, and point to additional resources for in-depth reading in areas of interest. Definitions and acronyms for many of the commonly used data management terms are also listed.

  For executives: At a minimum, the key chapters are "Implementing a Data Strategy" and "Overview of Data Management Frameworks." The "Leading a Data Strategy" chapter is also highly relevant to anyone contemplating a data management-oriented organizational structure. Once an organization has committed to implementing certain data management domains as part of its data strategy, executives may want to familiarize themselves with those domains as well.

For practitioners: If you've been tasked with implementing or growing a data management domain (e.g., data governance), each domain chapter provides steps to design and execute a specific data management domain. The "Implementing a Data Strategy" chapter provides context for how a data management domain is tied to the business strategy and is therefore a useful tool to convey to the management team the benefits of a data management strategy as well as the cost of a lack of one.

Introduction

Data is in the news. Everyone is talking about it. Organizations want more data, and individuals are increasingly vocal about how their data is being used. In many ways, organizations and individuals are diametrically opposed in how to use data. To be most effective, organizations want as much data as possible, as timely and precise as possible. Individuals, on the other hand, want control over how data about them is used and may not want to supply certain data at all.

Organizations use data so that they can improve their services and products. In private industry, this translates into using data to improve customer service, reduce costs, gain increased profits, and manage risks. In the public sector and in some industries, regulatory compliance is also a driver of data management. To effectively achieve business goals, organizations must understand the data they have, the additional data they want, and how to effectively organize all this data to yield the desired business outcomes. It is almost intuitive that if data is poorly organized and managed, it has little value.

Most organizations today, whether public or private, recognize that their data holds the potential for value. Recognition of the value of data has launched a frenzy to collect and store reams of data with the thought that it may harbor potential future value. Organizations openly talk of treating data as an asset.

In some ways, we do treat data as though it is an asset. For example, organizational data is routinely hacked to gain knowledge of someone else's intellectual property.[2] Individual data is so valuable that it is being traded on the black market in stock-market fashion.[3] These two examples demonstrate that at least some people consider data so valuable that they are willing to put forth significant time and effort, not to mention risk prosecution, to obtain data that is not theirs.

In other ways, we are just starting to treat data as an asset. Though we store incredible volumes of data, our storage bins sometimes resemble a junkyard rather than a well-organized, well-understood inventory of data assets. We are increasingly tempted to collect and store data with little thought about how that data might be used, or how it might help our business be more effective. Our thinking is to store everything we can to make use of it at some point in the future as new questions

---

[2] See, for example, https://www.fbi.gov/investigate/white-collar-crime/piracy-ip-theft.

[3] See, for example, http://www.symantec.com/connect/blogs/underground-black-market-thriving-trade-stolen-data-malware-and-attack-services.

arise, including questions we haven't even thought of today. This hints to our intuitive understanding that data does have value but falls short of treating data as an asset. Sometimes we fail to consider that too much data can lead to wasted productivity; or that it is redundant, obsolete, and trivial;[4] or that it entails legal risk.

Not all our data is stored so haphazardly, of course. Financial, operational, logistical, product, biographical, and biometric data are just a few examples of data that must be well organized and carefully stored so that we can function as a society. Most of us want to be able to identify and transact with each other predictably and legally. We use a host of identifiers—like social security number, user ID, email address, and increasingly biometrics (fingerprints or facial recognition)—to ensure our identities. We have identifiers with our public institutions, our banks, our workplaces, our insurers, and so on. We store address information, account balances, health data, and other data that is important to us in relatively consistent, structured ways because we rely on the quality of this data to run our businesses and perform our daily tasks.

To perform our daily tasks, organizations in which we work and with which we interact must also understand our data and data that is important to us. For example, our banks must record our deposits and withdrawals correctly, our medical institutions must have accurate data on our health history, our workplaces must manage sufficient data to provide our compensation and benefits, and businesses must have accurate information about the products and services they offer. Organizations work hard to manage this data carefully. They try to keep it accurate, secure it from being accessed wrongfully, and reflect updates back to us quickly. This is hard work. It requires the growing employment of software, computers, storage units, and information workers.

As hard as it is for us as individuals or for an organization to keep data well organized, it is nearly impossible for all this data to be kept in synch across many individuals or organizations. Just think of how difficult it is for us to keep up with all the current phone numbers of our friends. Even organizations that are specifically in the business of maintaining current data about us—the same address, financial, and purchasing data that is so carefully stored and maintained—struggle with the accuracy of this information.[5]

The volume of data keeps increasing.[6] In addition, machines are generating more and more of their own data. Satellites, mobile phones, web logs, weather and transportation sensors, appliances, and even personal wearable devices are eclipsing the data we generate as humans.[7]

---

[4] Aiken, P., & Billings, J., *Monetizing Data Management: Finding the Value in Your Organization's Most Important Asset*, Technics Publications, 2013.

[5] See, for example, https://www.ftc.gov/news-events/press-releases/2015/01/ftc-issues-follow-study-credit-report-accuracy.

[6] See, for example, http://www.cisco.com/c/en/us/solutions/collateral/service-provider/visual-net-working-index-vni/vni-hyperconnectivity-wp.html.

[7] See, for example, https://www.ncta.com/platform/broadband-internet/behind-the-numbers-growth-in-the-internet-of-things-2/.

With so much data, organizations' focus is often mainly on analytics, the analysis of large amounts of data, new types of data, and new relationships between data. There is no question that analytics is contributing significantly toward solving important business problems such as fraud, evidence-based healthcare, smart manufacturing, transportation optimization, and cybercrime. According to Bain & Company, the business drivers for big data analytics comprise improving existing or building new products and services, improving internal processes, and transforming the business model.[8]

To make the best use of this data, we cannot simply store increasing amounts of data in junkyard fashion, depositing it in raw form for potential later use. What is hidden behind analytics is both the preparation it takes to extract meaningful insight from data as well as the stewardship required to manage the data that led to the insight in the first place. Preparing data so that it can be effectively analyzed can consume 50–80% of an analyst's time.[9] In fact, this type of preparation work is so common that terms such as "data wrangling" and "data munging" are used to describe it.

Furthermore, the data yielded through analytics must be stored and then integrated into the existing data fabric of an organization—and increasingly across organizations or even industries—to be most effective. The data gained from analytics is most valuable when integrated with existing, proprietary organizational data such as customer, product, and service. If an organization finds through its analysis of social media data, for example, that there is some dissatisfaction with one of its products or services, how does it reach out to the right customers to improve the product or service? There is increasing urgency to develop approaches, or strategies, to manage data.

The best way to do this is for organizations to align their data management practices with business priorities. With data so pervasive, old attitudes that managing data is strictly an information technology discipline are finally changing, and business operations is becoming increasingly interested in data. Searching the *Harvard Business Review* archive returns 95 case studies and 106 articles on data published in 2014.[10] That business operations is focusing on data is good because it is shifting data ownership within organizations away from information technology departments to operations. By hook or by crook, business operations is becoming accountable for ensuring the quality of the data on which business decisions are based.

Data exists, in the same way as other organizational resources, to support the enterprise's business needs. Only by linking the need for a resource to a business priority can we ensure value from that asset. With most assets, we think carefully about whether they provide value. We wouldn't purchase a new fleet of trucks or airplanes unless existing ones did not meet our needs. We would debate the pros and

---

[8] From *Big Data: The Organizational Challenge*. Bain & Company, Web, September 2013. http://www.bain.com/publications/articles/big_data_the_organizational_challenge.aspx.

[9] Lohr, S., "For Big Data Scientists, 'Janitor Work' Is Key Hurdle to Insight," *New York Times*, August 17, 2014.

[10] Search performed December 14, 2014, on HBR.org, selecting publications over the past year.

cons of these purchases as part of an asset management strategy and align the strategy with our business goals. Even if these assets were very cheap or free, we likely wouldn't acquire them unless we needed them for our business operations or we could profit by reselling them. Storing unnecessary assets is time consuming and expensive.

Data doesn't always get this same thoughtfulness today. We think of data as cheap to store, even though storing large amounts of data can be expensive. We think of data as time consuming to organize and difficult to interpret without proper context, but the necessity for quality data to support operational needs is indisputable. As workers, we already make many daily decisions based on data. We target services based on customer profiles and history, we manufacture to specific designs, we set goals based on previous successes and anticipated results, and we manage based on costs and revenues. Just as they would do with any valuable asset, organizations must deploy their workers to manage data as an asset. To do so effectively requires a data strategy similar to other types of corporate asset management strategies.

This is difficult. A recent survey suggests that only 13% of organizations have a formal data strategy that covers managing data and unstructured content.[11] This same survey reflects that primary drivers for improving information management include a desire to reduce costs, improve compliance, and improve service to customers. There is every indication that the trend of better data management will continue to increase as data plays a more significant part in our lives.

With the increasing importance of data as part of the operational business fabric, many data standards are evolving and data management certifications exist in multiple areas of data management. In the public sector, numerous executive orders, memos, and policies on data and information management are being put forth at the highest level, further reflecting the importance of managing data.[12] Industry is publishing a growing body of data and information management frameworks.[13] These frameworks exist and continue to develop to help organizations manage data in a systematic way.

Underlying data frameworks are data management domains— fields of specialty under the broader umbrella of data management. These domains include approaches to managing data that have proven useful in the real world. The list of domains includes data quality, data governance, data architecture, data warehousing, master data management, data interoperability, data privacy and security, and others.[14] These domains are applied with varying levels of maturity in industry and the public sector. Some domains, like data quality, are well understood and relatively ingrained into many business practices. But even a mature data management domain, like data

---

[11] Leganza, G., "Changing Your Approach to Information Strategy? You're Not Alone," Forrester Research, Inc., October 2, 2014.

[12] Reference Open Data, Data Act, Records Retention, m 13 13, m 12 18.

[13] See Data Management Frameworks in Appendix A for a discussion of these frameworks (DAMA DMBOK, CMMI Data Management Maturity Model, TOGAF, DoDAF, etc.).

[14] See Part III for a detailed discussion on many of these domains.

quality, is often applied inconsistently at the enterprise level. Instead, it is applied at an application, project, or perhaps departmental level. Too often, a data management domain is applied as a reaction to a data issue such as inconsistent reporting or customer dissatisfaction. As a result, data management domains are often applied in patchwork fashion across parts of the organization and inconsistently applied across the enterprise, resulting in limited success and sometimes abandonment.

Most organizations do not include data management experts in their strategic planning, as they do in other areas such as finance, human resources, marketing, and production. Certainly, Chief Information Officers (CIO) have existed since the late 1980s/early 1990s, and today's CIOs are more often being included in strategic decisions. However, many CIOs are still at least one level down from executive decision makers, reporting to the Chief Financial Officer (CFO), for example. Having a CIO as part of the executive team has proven helpful for organizations that want to be differentiators.[15] CIOs, though, have many technology areas to attend to and thus are often forced to focus on the information technology infrastructure such as hardware, networks, and software applications.

CIOs' inability, or failure, to adequately address data has led to the creation of the Chief Data Officer (CDO) role, a position dedicated to overseeing data management. Ideally, the CDO is responsible for data management at the enterprise level within an organization. However, it is common for organizations initially to define the CDO as a mid-level manager with a limited (or even with no) budget, team, or authority.[16] In many cases, the CDO reports to the CIO, thus putting the CDO even further down the hierarchy from strategic decision makers.

The CDO reflects the recognition that someone high up in the organization is needed to guide the management of an asset that is rapidly growing in importance in all organizations. However, the CDO role is a relatively new position, first surfacing in the early twenty-first century. Even though information technology has been around for a half century or more, the recognition of the importance of managing data at an enterprise level only emerged within the last 15 years. What is the reason for that? This is partly due to the evolution of managing information, which initially focused on the hardware and then applications used for automating manual tasks.

---

[15] Banker, R. D., Hu, N., Pavlou, & P. A., Luftman, J., "CIO reporting structure, strategic positioning and firm performance," MIS Quarterly, Vol. 35, Is. 2, June 2011.

[16] See, for example, Botega, J., "Chief Data Officer Role Shifts to Offense," *Wall Street Journal*, April 7, 2015.

Part I
Data Strategy Considerations

Chapter 1
Evolution to Modern Data Management

Over the past decades, information technology management has evolved to a realization that data, not just systems and software applications, must be managed. This evolution began with the desire to automate manual tasks. It progressed to integrating independently automated tasks, advanced to large-scale centralized data management applications, and finally evolved into several closely related data management domains, including data quality, data governance, data architecture, master data management, analytics, and others[1] that can be managed in alignment with business goals.

With the initial use of computers in industry, organizations saw the benefit of managing manual tasks in a more automated way. As mainframe computers became cost effective, organizations began using them to automate tasks such as weather forecasting, tax returns, and air traffic control.[2] Then, in the 1980s, industry saw a significant shift away from mainframe computers, first toward minicomputers and eventually to decentralized, personal computers and servers. Along with this trend, business goals focused on moving away from expensive mainframe vendor lock-ins and toward cost-efficient automation of manual tasks. The gains achieved simply by automating functions on a personal computer were significant and allowed for individual creativity in problem solving.

With the shift to smaller computers, it eventually became clear that, although business productivity within vertical areas had improved significantly, the ability to integrate information from independent efforts was becoming increasingly difficult and increasingly important. By the mid-1980s, organizations became worried that they were not maximizing returns on their substantial investments in information technology. For example, in 1986, the U.S. Congress openly stated its concern about

---

[1] For a more complete set of data management areas, see *The Data Management Body of Knowledge (DMBOK) Guide*, Data Management International (DAMA), Technics Publications, Inc., 2009.
[2] From Methany, M. *Federal Cloud Computing: The Definitive Guide for Cloud Service Providers*. Syngress Publishing, 2012. See "A Historical View of Federal IT."

© Springer International Publishing AG 2018
M. Fleckenstein, L. Fellows, *Modern Data Strategy*,
https://doi.org/10.1007/978-3-319-68993-7_1

underdeveloped "Information Resource Management" practices in the federal government, intended to bring together disparate functions such as computers, telecommunications, and office automation.[3]

This realization led to the centralized management of IT infrastructure and the creation of the Chief Information Officer (CIO) role in the late 1980s/early 1990s. By integrating all information technology initiatives, it was envisioned, information would also be integrated. By then, the industry understood that IT software and system integration[4] alone was insufficient, and data integration had an important role to play. As a result, the industry shifted away from system integration toward application integration. Large-scale efforts to integrate enterprise information led to enterprise applications such as the data warehouse, customer relationship management (CRM) applications, and enterprise resource planning (ERP) systems. The idea was to streamline the business process by managing key data in enterprise applications.

With the shift to application integration, business operations had a larger role to play in managing data. For example, business operations and IT began working together when developing applications as part of a more formalized software development life cycle that relied heavily on business input, especially during requirements and testing phases. Data management became sufficiently popular that industry bodies began to form, for example, the Data Management Association (DAMA) in the 1980s and The Data Warehouse Institute (TDWI) in the 1990s.

Business' focus was at the application level, however. Different departments focused on the data important to them. Marketing, Finance, Operations, Human Resources, Customer Service, multiple lines of business, and other organizational components focused (and continue to focus) on department level data. In fact, even today, each department often treats its data as though it actually owns the data. Fundamentally, it is understandable that business units acted as though they own their data. It was in their interest to make data work for them efficiently and even to keep a tight leash on data as a competitive advantage. Of course, this hampered data management at the enterprise level. Data, if managed effectively, should be an enterprise asset, and organizations should differentiate between data accountability and data ownership.

Early in the twenty-first century, focus shifted to storing much more data due to the ability to store data on much less expensive commodity hardware. Servers could simply be strung together on an as-needed basis to adjust storage requirements. All of a sudden, it became possible to deposit non-integrated, raw data from many sources in a commonly accessible way and to execute algorithms against these massive data lakes in an effort to find patterns and relationships. Data scientists,

---

[3] U.S. Congress, Office of Technology Assessment, Federal Government Information Technology: Management, Security, and Congressional Oversight, OTA-CIT-297 (Washington, D.C.: U.S. Government Printing Office, February 1986).

[4] Wikipedia defines system integration as "linking together different computing systems and software applications physically or functionally, to act as a coordinated whole". https://en.wikipedia.org/wiki/System_integration. This differs from data integration, in which the focus is on ensuring data is used consistently across the enterprise.

with their ability to wrangle information from large pools of discrepant data, became a sought-after resource.[5] Organizations felt that collecting loads of data, such as individual behavior patterns, could help them better target those individuals, whether to increase sales or to spot crime. In parallel, and on even a bigger scale, industries began collecting machine-generated data in an effort to improve both the machines themselves and the processes associated with them.

[5] Davenport, T., & Patil, D. J., "Data scientist: The sexiest job of the 21st century," *Harvard Business Review*, October 2012. https://hbr.org/2012/10/data-scientist-the-sexiest-job-of-the-21st-century/.

Chapter 2
Big Data and Data Management

Big data is used to describe data so large, so complex a mix of structured and unstructured data, and so fast changing that it cannot be managed by conventional means; big data is often described in terms of the 3 V's—volume, variety, and velocity. Due to big data's size, our demand for real-time information, and the many different ways in which data might be stored, including within documents human ability to effectively manage data is further being challenged.

The ability to store data more cheaply than ever before fueled the desire of private and public organizations alike for massive amounts of data. The mantra shifted from ETL to ELT. "ETL" stands for "extract, transform, and load" and refers to how tools, used with structured data, first extract data from a source, then transform it to match its target environment, and finally load it. "ELT" was coined to refer to extracting data from the source, loading it into the target in raw form, and transforming it later, if and when needed, by applying analytics. As Google predicted flu outbreaks sooner and more accurately than the Centers for Disease Control could by using search data on flu-related topics,[1] organizations felt that if they did not take advantage of harnessing all possible data, they might be left behind in the big data revolution. Companies and public institutions wanted to extract and load as much raw data as possible and to have it ready for analysis and transformation when the time was right.

In response to this anticipated need, the marketplace has reacted by targeting business users in multiple ways. This market response, though a step in the right direction, has not embraced data management as an integral part of its message. Data analytics and data science degrees and certification offerings are on the rise. However, they typically focus on analytics rather than data management. Data preparation tools that allow business users to manipulate, integrate, and visualize

---

[1] See https://www.google.org/flutrends/about/. Google no longer publishes these trends but makes historical data available.

© Springer International Publishing AG 2018
M. Fleckenstein, L. Fellows, *Modern Data Strategy*,
https://doi.org/10.1007/978-3-319-68993-7_2

data more directly are pushing data wrangling to the business. This is helping to pique the business' interest in data, but it risks significant duplication of effort across the enterprise and a high level of data inconsistency if the data is not adequately governed.[2] Data brokers—which collect information such as consumer information from a wide variety of sources to yield marketing, risk-mitigation, and people search results—are increasingly selling syndicated data, though their accountability regarding the quality of information is sometimes in question.[3]

Considerable doubt has been raised regarding the ability to extract value from big data without a well-thought-out strategy tied to a business goal. One of the main reasons cited for the failure of big data analytics projects is the organization's inability to manage data it already has.[4] Extracting value from massive data is significantly more complex than extracting value from existing, internal data. Bain & Company cites multiple reasons why many big data analytics projects fail, including an over-reliance on big data technologies to attain value, an "overinvestment in unproven data sources, and inattention to valuable data sources closer to home."[5] Through this realization, the initial excitement over collecting reams of data is leading to an awareness that data must be well managed in order to extract value from it.

Gartner Research uses a hype cycle to track and predict industry technology trends. The hype cycle is represented by a curve, beginning with the "innovation trigger," representing a technology's introduction to the marketplace. The curve rises steeply to an apex, reflecting a technology's "peak of inflated expectations." The curve then declines just as steeply, reaching its "trough of disillusionment," before gently rising through its "slope of enlightenment" to its "plateau of productivity," where maturing technologies are reflected.

When the adoption of a trend goes beyond 20% of the wider IT market, Gartner retires the hype cycle for a given trend. In its 2015 report, "The Demise of Big Data, Its Lessons and the State of Things to Come," Gartner Research retired its hype cycle for big data.[6] The report envisions side-by-side modes for traditional solutions and big data, one being stable for production and enterprise-ready (traditional data infrastructure), the other allowing for experimental solutions and more rapid iterations (big data infrastructure). It concludes that "new emphasis will be found in how

---

[2] Van der Muelen, R. "Managing the Data Chaos of Self-Service Analytics," Gartner Research, December 17, 2015. http://www.gartner.com/smarterwithgartner/managing-the-data-chaos-of-self-service-analytics/.

[3] Federal Trade Commission, "Data Brokers—A Call for Transparency and Accountability," May 2014. Examples of data brokers include Acxiom, Corelogic, Datalogix, eBureau, ID Analytics, Intelius, PeekYou, Rapleaf, and Recorded Future.

[4] See, for example, Ross, J. W., Beath, C. M., & Quadgraas, A., "You may not need big data after all—Learn how lots of little data can inform everyday decision making," *Harvard Business Review*, December 2013.

[5] Almquist, E., Senior, J., & Springer, T., "Three promises and perils of big data," Bain & Company, 2015. http://www.bain.com/Images/BAIN_BRIEF_Three_promises_and_perils_of_Big_Data.pdf.

[6] Heudecker, N., Beyer, M., & Edjlali, R., "The Demise of Big Data, Its Lessons and the State of Things to Come." Gartner Research, August 19, 2015.

point solutions can be integrated into existing infrastructures, rather than building entirely new infrastructures around these point solutions," and predicts much larger data management markets.

The Executive Office of the President, via the National Science and Technology Council, published "The Federal Big Data Research and Development Strategic Plan" in May 2016.[7] This report focuses on many aspects of how to make big data most useful within the federal government and for the public. Among the topics the report addresses are adopting next-generation techniques and technologies, building an enhanced cyber-infrastructure, and improving big data education. A more careful reading of the report, though, exposes many references to data management, which is also required to achieve big data proficiency. Here are some excerpts:

- "… standardize access to data resources …"
- "… developing data and metadata standards in order to improve interoperability …"
- "… large-scale warehoused historical data …"
- "… development of standards, and data sharing and data integration approaches …"
- "… share data across disciplines and among agencies …"
- "… dedicated to promoting a culture of data sharing and open data for government …"
- "… requires data stakeholders to play an active role in data stewardship …"
- "Data sharing includes the curation and sharing of data itself but, equally importantly, the metadata and the APIs to the data."
- "Develop Best Practices for Metadata to Increase Data Transparency and Utility"
- "… tools that automate the capture of data provenance …"
- "A standardized language system, or ontology, for describing data processes is essential to enable better sharing of data."
- "… address the issue of data archiving …"
- "Defining data privacy and security measures will be critical elements …"
- "… rules of the road are needed for data governance …"
- "… ensuring that data is readily available for use while guaranteeing data confidentiality …"
- "… ensure that the privacy of a particular dataset's contents is protected …"

Companies and public institutions are just beginning to conclude that, before engaging in the race to big data, they must give thought to how a big data initiative will fit into their existing business and data infrastructure. How will it help solve a business problem, and how will the data extracted be effectively integrated with what already exists? They are realizing that, although exploring big data has an experimental side, big data must be governed, shared, secured, archived, contextualized, and understood.

---

[7] See "The Federal Big Data Research and Development Strategic Plan,"https://www.nitrd.gov/PUBS/bigdatardstrategicplan.pdf.

Astonishingly few organizations are realizing the value their information holds. A joint study of 1800 large and small businesses by PricewaterhouseCoopers and Iron Mountain concluded that only 4% of these companies are able to exploit their data to its greatest extent.[8] The study refers to this small group as the "elite." It notes several key practices that elites exhibit. The top two are: get your [data] governance right and treat information as a valuable asset.

---

[8] See "Seizing the information advantage How organizations can unlock value and insight from the information they hold," PwC, September 2015. http://www.ironmountain.com/Knowledge-Center/ Reference-Library/View-by-Document-Type/White-Papers-Briefs/S/~/media/Files/Iron%20 Mountain/Knowledge%20Center/Reference%20Library/White%20Paper/S/Seizing%20The%20 Information%20Advantage.pdf.

Chapter 3
Valuing Data As an Asset

We frequently hear the slogan "manage data as an asset." The implication is that data has worth, and as such, should be treated as a valuable asset. But what is required to manage data as an asset? Organizations understand that data is vitally important to their enterprise, to their ability to manage their finances, execute customer service, and improve their operations. Yet what it means to manage data as an asset is too rarely discussed and not well documented, and most organizations don't account for their data assets as they do for their other assets. In fact, managing data as an asset has many similarities to managing other assets. Of course, there are some differences because data is intangible and consumed differently than physical assets. However, similarities abound.[1]

Formal asset valuation has evolved over a lot of time, and it continues to evolve. The concept of financial accounting dates back some 7000 years. More recent concepts, such as valuing inventory and depreciating assets, did not manifest themselves in accounting practices until the mid-nineteenth century during the Industrial Revolution.[2] Even more recently, the importance of intangible assets is continuing to become increasingly significant. This class of assets includes intellectual property like patents and copyrights, and, if measured in terms of revenue potential, also data.

Organizations value their assets for many reasons, including consistent financial reporting, mergers and acquisitions, customer service, capital budgeting, and taxes. Today, tangible assets like buildings, machinery, land, and inventory are valued based on their cost, their current market value, or their revenue potential. The basis of how asset value is assigned is rooted in such areas as lenders' desires to know the value of collateral against which they lend money and governments' tax assessments, which use the value of assets to generate tax revenue. Recently, an increasing

---

[1] For a comparison between physical inventory management and managing data as an asset, see the Physical Asset Management vs. Data Management section.

[2] Wikipedia. "History of Accounting." Web. http://en.wikipedia.org/wiki/History_of_accounting. Accessed Nov. 2014.

© Springer International Publishing AG 2018
M. Fleckenstein, L. Fellows, *Modern Data Strategy*,
https://doi.org/10.1007/978-3-319-68993-7_3

number of valuations are also based on revenue potential. This can be seen, for example, with stock valuations of start-up companies and with intangible assets such as intellectual property.

In recent years, there has been a growing tendency to assign value to intangible assets—like patents, copyrights, trademarks, and brands—as part of the organizational makeup. In one study, Dr. Margaret Blair, of the Brookings Institution, examined the degree to which value has been tied to organizational intellectual property between 1978 and 1998. Dr. Blair reports that, over time, intangible assets increasingly determined corporate value. In studying all nonfinancial, publicly traded firms in the Compustat database, Dr. Blair showed that in 1978, 80% of firms' value was associated with its tangible assets and 20% with its intangible assets. By 1988, the makeup had shifted to 45% tangible assets and 55% intangible assets. By 1998, only 30% of the value of firms studied was attributable to their tangible assets, whereas 70% was associated with the value of their intangibles.[3]

It's not a stretch to say data should be included as part of organizational intellectual property. In fact, the Internal Revenue Service (IRS) guidelines for valuing intangible assets lists "technical data" as one type of intangible asset.[4] According to the IRS, the value of an intangible asset can be determined in the same way as tangible assets: using a cost basis, gauging its value in the marketplace, or based on revenue potential of the asset in question. The rules allow auditors to apply any combination of these approaches, provided the auditor has sufficient documentation to justify the valuation. These approaches could be applied to data valuation. However, at the time of this writing, most organizations do not estimate the value of their data in this way.

There is no agreement on data valuation as yet, but some attempts have been made. One example is a paper authored by Daniel Moody and Peter Walsh.[5] The paper looked at different approaches that had in part been previously researched to value information, including the different accounting valuation models based on cost, market value, and revenue potential. Another valuation approach the authors examined, termed "Communications Theory," attempted to measure the value of information based on the amount of information communicated. This, they correctly concluded, leaves out the value of the content and is not a useful approach to data valuation. The report concluded that the best cost approximation of data is based on future cash flow, predicting today's industry trend.

---

[3] Blair, M. M., "Unseen Wealth," Brookings Institution, 2001. Note: Dr. Blair defines the value of intangible assets as the difference between a company's market value and the value of the company's tangible assets. Not everyone agrees on this formula. However, there is agreement that intangible assets are growing as part of overall corporate asset make-up. See, for example, Harrison, S. S., & Sullivan, H. P., *Edison in the Boardroom: How New Leading Companies Realize Value from Their Intellectual Property*, John Wiley & Sons, December 2006, "A Brief History" section.

[4] Internal Revenue Manual—4.48.5 Intangible Property Valuation Guidelines, Web. Autumn 2014. http://www.irs.gov/irm/part4/irm_04-048-005.html.

[5] Moody, D., & Walsh, P., "Measuring the Value of Information: An Asset Valuation Approach," ECIS, 1999.

The report had another interesting conclusion on why data may not be formally accounted for as an asset on corporate books. The authors concluded that it is financially advantageous for companies to treat the cost of information as an expense rather than an asset. The reason for this is simple. By treating data as an expense, companies can avoid showing data on their balance sheet and the associated tax implications. However, the paper also determined that, aside from the financial valuation of data, there are practical reasons for valuing data, including greater accountability, measuring IT effectiveness, and helping to justify the cost of information systems.

A more indirect approach to valuing data as an asset is also exemplified in a book by Tony Fisher on how and why to treat data as an asset.[6] The book does not state outright how data should be valued as an asset, but it makes the case that data quality and data governance directly benefit the bottom line. Fisher builds the case that organizations' effective use of data to mitigate risk, increase revenue, and control cost is a key differentiator between successful organizations and less successful ones. The book defines risk mitigation as successfully addressing compliance and regulatory issues. Definitions for increased revenue or contained cost are more self-explanatory. It uses many examples to highlight these concepts. For example, it uses Wal-Mart's instant feedback up and down the supply-chain as an example for increased revenue. Similarly, the book uses a manufacturing plant's ability to adjust its machinery to new demands, based on good quality and well-managed data, as an example of effective cost control.

In his book, Peter Aiken, presents numerous examples of how, when data management is effectively applied, organizational risks and costs are reduced.[7] In addition, the book highlights case studies that result in improved national security and saving of lives through good data management. Though it is essentially impossible to attribute a monetary value to these examples, it is intuitive that data must have significant value if it helps with national security and saving lives.

Although there is no formal agreement yet on a method to value data as an asset, more and more people and institutions are giving the matter thought. Douglas Laney, an analyst and author with Gartner, for example, has introduced the concept of "Infonomics" in an effort centralize discussion on valuing data as an asset. One of the concepts he suggested early on is for organizations to keep an internal balance sheet to track the value of their data assets.[8]

Clearly organizations recognize that data is an asset. They employ increasing resources, both internal as well as outside experts, to help them manage data at considerable expense. Organizations understand intuitively that incurring data management costs, expensive as they are, still saves them money, reduces their exposure to risk, and may significantly increase their revenue.

---

[6] Fisher, T., *The Data Asset—How Smart Companies Govern Their Data for Business Success*, John Wiley & Sons, 2009.

[7] Aiken, P., & Billings, J., *Monetizing Data Management*, Technics Publications LLC, 2013.

[8] Laney, D., "Introducing Infonomics: Valuing Information as a Corporate Asset," Gartner Research, March 21, 2012.

In addition, managing data well leads to significant benefits that are hard to quantify. These benefits include crime prevention, better healthcare, improved transportation, more high-quality information, better communication, and even the saving of lives. These benefits are significant drivers in our quest to manage our data better.

It remains unclear whether data will ever be valued as an asset in the organization's financial statements or whether it will continue to be treated as an expense. Increasing dialog around the valuation of data as an asset makes it likely that data will be managed more and more formally. As the next section shows, the similarities between data and a physical asset are striking. As such, it is a given that data will successively be treated more and more formally.

Chapter 4
Physical Asset Management vs. Data Management

With the growing significance of data as a key component of doing business, organizations are treating data more and more like an asset. Although organizations realize that data holds value, no formal or agreed-upon approach currently exists for data valuation. Thought leaders in the data space have proposed several different approaches to data valuation. They include traditional asset valuation concepts based on cost (e.g., the cost of third-party data), fair market value (i.e., the amount an entity is willing to pay for data or an organization that brings with it access to data), and future revenue (e.g., insight into ongoing consumer behavior through data). More indirect approaches to data valuation highlight risk and cost associated with lack of data quality and data management. These approaches express the value of data in terms of costs incurred when an organization is unable to comply with regulations or adapt to changing demand, due to the poor quality of data and data management.

Another way to look at the value of data is by comparison to how physical data is managed, specifically inventory. Although this approach does not provide an explicit value to data items, it allows us to approximate the value of data through the resources required to manage it. That is, just like physical inventory management requires manpower and infrastructure, so does data management. In many cases, the analogy is striking.

The Institute of Asset Management (IAM)[1] divides asset management into 39 subject areas. Each subject area encompasses a specific step required for asset management. These subject areas are fit into six groupings that include strategy and planning, operational decision making, lifecycle management, asset information, organizations and people, and risk and review.[2] Sections of the IAM guideline

---

[1] IAM proclaims its mission as: "The IAM is a not for profit membership organisation that exists to advance for the public benefit," See https://theiam.org/about-us/work-organisation.

[2] The Institute of Asset Management, "Asset Management—An anatomy," ver. 2.0, p. 17. Institute of Asset Management, 2014. Note that the IAM has adopted the ISO 55001 Asset Management standards.

© Springer International Publishing AG 2018
M. Fleckenstein, L. Fellows, *Modern Data Strategy*,
https://doi.org/10.1007/978-3-319-68993-7_4

include detailed approaches to evaluating trade-offs between short- and long-term goals; among costs, risks, and performance outcomes; and between capital investments and subsequent maintenance costs. For example, the guideline emphasizes the need to understand the costs and risks associated with an asset over its life cycle. Many of these principles could also be applied to data valuation.

Most organizations make educated guesses, at best, with respect to data valuation. Managing data as an asset is encouraged with increasing frequency in technical literature and by business leaders. Executives, managers, and line personnel all try their best to manage data within their organizations' data management framework.[3] At each level of the enterprise, they attempt to organize data as best they can—conscientious data input by line workers, careful coding by software developers, attention to data reporting by managers, and careful planning on the basis of data by executives. However, in each case, people are bound by the limitations of their data management framework. For example, if a line worker doesn't have the proper knowledge or tool and consistent processes are not in place to properly enter or integrate data, either data does not get loaded or it gets loaded incorrectly. Such errors work their way up the management chain and often lead to gaps and inconsistencies—resulting in a significant manual data reconciliation effort at best and erroneous data at worst—in the data on which executives base their planning.

4.1 Cost

To examine parallels between inventory management and data management, we begin by comparing the cost of acquiring and managing a physical asset with that of acquiring and managing data. Acquisition costs in both cases are significant in and of themselves. In the case of physical assets, people who manage the purchase must be paid, inventory must be allocated to the right location, and the product itself has a cost. Similarly, with data, resources are necessary for understanding exactly what data needs to be acquired, for leveraging software and hardware needed to obtain and store new data, for accommodating data infrastructure such as a data entry portals and databases, and for planning how data will be integrated with other, existing data in the enterprise data infrastructure. These processes all contain significant up-front costs. It is quicker and cheaper initially for organizations to create on-the-fly data infrastructures. Often data is placed in a spreadsheet, or a new data store is quickly stood up, or, with the advent of big data, data may simply be gathered and stored for later use.

---

[3] Data management frameworks outline the data management disciplines required for an integrated approach to data management best practices, e.g., data quality, data governance, data architecture, and master data management. One framework example is the Data Management Association (DAMA) Data Management Body of Knowledge (DMBOK). See https://www.dama.org/content/body-knowledge.

Table 4.1 Inventory vs. Data management: cost

Physical inventory management concepts[a]	Data management concepts
Inventory costs	Data management costs
• Cost of ordering and acquiring inventory, including salaries of persons involved	• Cost of obtaining and loading data, accommodating data infrastructure and purchasing syndicated data, including salaries of persons involved
• Holding cost of inventory, such as rent, equipment needed to handle inventory, warehouse staff	• Cost of software licenses, data stores, and database and tool administrators
• Losses and wastage	• Losses due to poor data quality

[a]Examples used for Physical Inventory Management Concepts in Tables 4.1, 4.2, 4.3, 4.4 and 4.5 come from Muller, M., "The Essentials of Inventory Management," 2nd Ed., AMACOM, a division of The American Management Association, 2011

The cost of data maintenance is not trivial either. Here too a spreadsheet or local data store are inexpensive approaches to managing data initially, but when reporting and planning demands require data to be integrated at a broader level, costs can quickly add up. For example, managing newly acquired data in a local, siloed data store can lead to unmanaged replication of the same data across multiple data stores throughout the organization. Each copy of the data may then be independently updated, leading to data discrepancies, often without a good understanding of provenance. If data redundancy is unmanaged, data discrepancies are likely to cost the organization significantly in terms of aligning nonmatching data. If exposed beyond the organization, these kinds of data quality issues can harbor hidden costs such as organizational reputation and may even have legal ramifications, which can be very expensive and difficult to quantify. Table 4.1 summarizes our comparison.

To mitigate the cost of managing information, an organization must decide on the strategic importance of each of its data assets. Just as with physical assets, not all data is equal in value. In the words of the IAM's Asset Management guide, "Simple, non-critical [asset management] decisions can and should be made with (educated) common sense, whereas higher impact decisions, with multiple influences, options, timings or inter-dependencies require greater systematic, multidiscipline and auditable optimisation methods"[4]. The same rule of thumb can and should be applied to data. Some data will be worth more to an organization than other data. Key data important to an organization as a whole must be managed more robustly than localized data. Determining what data to manage more robustly and what data to manage more informally is tricky, will vary for each organization, and will evolve over time. Some data will be required in raw form, and other data will have to be highly refined and integrated.

---

[4]The Institute of Asset Management, "Asset Management—An anatomy," Ver. 2.0, 2014, p. 10.

Table 4.2 Inventory vs. Data management: quality fit for use

Physical inventory management concepts	Data management concepts
Types of inventory	Types of data
• Raw material	• Raw data
• Finished product/consumables	• Cleansed and validated data ready for consumption
• Work in progress	• Partially cleansed data
• Service, repair, replacement and spare parts	• Data profiling, Data cleansing, metadata

4.2 Quality Fit for Use

Continuing our comparison between inventory management and data management, we can also see similarities in classifying types of inventory. Inventory management classifies assets into categories such as raw material, work in progress, finished product, and spare parts. Similarly, for data, business managers need to know what version and quality of data they are retrieving. Is it raw, unscrubbed data or data cleansed and ready for consumption? Perhaps both types are needed at different points in time. For example, an organization may want a record of an unscrubbed address as a reference to exactly how the customer entered the address; but it may want a cleansed address to better fulfill an order or for billing. An organization may want to scrub order fulfillment and billing address data on an ongoing basis. Data profiling and data cleansing are used to "service" and "repair" data. Metadata, data that describes other data, functions like a data "spare part" in that it is important to help find the right data and differentiate one type of data (e.g., an unscrubbed address from a cleansed address) from another. Table 4.2 summarizes our comparison.

4.3 Stewardship

The inventory and data asset management similarities continue as we examine who is responsible for managing physical and data assets. Just as with inventory management, it takes a team of people at all levels of the organization to manage both inventory as well as data. In inventory management, business managers are responsible for managing particular parts of the inventory. For their product domain, they ensure supply meets demand, manage quality and field issues, and foster product improvements based on customer feedback. They manage a supply chain and are supported by a team ranging from warehouse workers, to marketers and accountants. Similarly, formal data governance is a data management domain specifying who has responsibility for specific data. A key component of data governance, a data steward is someone who has accountability for managing a piece of data to fulfill a business purpose. Data stewards, like their counterparts in physical asset management, work together with a support team that includes data architects, the information technology

Table 4.3 Inventory vs. Data management: stewardship

Physical inventory management concepts	Data management concepts
Inventory stewardship	Data stewardship
• Transfer of ownership by finance when product leaves the dock or arrives at inventory site	• Data ownership by the enterprise; data sharing and interoperability management
• Inventory stewardship by business managers	• Domain based responsibility for data by a data steward
• Inventory warehouse operations by inventory manager and his or her team	• Coordination with data architects, IT, business SMEs, and others; issue escalation path to data governance council

(IT) department, business subject matter experts (SMEs), and others. Table 4.3 summarizes our comparison.

Typically, a data steward is responsible for a data domain (or part of a domain) across its life cycle. He or she supports that data domain across an entire business process rather than for a specific application or a project. In this way, data governance provides the end user with a go-to resource for data questions and requests. When formally applied, data governance also holds managers and executives accountable for data issues that cannot be resolved at lower levels. Thus it establishes an escalation path beginning with the end user. Most important, data governance determines the level—local, departmental or enterprise—at which specific data is managed. The higher the value of a particular data asset, the more rigorous its data governance.

In inventory management, different types of inventory are stored in designated places. This helps business managers optimize access to each type of inventory based on demand. Similarly, managing where key data is stored and how it flows across the organization ensures high-quality data and helps mitigate data discrepancies, minimize incorrect information, and buffer future costs. An organization will want an approach to determine who is responsible for data at a given point in time, so that when questions arise, people will know whom to ask.

4.4 Architecture

Whether in physical inventory management or in data management, understanding the location of an asset is extremely helpful to stewards, managers, and consumers (end users in data). Disciplines such as optimizing inventory locations and stock tracking have data management parallels like authoritative data sources, data maps, and data models. In data management, these concepts fall under data architecture.

Data architects work closely with data stewards and help determine how data is best stored and how it flows across the organization. This is conceptually similar to tracking physical inventory. Inventory location, placement, and tracking are managed with design concepts such as using a grid system for types of products, co-locating products in the same family, specifically assigning a fixed inventory address for

Table 4.4 Inventory vs. Data management: architecture

Physical inventory management concepts	Data management concepts
Inventory location and stock tracking	Data architecture
• Location address (e.g., Address, Rack-Section-Tier-Bin, Room-Bldg-Rack-Bin)	• Authoritative data sources, data maps, data models
• Locator systems (e.g., fixed location, zoning, bulk storage grid system, random)	• Databases and data stores, managed redundancy (e.g., operational, data warehouse)
Identifiers	Identifiers
• SKUs	• Keys and indexes
• Bar codes	• Tags and metadata

high-value inventory, locating frequently used inventory where it is most easily accessible, or special labeling and location for volatile products.[5] Similarly, data architecture applies design concepts like subject areas for types of data; data maps and data models for location, indexing, and metadata to quickly identify high-value information; authoritative sources for data quality; and master data management for managing replication, among others. Table 4.4 summarizes our comparison.

4.5 Obsolescence

Data architecture also helps with differentiating current data from useful historical data and from obsolete data. Like obsolete inventory, obsolete data has diminishing value for the organization. In inventory management, recapturing costly warehouse space is key. In data management, the cost of storage is comparatively relatively low, though storing large amounts of data online can be expensive. With data, the efficient use of resources—people and machines—benefit from an understanding of which data is current, historical, or obsolete. For example, excluding historical and obsolete data from the operational environment helps locate desired data more quickly and may also aid performance. Data is easier and faster to find and the likelihood that incorrect data is used is diminished. Unknowingly retrieving obsolete data can certainly incur significant cost as well. Table 4.5 summarizes our comparison.

4.6 Additional Considerations

Just as in physical asset management, multiple data management components work together to better manage data infrastructure. For example, organizations may store the same data, such as customer data, multiple times. Customer information is

---

[5] The Institute of Asset Management, Asset Management—An anatomy," 2014, https://www. theIAM.org.

Table 4.5 Inventory vs. Data management: obsolescence

Physical inventory management concepts	Data management concepts
Obsolete stock	Obsolete data
• Recapture space	• Online storage vs. near-line storage vs. archiving data
• Efficient use of machine and human resources	• Removal of obsolete data results in more efficient searches, data integration, and reporting
– Reduction of carrying costs	

stored in the operational database as a course of doing business; the same data may be found in a corporate data warehouse for analysis purposes. In some cases, the same data may be needed in multiple operational systems across different departments such as Marketing, Operations, and Finance. Data governance, data architecture, data warehousing, business intelligence and analytics, data quality, and master data management, when coordinated, help improve data quality and access, reduce manual reconciliation, and optimize data sharing.

Data sharing is also increasingly important. Corporations clearly benefit from the plethora of data available to them. Perhaps they are collaborating with supply chain partners to optimize inventory or services, or they may be using social media data freely available to them to drive business performance. Government agencies are increasingly on the hook to share data as well. Open data and data transparency acts, executive orders, memoranda, directives, policies, and guidelines abound, driving government to share data[6,7] In addition, different parts of government are increasingly required to share data digitally. For example, states must share data for Medicaid, a $415 billon program in FY2012,[8] with the federal government in order to get reimbursed. It's easy to see that the increased sharing of data is significantly optimized by applying data management domains like the ones mentioned earlier.

More and more organizations are also purchasing data to augment their own information. In fact, entire industries of data brokers have developed around selling syndicated data.[9] Data brokers collect information, such as consumer information, from a wide variety of sources to yield marketing, risk-mitigation, and people search results. When purchasing syndicated data, approaches to integration and

---

[6] See, for example, White House Memorandum, "Open Data Policy—Managing Information as an Asset," https://obamawhitehouse.archives.gov/sites/default/files/omb/memoranda/2013/m-13-13.pdf, May 9, 2013. Accessed February 2, 2015. This memorandum refers to numerous other open data and data transparency documents.

[7] Numerous memoranda and Presidential directives have been archived. As of this writing, due to a change in administration, links to these memoranda and directives default to https://www.white-house.gov/sites/default/files/omb/assets/memoranda_2010/m10-06.pdf. Therefore, we surface the archived version of the documents when they cannot otherwise be found.

[8] See The Henry J. Kaiser Family Foundation, "Total Medicaid Spending," http://kff.org/medicaid/state-indicator/total-medicaid-spending/Accessed February 2, 2015.

[9] Federal Trade Commission, "Data Brokers—A Call for Transparency and Accountability," May 2014. Examples of data brokers include Acxiom, Corelogic, Datalogix, eBureau, ID Analytics, Intelius, PeekYou, Rapleaf, and Recorded Future.

interoperability of the purchased data with the legacy environment become important considerations. The less developed and coordinated data management domains are, the greater the likelihood of one-off automated data integration, manual data integration, or no proper data integration at all. To make matters even worse, different parts of an organization may purchase the same or similar data, perhaps even from different vendors. Once acquired, this data is then independently maintained across different local data stores. The cost of maintaining independent data stores and later integrating such data can be very time consuming and expensive, exacerbated by the possibility that each syndicated vendor may very well use proprietary data definitions.

Just as in physical asset management, successful teams of executives, managers, and operational people set rules, collaborate, and leverage technology to execute a data strategy.

Part II
Data Strategy

Chapter 5
Leading a Data Strategy

Clearly organizations are collecting, creating, and exchanging more and more data. They have a vested interest, and increasingly realized interest, in tapping the potential of this data to increase revenue, to decrease costs, and to help them manage risks. However, this requires a different way of thinking and a maturity of data management that many organizations don't yet have and must grow over time. Organizations can make a fair amount of progress in specific data management domains from grassroots efforts and IT-driven efforts, but organizations usually reach a point where to really move forward, to make that quantum leap of realizing the benefits from their data, business and IT need to collaborate, think about data as an asset and a business enabler, and apply some degree of discipline to define how to:

- Move the data maturity of the organization forward and
- Coordinate existing data-related projects to ensure they support each other, all while
- Furthering the business goals of the organization

In short, to take advantage of their data, organizations need an overarching data strategy. A data strategy should be a collaborative effort that includes both business representatives and representatives from IT to ensure that both the business objectives and technology capabilities are understood. But who should participate and who should drive and coordinate these efforts?

5.1 Process, Technology, and Data People

Ideally a data strategy should be driven by an executive who is a data person, but at a minimum, a data strategy team should include one or more data people, in addition to process and technology people. What's meant by "data person"? There are

© Springer International Publishing AG 2018
M. Fleckenstein, L. Fellows, *Modern Data Strategy*,
https://doi.org/10.1007/978-3-319-68993-7_5

different types of people in the world, including process people, technology people, and data people. This doesn't necessarily refer to a person's background or their experience exactly, but instead it refers to the way they think and the way they approach problems.

- *Process People*: Most people and most business people are "process people," that is, process-oriented people who think in terms of processes and business outcomes. Processes have inputs and outputs, but the data for process people is mostly an afterthought, as all too often are their data requirements. They've historically identified data requirements when pressed, but they weren't necessarily concerned that the same data for project 1 and project 2 be similarly named and described. In the past, many process people felt that the details of the data were someone else's issue, for example, IT's issue, but that attitude is finally beginning to change—the business is recognizing that data is a business concern. An interesting note is that many process people aren't all that aware that not everyone thinks the same way they do. This is similar to how right-handed people aren't really aware that much of the world around them is designed for right-handed people and is awkward for left-handed individuals.
- *Technology People*: Technology-oriented people are really a subset and outgrowth of process-oriented people. Technology people focus on the automation of tasks and the elimination of manual steps and manual bottlenecks and they think in terms of systems and applications. The better technology people have historically sought out functions and activities that are part of many business processes and aimed to reuse associated programs/utilities for efficiency. Technology people are arguably more concerned with data but sometimes in ways that are more form than function. They need data requirements and may even want a data model, but they aren't necessarily concerned that the same data for project 1 and project 2 are similarly named and described or that the data comes from an authoritative source. Too often, data is something to be obtained for the immediate purpose at hand, often copied from wherever is convenient, sometimes cleaned because, after all, you can't trust what may or may not have been done to the data previously, and then processed for the purpose at hand. When new data is produced as a by-product of the process, neither its downstream uses nor its integration with other similar data is given much thought.
- *Data People*: Data people understand processes and systems/applications views, but somewhere along the way they came to believe that data is the key to understanding an organization and its business. They came to recognize that organizational models change every other year, processes and business channels change regularly, and systems come and go as technology changes, but an organization's data remains through it all. Data people may come from IT or be on the business side, for example, in finance, regulatory reporting, or business analytics, but they have come to understand that data has a life cycle all its own and goes through state transitions over its life. Data is imported or created by one process, may be updated by many processes and by different business events, is used by many processes, and often must be integrated and combined with other data for downstream processes including reporting and analytics, which may identify

business opportunities for historical data long after the data is created or no longer believed relevant to business operations. By looking across the life cycle of an organization's key data, the data person gains an understanding of the complexity of the organization's data environment; the cost of poor data; the money wasted on unmanaged redundancy, knowledge worker time, business reconciliations, and so on; the lost business opportunities because customers, business partners, and the market aren't well understood; and the extent to which the organization's risks are unclear or unknown.

In truth, all three of these perspectives—process, technology, and data—are needed to create a good data strategy. Each type of person approaches things differently and brings different perspectives to the table. Think of this as another aspect of diversity. Just as a multicultural team and a team with different educational backgrounds will produce a better result, so will a team that includes people with process, technology *and data* perspectives.

Unfortunately, data people are relatively rare. Based on personal experience, 90% or more of the world's population are either process people or technology people. Chief Executive Officers (CEOs), Chief Operating Officer (COOs), and business people in general are often process people. Chief Financial Officers (CFOs) and individuals working in areas such as risk, compliance or regulatory reporting, or business analytics are more likely than most business people to be data people and understand the value of data. CIOs are invariably technology people but nevertheless may be the default starting point for an executive to lead a data strategy. This is in part because data has in the past been seen as an IT concern and also because CIOs often have data people working for them.

The remainder of this chapter discusses the CIO option and discusses an emerging alternative presented by the role of the CDO.

5.2 CIO Role

The CIO role is primarily focused on technology. Ross and Feeny provided a good summary of the evolution of IT and the CIO through three eras: mainframe, distributed, and web-based.[1] The head of IT, pre-CIO, was a lower level operational role focused on keeping (usually mainframe) systems running. The CIO title emerged during the late 1980s/early 1990s at a time when IT was evolving away from mainframe computers toward distributed client-server solutions. With this shift came a dramatic increase in the complexity of IT and corresponding needs to staff for changing technologies and specialized skillsets and to evaluate a much larger pool of technology vendors. Later came the needs to incorporate various degrees of outsourcing, to integrate commercial off-the-shelf (COTS) software, to integrate with

---

[1] Ross, J. W., & Feeny, D. F., "The Evolving Role of the CIO," Center for Information Systems Research, Sloan School of Management, MIT, August 1999.

business partners, and so on. As business became more reliant on IT, and IT was increasingly seen as a competitive advantage, the need for an executive officer over IT became more apparent and the CIO-role was seen as the answer. Though the CIO continued to have operational responsibilities, the CIO also began to have responsibility for developing an IT strategy and later to ensure that it aligned with the business' strategy. During this period, the CIO took on multiple roles:

- Organizational designer
- Technology adviser
- Technology architect
- Informed buyer

Successful CIOs began to focus on the role of technology adviser, building relationships with other members of the C-suite, and building strong teams to address the other roles, for example, by creating the Chief Technology Officer (CTO) position to focus on the technology architect and informed buyer roles. Throughout these changes, the CIO role has remained focused on technology.

During the distributed era, data was considered an IT responsibility and data quality issues were considered IT problems. The reality, however, was that in many organization during this period, no one was accountable for, responsible for, or effectively managing data, including the CIO. When systems were few and primarily mainframe, "what's the authoritative source" wasn't even a question that needed to be asked. During the distributed era, however, IT systems proliferated without control and unmanaged data redundancy became rampant. In some cases, individual business units developed or bought their own duplicative systems. But, in other cases, new systems were developed under the CIO to replace legacy systems, but the legacy systems weren't retired and projects gave little thought to integrating data for downstream consumers, who often had to integrate the data themselves.

By the late 1990s/early 2000s, data people within IT realized that they had an absolute mess on their hands and slowly began to convince IT leaders, if not initially the CIOs, who responded by creating data management groups. These groups began to model the data, define modeling standards, assess data quality, and identify authoritative sources, often in grassroots efforts associated with data warehouses. Unfortunately, these groups were often buried deep within IT and were too low in the organization to influence executives, even the CIO. Given that IT was historically focused on cost reduction, these early data groups were sometimes perceived by CIOs as costs without any appreciation for the business value provided. In the 2000s, the creation of data architects and their integration into Enterprise Architecture groups, together with the early efforts at IT-driven data governance, sometimes achieved more visibility and some CIOs began to "get data." Even with CIO support, however, data efforts under the CIO have had limited ability to impact the business.

To be fair, even when the rare CIO has an appreciation for data, there may be only so much the CIO and IT can do without the active participation of the business because many data problems are "fundamentally business problems,"[2] symptoms of

---

[2]Lee, Y., Wang, F., Madnick, S., Want, R., & Zhang, H., "A cubic framework for the chief data officer: Succeeding in a world of big data." *MIS Quarterly Executive*, March 2014.

organization or process dysfunction. After all, data is created by business processes and "the quality and integrity of that data often depend more on business processes and rules than on technology"[3] used to capture the data. Only the business area can really define what a data attribute means, what its valid values are, what legal and contractual restrictions might exist for the use and disclosure of the data, the likely uses for the data, what level of data quality is acceptable for those uses, and what the integration requirements are. A report by Oracle, based on a survey of 333 C-level executives spanning 11 industries, found that up to 14% of a company's revenue is lost when they fail to adequately manage and leverage their data.[4] A Gartner survey from 2013 indicated that poor quality data was costing surveyed organizations on average $14.2 million annually.[5] It's for these reasons that data is increasingly recognized as a business concern and for these reasons that data governance ultimately must move under the business to be successful and strategic data efforts such as master data management must have strong business sponsorship and participation to be successful.

If an organization isn't mature enough to recognize that data is a business concern, the CIO of course may be the logical executive to advance an organization's data practices and capabilities. Unfortunately, by that same measure, such an organization probably isn't mature enough for an overarching data strategy and might be better off pursuing strategy at the next level down. In this case, the CIO might be better off by first pursuing strategy for one or more components of data management to address gaps in the organizations data management foundation. For example, they might pursue a strategy to stand up a data architecture function or metadata management. Both data architecture and metadata are foundational capabilities to the organization, and the CIO has a better chance of influencing either on his or her own. These and other components of data management are discussed later under the Data Management Domains section.

When an organization is ready for an overarching data strategy, however, the CIO still may be the default starting point for an executive to lead a data strategy in part because data has in the past been seen as an IT concern and because CIOs often have data people working for them, for example, the head of a data management group, senior data architects in an EA group, or the head of a BI or Analytics Center of Excellence. Although the participation of the CIO and IT in creating an overarching data strategy is important, the average CIO might not be an ideal candidate to take the lead on an overarching data strategy for several reasons. First, as discussed earlier, CIOs are most often technology people who rarely have data management backgrounds and have traditionally lacked an appreciation for the importance and business value of data,[6] though there are some indications this latter point is changing.

---

[3] Bowen, R., & Smith, A. R., "Developing an enterprise-wide data strategy," *Healthcare Financial Management*, April 2014.

[4] *Ibid.*

[5] Logan, D., Raskino, M., & Bugajski, J., "Business Case for the Chief Data Officer," Gartner Research, October 16, 2014.

[6] Logan, D., & Raskino, M., "CIO Advisory, The Chief Data Officer Trend Gains Momentum," Gartner Research, January 13, 2014.

Second, even in those instances in which a CIO does "get data," having the CIO lead a data strategy effort, unfortunately, may cement the outdated attitude that data is an IT issue rather than a business concern. Last, if the business doesn't view the CIO as a strategic partner, the entire effort may be labeled "just an IT thing" that fails to garner business participation and by-in.

The "Evolution of the CIO Role" as depicted by Ross and Feeny[7] in 1999 showed the CIO evolving from a functional head who delivered on promises, to a strategic partner who aligned IT with the business, and then to a business visionary who would drive the strategy of the business. Certainly, in some organizations, the CIO has indeed become a strategic partner, but that is still not the case in many other organizations in which there remains a distrust or outright dysfunction between business and IT. It's now eighteen years later, and there is much doubt whether CIOs will ever become business visionaries as Ross and Feeny envisioned. Successfully positioning themselves to collaboratively lead data strategy could move them in this direction, but that doesn't seem likely. Given current trends in outsourcing, software as a service (SaaS) offerings, the advent of cloud computing, and the emergence of new roles such as the CDO, there is doubt whether the CIO role will survive in the long term. Two interesting indications when taken together are:

- Though some CIOs will surely view the CDO as competition, "most CIOs and senior IT leaders interviewed by Gartner are supportive of the business case for a CDO and understand the need."[8]
- When Paul Barth, keynote speaker at a Chief Data Officer Forum, suggested that "the CIO role was becoming less and less relevant to organizations" and "asserted that the CIO role would go away within ten years," "to his surprise most of the CIOs in the audience as well as the chief data officers agreed with him and said that they envisioned this as well!"[9]

5.3   Emerging CDO Role

Wikipedia defines the CDO as follows:

A chief data officer (CDO) is a corporate officer responsible for enterprise-wide governance and utilization of information as an asset, via data processing, analysis, data mining, information trading and other means.

---

[7] Ross, J. W., & Feeny, D. F., "The Evolving Role of the CIO." Center for Information Systems Research, Sloan School of Management, MIT, August 1999.

[8] Logan, D., Raskino, M., and Bugajski, J., "Business Case for the Chief Data Officer." Gartner Research, February 29, 2016.

[9] R. Bean (NewVantage Partners) interviewed by D. Kiron. "Organizational Alignment is Key to Big Data Success." *Sloan Management Review*, MIT, January 2013.

Another perspective, a cubic framework,[10] defines the CDO role in terms of three dimensions: collaborative direction that may be either inwardly or outwardly focused, data space that includes traditional data or big data, and value impact that focuses either on service or strategy.

Depending on where a CDO falls on these dimensions, the authors of" A Cubic Framework" assert that the CDO will hold one of more of eight roles they define but only one primary role at a time:

1. Coordinator
2. Reporter
3. Architect
4. Ambassador
5. Analyst
6. Marketer
7. Developer
8. Experimenter

Though we agree that CDO's primary role will change over time, it's doubtful the typical CDO will have the luxury to focus on only one of these roles, for example, that of ambassador, and more likely that CDOs will have to balance multiple roles simultaneously, for example, a combination of ambassador, coordinator, and architect. Interviews of people with the "Chief Data Officer" title suggest that many if not most are data people, which is encouraging to hear.[11] Specific responsibilities for the role vary widely, but according to Gartner, by late 2015, the CDO's responsibilities usually included data governance and data strategy and may include other data management capabilities such as analytics, master data management (MDM), or data quality.[12]

Why couldn't business-driven data governance, combined with traditional data-related managers, achieve the same results as a CDO (A Cubic Framework)? In fact, Enterprise Information Management (EIM) groups tried this approach in the 2000s and still found it lacking. The increasing recognition that data is a business concern led to the development of EIM groups who reported up through the COO or CFO, rather than IT. These were quasi-business/quasi-IT organizations. They focused on data governance and enterprise data requirements. In some cases, they assumed data-related functions from IT, like data architecture and data quality groups. In some cases, they tried to tackle data strategy. To be successful, the heads of these organizations had to be very collaborative, working across the business area as well as

---

[10] Lee, Y. W., Madnick, S. E., Wang, R. Y., Wang, F. L., & Zhang, H., "A cubic framework for the chief data officer: Succeeding in a world of big data." *MIS Quarterly Executive*, Composite Information Systems Laboratory (CISL), MIT Sloan School of Management, March 2014, http://web.mit.edu/smadnick/www/wp/2014-01.pdf.

[11] Shaw, T., Ladley, J., & Roe, C., "Status of the Chief Data Officer: An Update on the CDO Role in Organizations Today." Dataversity Education, LLC, Fall 2014.

[12] Belissent, J., "Better Your Business Performance with a Chief Data Officer," Forrester Research, Inc., September 2015.

closely coordinating with IT. These leaders should be thought of as proto-CDOs. They may have fulfilled much of the new CDO role but without the title or clout. Too often, they were VPs and so didn't have a seat at the C-suite executives table that is needed to impact the organization's direction and culture.

When the CDO title first began appearing, an initial concern was that existing data leaders, such as EIM VPs, would be given the title but would be CDOs in name only because they were still placed too low in the organization to affect change. Although we have indeed heard of individuals in this situation, with the title but too low in the organization, this may be changing:

- Forrester Research indicates that as of late 2015, 33% of CDOs *world-wide* reported to the CEO, 32% to the CIO, 12% to the COO, and surprisingly 13% reported to the Chief Information Security Officer (CISO).[13]
- The Gartner information from late 2015 indicated that in the United States and the United Kingdom, COO, CFO, and CIO were most common, but they estimate that by 2020, fewer than 20% will report to CIOs.[14]

Gartner's "CDO Reporting Relationships Can Make or Break Your Information Management Program" discusses the impact of reporting relationships on CDO success.[15] "CDOs who are most likely to succeed report to COOs, CEOs, or CFOs, provided those CFOs care about data other than financial reporting data." This is presumably in part because reporting up through any of these positions sends the message that data is a business concern. However, Gartner indicated it may also have to do with where CIOs are placed in the organizational hierarchy: "CDOs who reported to CIOs have generally failed to make as much headway as those with reporting lines to other line-of-business functions. Many CIOs report to an executive other than a CEO. In the past 15 years of our CIO survey, Gartner has found that between 36 and 41% of CIOs report directly to the CEO. This number has been remarkable stable over time. The newly created CDO positions were then at least four levels of management removed from board decision making." Gartner's assessment was that "A CDO who is three or more layers of management removed from the CEO is a pro forma appointment, not an effective executive."

One of the advantages of having a C-level officer for data is that this person "can be held accountable for a failure of leadership in resolving data problems" (A Cubic Framework). This is true to an extent. Realistically, however, although an executive at that level does have more accountability and ability to influence change, he or she still must sway their business peers to effect change. The CDO role, by definition, has to be a collaborative and persuasive role. Although the CDO can spearhead data strategy, it must be done with active business and IT participation. This is one of the reasons it makes sense to put data governance and strategy together under the CDO.

---

[13] *Ibid.*

[14] Logan, D., Popkin, J., & Faria, M.., "First Gartner CDO Survey: Governance and Analytics Will Be Top Priorities in 2016." Gartner, January 6, 2016.

[15] Logan, D., & Bugajski, J., "CDO Reporting Relationships Can Make or Break Your Information Management Program," Gartner Research, February 25, 2015.

The CDO "enhances the effectiveness of existing governance by putting data on the organization's business agenda" (A Cubic Framework). In turn, chairing data governance bodies and managing Data Governance Operations provides the CDO with resources to drive the creation of a data strategy, as well as a collaborative mechanism to validate the strategy and socializing it.

Interest in the position has climbed quickly since the first recognized CDO was created at Capital One in 2003 (A Cubic Framework). Ten years later, the role was common in banking and financial services, with almost all major U.S. banks, asset management companies, and credit card companies having named a CDO. By the end of 2014, CDO positions also had been created in healthcare organizations, U.S. federal and state governments, and U.S. military organizations (A Cubic Framework). By the end of 2015, 45% of companies and governments worldwide had appointed a CDO.[16]

Gartner estimates the role will continue to grow and that by 2019, 66% of large organizations will have a CDO, but only 20% will be successful (First Gartner CDO Survey). Success depends on many factors, of course, but examples include reporting relationships as previously discussed, support from other C-suites, and the data management maturity of the organization. Those CDOs who have the support of the CIO have been more likely to be successful. By "undertaking business duties and responsibilities for information asset management, [the CDO can] help the CIO address longstanding problems stemming from a business's indifference to information value, reliability, usefulness, veracity, and quality." (CDO Reporting Relationships) Success also depends in part on the information management maturity of the organization, which raises the question whether an organization should pursue a formal CDO role until they reach a certain level of maturity. As of 2016, Gartner felt that "few companies have the required maturity level to embrace, support, and exploit the CDO role."[17]

5.4   Alternative Executives to Lead a Data Strategy Effort

Although the number of CDOs is increasing, not every organization will have a CDO role in the near term. This role is likely to be more common in very large organizations and more common in specific industries such as those that are regulated or subject to significant litigation.[18] If your organization doesn't have a CDO or equivalent with a different title, there may be other possibilities to consider to lead a data strategy effort.

---

[16] Belissent, J., "Better Your Business Performance with a Chief Data Officer," Forrester Research, Inc., September 2015.

[17] Logan, D., Popkin, J., & Faria, M., "First Gartner CDO Survey: Governance and Analytics Will Be Top Priorities in 2016," Gartner Research, January 6, 2016.

[18] Logan, D., Raskino, M., & Bugajski, J., "Business Case for the Chief Data Officer," Gartner Research, October 16, 2014.

CFOs' reach and influence extends across the organization. Additionally, CFOs usually understand the importance and value of data, and in regulated industries, CFOs may have some legal accountability for data. For these reasons, CFOs are good candidates to sponsor or chair an executive data governance forum and could be good candidates to lead an overarching data strategy. One advantage of at least including the CFO and his or her organization is that the CFO may be able to help quantify potential costs of poor data.[19] Given the nature of the CFO's job, however, a CFO-led data strategy is more likely to focus internally, on traditional data and service delivery.

If your organization has a Chief Risk Officer (CRO), common in some industries such as banking and financial services, he or she could be a good candidate. Like the CFO, a CRO's influence often extends across the organization and the CRO usually understands the value of data to the organization. Also like the CFO, however, a CRO-lead data strategy is more likely to focus internally, on traditional data and service delivery.

---

[19] Bowen, R., & Smith, A. R., "Developing an enterprise-wide data strategy," *Healthcare Financial Management*," April 2014.

Chapter 6
Implementing a Data Strategy

Today there is much excitement about using analytics against reams of data to gain better insight. The hope is that more data will keep us from guessing about what is most suitable for our target audience because it allows us to focus on nuanced solutions tailored to our audience. Similarly, there is excitement about accessibility to data. Between storage in the cloud and access by way of mobile devices, the promise of information at our fingertips becomes more and more real. Entire cities are even building public infrastructures to facilitate this type of instant access. For example, in 2014, Google provided the city of San Francisco with complimentary wi-fi access in select public places.[1] In an even more recent example, New York City began converting its outdated phone booths to a city-wide net of ultra-high-speed, free, wi-fi kiosks, in 2016.[2]

Our appetite for data keeps increasing. Not only do these trends provide individuals with access to more and more data, they also provide organizations with substantial knowledge on how we as individuals use data. In the NYC example, access to the wi-fi network is funded through targeted advertisements to individuals based on their network usage pattern, made possible by analytics.

There is no question, that executing automated algorithms against large datasets is an important component of managing data. Doing so is fundamental to managing increasing volumes of data and to responding quickly to end users' desires for information. The algorithms used to extract value from data are developed by data scientists—highly specialized individuals who understand statistics, software development, and ideally the business context against which they are developing software. As mentioned earlier, data scientists spend considerable time and effort preparing their data—or "wrangling" their data—for analysis.[3] That is an expensive

---

[1] See http://sfgov.org/sfc/sanfranciscowifi.

[2] See https://www.link.nyc/.

[3] Lohr, S., "For Big Data Scientists, 'Janitor Work' Is Key Hurdle to Insight," *New York Times*, August 17, 2014.

© Springer International Publishing AG 2018
M. Fleckenstein, L. Fellows, *Modern Data Strategy*,
https://doi.org/10.1007/978-3-319-68993-7_6

proposition. It also requires increasing numbers of data scientists. Industry is responding by creating tools such as data preparation tools that allow business users to get more direct access to data.[4] These tools allow business-oriented end users to manipulate source data directly, with the promise of eliminating the technical middlemen. In actuality though, these data management tools are designed to push the data wrangling to business users. In other words, these tools expect the business community to cleanse, map, unify, and enhance the data, reasoning that business users are well equipped for this.[5]

Involving business users to a greater extent in data management is a really good idea per se. Too often data has been and continues to be relegated to IT to manage. Based on our experience, preparing data for continued, systematic use requires both IT as well as business end users. Most notably, the business community's hiring of data scientists is attracting lots of attention in the data world. However, to effectively manage data, a variety of other specialists are needed in such areas as data quality, data modeling, data architecture, and data management technologies.[6]

In addition, "data wrangling," whether it is performed by data scientists or by business end users, is a somewhat misleading term because it implies an informal "rounding up and herding of cattle" approach to managing data. Such an informal process may not lend itself well to managing data at scale. The point is that data needs to be organized into a consistently consumable product that is scalable to the enterprise level. In fact, the rise of data standards across all spectra of industry reflects that the need for organization and management of data extends well beyond the enterprise and across entire industries. In our view and experience, this level of data organization requires a coordinated approach to data management through the implementation of a data strategy.[7] How, then does a data strategy attempt a coordinated approach toward data management?

The book titled *Data Strategy* published in 2005[8] puts it this way: "Working without a data strategy is analogous to a company allowing each department and each person within each department to develop its own financial chart of accounts. This empowerment allows each person in the organization to choose his own numbering scheme. Existing charts of accounts would be ignored as each person exercises his or her own creativity." It is easy to see that this would be a mess. The book goes on to highlight how to counteract such a mess from happening. It lists the components of a data strategy as a series of specific data management domains (e.g., data quality, data integration, metadata, security, and privacy), roles and responsibilities within

---

[4] See, for example, Lakshmi, R., et al. "Market Guide for Self-Service Data Preparation for Analytics," Gartner Research, March 5, 2015.

[5] Goetz M., Leganza G., & Evelson B., "Vendor Landscape–Data Preparation Tools, Forrester Research, Inc., February 2016.

[6] Redman, T. C., "Manage Data with Organizational Structure," HBR Blog Network, https://hbr.org/2012/11/manage-data-with-organizationa/, November 26, 2012.

[7] A data strategy may sometimes be referred to in slightly different terms, e.g., data management strategy, or as a component of Enterprise Information Management (EIM). See the Definitions and Acronyms in Appendix D for additional detail.

[8] Adelman, S., Moss, L., & Abai, M., *Data Strategy*, Addison-Wesley Professional, June 15, 2005.

these domains, associated performance measures, and return on investment (ROI). This book made a good start at highlighting some data management domains and their importance.

Another book, *Making EIM Work for Business*,[9] makes a strong case for organizing information by managing it as an asset, much in the same way we manage physical assets. Enterprise Information Management (EIM) is defined as "a program to treat data and all other types of enterprise information as assets." There is much to be said for managing data and information more formally just like physical assets. Managing physical assets means tracking them very closely. Organizations track the cost and revenue throughout physical assets' life cycles. This helps organizations more accurately build the potential cost, revenue, and risk related to physical assets into their overall business strategy. This is not something organizations currently do with data primarily because guidelines and rules surrounding data valuation as an asset are immature. However, it is a good idea, one that is likely to evolve, and would be very useful to a data strategy.

The concept of managing data in the same way as physical assets is still evolving, but several data management domains that do encompass aspects of treating data as an asset have evolved. These data management domains help to define and track data consistently and authoritatively. They focus, for example, on defining data succinctly; ensuring its quality; keeping data secure and ensuring its privacy; conveying how data is stored, exchanged, and consumed; and creating more formal roles and responsibilities for managing data. Each of these data management domains applies useful techniques for managing the various aspects of data.

Much of this book is focused on key data management domains that are integral to a data strategy. This book highlights several, but not all, data management domains. We chose these domains because we find ourselves involved with them frequently, consider them particularly relevant, and in some cases, are able to offer insight in addition to what can be found elsewhere. For the reader who wants to explore additional data management domains not covered in this book, we discuss several data management frameworks and include references to them in the appendices.

With names like data quality, data architecture, data governance, data privacy and security, data sharing, analytics, and master data management—to name a few—these data management domains are likely terms many of us hear more and more frequently. We understand that these terms are indicative of improved, underlying organization and management of data, and we know from personal experience, industry literature, and stories from our co-workers, about the challenges associated with data management. Yet, data management is often overlooked for many reasons, including that:

- Until recently, data management has often been blindly consigned to the IT department.
- Until recently, data management was often defined very narrowly to include only a limited set of responsibilities like data modeling and metadata repository management.

---

[9]Ladley, J., *Making EIM Work for Business*, Elsevier Inc., 2010.

- Organizations do not feel comfortable with data management because formal data management is just beginning to be ingrained into corporate culture.
- Data management practices are expensive to implement.
- Organizations have already spent significantly on tools they were promised would help better manage data, including sophisticated databases, customer relationship software, and enterprise resource management tools.
- Organizations understand intuitively that they must treat data as an asset (because loss of their data can spell disaster), but data as an asset is squishy, and the laws, standards, and guidelines on data management are immature and not consistently documented.
- There is a misperception that big data and analytics supplant the need for a data strategy and data management, rather than being part of both.
- Although business is becoming increasingly interested in data, the techniques necessary for a data strategy and for data management are unclear to the business.

We have all witnessed data management struggles like manually manipulating data every month to generate an enterprise-level report; or integrating data from one part of the organization with another organizational component; or having no clear understanding of our customer; or not being able to reproduce a snapshot of our environment from a year or two ago (versus the current state of business). Many other examples exist. Sometimes the inability to manage data is as fundamental as not even having a good inventory of data assets.[10] This costs organizations money and increases operational risk. It can even result in embarrassment for the organization, for example, in cases where customer-facing data is wrong. Accordingly, data management continues to evolve toward more formality.

Each data management domain contributes to a successful data strategy in important ways. Something as simple as having a business glossary, a registry of consistently applied terms for data representations of products and services, can be very useful. The same can be said of other data management domains or even components thereof. For example, improving the quality of data input, maintaining data models, having an enterprise data warehouse, or applying a data sharing standards are all worthwhile endeavors. The list goes on. However, it is the coordinated approach of data management domains that yields even greater benefits. As a result, a coordinated approach to data management helps an organization better assess the value of its data and, in turn, align its data strategy with its business strategy.

Together, data management domains offer a consolidated way to manage and fully leverage data, in other words, a data strategy. Each domain is dependent on other domains to succeed. Even when implementing a data management domain in relative isolation, an organization will be forced to apply aspects of other data management domains if it wants to be successful. *This point is worth repeating:*

---

[10]We refer here to data architecture components that can include data models, a business glossary, and data lifecycle diagrams, techniques we address later in this book. Such components provide a good picture of what data an organization has. For more detail, refer to the Data Architecture chapter.

Successfully implementing even an isolated data management domain requires also implementing parts of other data management domains.

Consider, for example, master data management. A simple case may be applying a master data standard to a value list for a particularly important value set, say, country code or facility location. Mastering this data not only involves gaining agreement on the value set, but also agreeing on a process to manage changes to the dataset (data governance), on where to store the dataset, and on how to disseminate the information (data architecture). In each case, the scope of data governance and data architecture would be very narrow and limited to the targeted master data. This is both necessary and good. It is necessary because without the application of these additional two data management domains, master data management cannot be successful. It is good because it allows for a very incremental approach to building a coordinated approach to data management. Beginning with a narrow focus allows the allocation of fewer resources and an approach that is easily adjusted to optimize success.

Another example might be data sharing. In this use case, the team must consider what data can be shared, with whom the data will be shared (data quality, data security, and privacy), and to what extent the data might have to be transformed to accommodate a mutual standard (data architecture). These are just two examples of many.

It is common for a data strategy to begin with a small, coordinated subset of data management domains. Such a data strategy might have its primary focus in even a single data management domain, but with an understanding that other domains must also be addressed to be successful. This type of approach is poised to succeed, grow, and mature over time. Depending on what is already in place, a data strategy may be crafting a coordinated approach among existing but siloed efforts to build a unified approach within the organization. Very likely it will include the formalization of informal current initiatives such as data stewardship.

How does an organization decide where to begin? A data strategy that encompasses all aspects of data management is uncommon for several reasons. First, and of greatest importance, a data strategy must take the most critical business needs into account. The business will want improvements to its process and bottom line sooner rather than later. By default, this means focusing on the data management domains and specific subsets of critical data that will solve the most pressing business issues quickly. Second, it is important for any organization to understand the data management infrastructure already in place because this can be leveraged quickly. Several important business needs may be rapidly met if an organization's data management infrastructure is sufficiently mature. Third, an all-inclusive data management strategy is an overwhelming task requiring enormous amounts of time and resources. Such a broad approach to data management will have trouble isolating critical business issues and orienting the data strategy accordingly. This makes it very expensive without a clear understanding of the benefits. It is fraught with risk of failure versus an incremental approach that can be adjusted along the way. It is important for an organization to be clear about its need for and expectations of data management as well as to scope efforts accordingly.

Thus we will examine the approach to a data strategy for a given organization based on these three factors:

- What are the organization's most pressing business problems?
- What is the organization's current data management environment, and what pain points is the organization experiencing in this infrastructure?
- What is the scope of the data strategy an organization wants to tackle?

6.1   Business Strategy As a Driver for Data Strategy

Let's begin with a short primer on business strategy. A business strategy exists to maximize profit, minimize cost, and manage risk. This does not necessarily translate into spending the least amount of money possible or making the most amount of money without contextual awareness. Organizations begin by asking themselves questions about their goals and often develop approaches based on their values, vision, and purpose to differentiate themselves. This allows organizations to target and serve a specific customer base. For example, if one of an organization's values is to provide superior customer service, there is an associated up-front cost that the company might aim to recoup through things like loyalty and higher end products and services.

In the public sector and in certain industries like banking and healthcare, compliance is a major driver. To highlight this perspective, Leandro Dalle Mule and Thomas Davenport argue that a data strategy can be separated into "offensive" and "defensive."[11] Data defense, the authors argue, is about minimizing risk and focused on data management areas such as data privacy, data security, data quality, and data governance. Alternatively, data offense focuses on increasing the organization's competitive position, resulting in increased revenue, profit, and customer satisfaction. Hence, an organization that has a business strategy more focused on revenue and profit might develop a data strategy that is more offensive, whereas one with a business strategy more geared toward compliance might develop a data strategy that is more defensive. The authors clearly state that all organizations need both defensive and offensive data strategies, but that the balance of where emphasis is placed depends on the business model. They also emphasize that the importance of managing data strategically has become central to any business and is growing.

In an ironic twist, author Brian Tracey, in his book *Business Strategy*, states that the first phase to determining a business strategy is to answer a key set of questions by evaluating data.[12] The clear implication here is that, in order to formulate a good business strategy, good data is required. Access to good data, in turn, requires thoughtful data and information management. To this end, the strategist can either

---

[11] Dalle Mule, L., & Davenport, T., "What's your data strategy?" *Harvard Business Review*, May-June 2017.

[12] Tracey, B., "Business Strategy (The Brian Tracey Success Library)," AMACOM, April 22, 2015.

tap its own data or perhaps purchase it externally, though purchasing data arguably depreciates its competitive advantage.

Michael E. Porter's five-forces competition model is a common approach to modern-day strategic thinking. This model is a framework that allows analysts to estimate the level of competition in an industry. Porter's five forces include:

1. The threat of substitute products or services
2. The threat of established rivals
3. The threat of new entrants
4. The bargaining power of suppliers
5. The bargaining power of customers[13]

By evaluating a multitude of factors within these five forces, a company can help answer questions as to whether or how it might operate in a specific market. It is easy to see that with this model, too, good data is crucial to effectively evaluating an organization's strategic business approach.

Many techniques—like value chain analysis, product differentiation, market forecasting, and others—help organizations formulate a strategic position. Some of these techniques—like policy analysis, compliance, or legal analysis—may be more qualitative in nature. Many, though, are quantitative and require access to good data. And even in the case of qualitative analyses, obtaining access to the right content rests on well-organized information, lest an outdated or incorrect policy or legal basis be used to formulate a strategy.

Companies will seek out specific niches of customers, products, or services. Each organization will a have its own approach to marketing, maybe even giving a product or service away for free in order to draw attention to other products and services. It may strategically enter markets based a litany of factors from perceived advantages in barriers to entry to expected cost/revenue/risk benefits. Some companies are disruptors and create new marketplaces; others leverage economies of scale; still others use their know-how to enter markets with new technologies, better services, or lower prices. In each instance, reliable access to good data and information is key.

In the case of the federal government, the Government Performance Results and Modernization Act of 2010 (GPRA Modernization Act)[14] requires all agencies to produce a strategic plan at the beginning of each Administration. These plans must outline long-term goals and the actions the agency intends to take to achieve these goals. The act explicitly acknowledges that agencies' "missions, programs, and strategies" are statutory in nature. Thus agencies are limited in their creativity to exploit new opportunities. Primarily they are expected to be descriptive of meeting their statutory obligations as well as respond to analyses of their operating environment.

---

[13] See "Porter's Five Forces Analysis," https://en.wikipedia.org/wiki/Porter%27s_five_forces_analysis

[14] See "GPRA Modernization Act of 2010," https://www.gpo.gov/fdsys/pkg/BILLS-111hr2142enr/pdf/BILLS-111hr2142enr.pdf.

The approach an agency is expected to take in publishing its strategic plan is outlined in Section 210 of the Office of Management and Budget (OMB) Circular A-11.[15] Each agency posts its goals on the public-facing website Performance.gov. In doing so, each agency is meeting the Open Government Directive[16] to make its processes and information transparent, inclusive of public participation, and collaborative in working with agency partners. Interestingly, here too one of the cited objectives is to "Improve the Quality of Government Information," directly implicating the tight-knit relationship between an agency's strategic objective and its ability to manage data.

Circular A-11 also references the Open Data Executive Order,[17] which mandates that federal agencies manage "government information as an asset." More specifically, the Open Data Executive Order states that agencies collect and create information in a way that supports downstream processing and dissemination. In addition, this Executive Order cites several related guidelines and mandates, all significantly addressing how data and information must be managed.[18] Thus managing data is a de facto part of federal strategic plans.

Also mentioned the OMB circular is the alignment of openness of information consistent with the Federal Records Act. The original act, enacted in 1950, addresses the requirement to manage the creation, maintenance, and disposition of federal records.[19] In 2014, the act was amended to address conditions under which presidential records are made public and to limit the emailing of records using nonofficial email accounts.[20] This law too, by specifying how information is managed, directly relates to the proper organization and management of data because records are tagged with metadata and the quality of tagging can determine the success or failure of complying with the proper access to and management of records.

It is imperative for a data strategy to align with the business strategy and to prioritize its goals around the most pressing operational needs of the organization. As we have seen, each business is likely to have a somewhat different strategy, and in each case, the strategy is likely to be significantly aided by data. Similarly, governmental strategies are based on statutes and operational efficiency. They must not only document how well they are performing, but they also have mandates to share this data widely and leverage it effectively. In either case, an organization

---

[15] See OMB Circular A-11 (2015), https://obamawhitehouse.archives.gov/omb/circulars_a11_current_year_a11_toc.

[16] See Presidential Memorandum on Open Government Directive, December 8, 2009, https://obamawhitehouse.archives.gov/sites/default/files/omb/assets/memoranda_2010/m10-06.pdf.

[17] See Presidential Memorandum "Open Data Policy—Managing Data as an Asset," May 9, 2013, https://obamawhitehouse.archives.gov/open/documents/open-government-directive.

[18] Refer to the Records Management References section in Appendix C for a more exhaustive list of federal data management-oriented guidelines.

[19] See Federal Records Act of 1950, https://www.gpo.gov/fdsys/granule/USCODE-2011-title44/USCODE-2011-title44-chap31.

[20] See "Presidential and Federal Records Act Amendments of 2014," https://www.congress.gov/bill/113th-congress/house-bill/1233.

attempting to align its data strategy with its business strategy must also ask itself the fundamental question: What data does my organization need to develop and execute its business strategy?

At this point, we have a business strategy and understand our business goals. We also have an idea of major pain points and their priority to the business, and we now fully understand that data is key to addressing them. To focus on the best data management technique(s) in addressing one or another pain point, we can begin by breaking the question into more succinct data management domain-specific questions. This will allow us to narrow the focus of a given pain point and employ the right data management domain(s) to address it. The following list of sample questions offers more detailed context. Though not exhaustive, the list provides examples of key data management questions that, when addressed, are likely to positively impact the business.

Data Architecture

- What data exists within my organization and where is that data located?
- What are the authoritative sources for key information within my organization?
- How critical to my business are near-real-time information and event-driven processing?
- What need does my organization have that requires us to analyze very large amounts of data?
- How important is it for my organization to be able to reconstruct historical data?

Data Governance

- What data is most important in running my daily business? Who is responsible and accountable for it?
- How can my organization reduce the risk of making business decisions based on poor or incorrect data?
- What need and capability does my organization have to revert to manual processing as a secondary process, and how will we manage associated data?
- What are the right metrics to focus on and the right data to support those metrics?

Data Quality

- What is the required degree of data quality for different data in my organization based on how we use that data?
- How can my organization meet its need for data accuracy, timeliness, completeness, relevance, understandability, believability, and so on?

Data Privacy and Security

- What level of privacy must/should my company's data conform to?
- How does my organization accommodate timely access to confidential data and information?

Data Integration

- What data is my organization sharing or planning to share, and with whom? What data is my organization mandated to share? What useless data is my organization sharing?
- How many different lines of business exist within my organization, and to what degree does data in one overlap with data in another? To what degree is the same data re-stored across lines of business?
- What data does my organization plan to obtain from a third-party and how will this data be integrated?

Metadata Management

- What is the need for my organization to manage digitized content?
- Does my organization need to combine structured and unstructured data?
- How can my organization comply with legal obligations to find required information (e.g., documents, emails, structured data) and also limit legal liability by destroying data and information no longer needed?

Master Data Management

- How can my organization unify key reference data, like country code or facility, at the enterprise level?
- How does my organization accommodate a person-centric view of information?
- What information sources should my organization leverage to build a robust master profile, and how should that data be disseminated?

Answers to these types of questions will help draw out the data management domains best suited to support addressing the most pressing business needs. Typically, aspects of more than one data management domain are needed as part of an effective data strategy. An organization must start with an approach that solves one or more business issues. As we will see, the maturity of an existing data management infrastructure and available resources are also significant factors in this decision.

6.2   Existing Data Management Infrastructure As the Driver of Data Strategy

In addition to aligning its data management priorities with its business needs, an organization can evaluate its existing data management infrastructure. To do so involves assessing and leveraging the artifacts, processes, and tools already in place. Understanding the data management infrastructure and knowing what is working and what needs improvement will further help an organization formulate its data strategy.

Many organizations have made some headway with data management, either formally or informally. Often this progress exists within individual departments or even projects. Consider, for example, data models. Physical data models at the system level almost always exist. Such physical models can be automatically reverse engineered into bare-bones logical data models. Often, logical data models already exist as well. Logical data models may contain additional information, such as descriptions, metadata, and possibly business rules that are useful to data management. Data models or their components may also exist at higher levels. For example, some organizations have an enterprise data model that portrays the organizational data standards to which all data models should comply. Or, perhaps a set of common subject areas or one or more business glossaries exist locally and can be leveraged.

Another artifact that can be leveraged is a master system inventory. Such an inventory can sometimes be generated automatically from things like a service bus or information stored in database system tables. It may even be possible to depict this output graphically and show all connections each system has with every other system. Documenting how data stores and/or applications are connected provides data architects with a starting point for how data may flow across the organization. This can serve as a useful basis for a data asset inventory.

Sometimes data standards have been implemented at the local level. Such standards may also foster the documentation of a data asset inventory in that they specify how different parts of the organization refer to data terms and potential business rules that are applied. This may even be an opportunity for a department within a large organization to share its artifacts with the enterprise. For example, this type of local initiative, with a set of robust metadata standards, was worked out and documented and then made publicly available by the Bureau of Fiscal Services.[21]

Other examples of data management assets that are sometimes already in place include well-functioning and well-documented enterprise data warehouses, data marts, and business intelligence applications. These are the likely sources of key enterprise-level reports. Analyzing these reports typically yields an understanding of an organization's perceived authoritative data sources. Because data warehouses reflect historical snapshots of key data over time, examining their data models often also provides a good understanding of the type of data that matters most to the business. Examination of the extraction routines used to populate a data warehouse can yield important data lineage information. Furthermore, business intelligence tools often include a business semantic layer that frequently renames data fields in more user-friendly terms. Reviewing these terms provides a good indication of potential naming standards that make sense to the business.

More types of data management assets are possible and are covered in each data management chapter in greater detail. Such data assets provide a good basis for any data strategy initiative. Often what is missing is an integrated, formalized approach

---

[21] See, for example, the Bureau of the Fiscal Service within the Department of Treasury has created a publicly available a data registry (https://www.transparency.treasury.gov/dataset/data-registry) in which they publish a long list of attributes and associated standards.

to data management. This includes a formal approach to localized tasks that people are already undertaking in an informal way to the best of their ability, given their other, full-time work load.

Sometimes organizations have in place people and processes that may not even appear to be related to data management. For example, an organization may have put a governance processes in place, such as an internal review board (IRB). Part of the board's function might be to ensure that the project meets specific criteria before going into production. However, this governance process may not adequately address data management. Its procedures may not ensure that data stewards are involved or review the use of data standards, use of authoritative sources, creation of sufficient and correct metadata, data integration with other initiatives, and so forth. However, it is quite possible that some of the same people involved in such an IRB can be effectively leveraged as part of a data strategy.

Similarly, other formal or informal data management is likely to exist within the organization, and in each case, some of the people and processes involved might be tapped as part of a more formal, comprehensive data strategy. Some examples might include:

- Many organizations have some employees, either on the business side or in IT, who are performing some level of informal data stewardship. This may be reflected by a business-side subject matter expert who is vigilant about data in his or her business domain, and how that data is recorded; or it might be a person from the IT department who has developed an effective way to compile enterprise-level quarterly reports, often including a series of automated and manual steps.
- An organization may have an enterprise architecture office that maintains many useful information management artifacts, such as a data dictionary, a conceptual enterprise data model, enterprise- or application- level logical or physical data models, a metadata repository, a data asset inventory, key business processes, and so forth. Responsibilities for the enterprise architecture office may be loosely defined and their resources tapped voluntarily on an informal, project-to-project basis.
- Many organizations have one or more data warehousing and business intelligence teams that integrate data from a host of systems and transform and prepare this data to facilitate consistent enterprise and ad hoc reporting. Each team may be protective of their data warehouse, and each warehouse may have some of the same data; however, coordination among these teams may be limited.
- An organization may have data scientists who use a multitude of data and information stores, both internal and external, to glean new data patterns. These data scientists fulfill their jobs very well, finding many new correlations among data; however, how the surfaced data integrates with the legacy data environment can be an afterthought, and repeated inquiry may warrant constant adjustment to the underlying availability of data sources.
- Virtually all organizations have a legal department, and they often have a need to quickly identify data and information in lawsuits and to accommodate freedom

of information act (FOIA) requests. They execute, monitor, and ensure proper privacy, information discovery, FOIA requests, information archival, and data exchange standards. This is done for paper records, digitized historical and current records, and even for emails. However, this is done in isolation. The information cannot be effectively integrated with other, more structured data that exists within application databases.

- In the public sector, the federal government is required to publish System of Record Notices (SORNs)[22] to disclose to the public how the government is using their personal data, and it is required to author privacy impact assessments (PIAs) for systems with sensitive data. These documents can clarify the data architecture. Authors of these documents may have a good understanding of how systems and data interact with each other.

- Data administrators, including database administrators (DBAs) who manage high data availability and application administrators who ensure data quality input in their product, are another option. Though these administrators work judiciously at the database and application levels, they have no incentive to manage data consistently at an enterprise level.

The amount of data management infrastructure, whether formal or informal, that exists within an organization is a pretty good reflection of the time and resources already being dedicated to data management. It may even be a sign of too many resources being allocated because efforts are not coordinated and must be reconciled, may be duplicated, or are not in line with the organization's data management priorities.

Having aligned data management priorities to business priorities, an organization will have a good understanding of which data management domains to focus on first. With this in mind and to fully understand what is already in place with regard to a specific domain, the organization may want to perform a maturity evaluation. In addition to highlighting an organization's level of data management maturity for a given domain, these models provide guidance on how to reach greater maturity, as well as related practice areas.

Another area to examine is data management tools. Big organizations, including many federal agencies, often have a large variety of tools to accommodate similar needs. This is no different with data management. Although it may be impractical to limit the organization to fewer tools, examining how these tools define and use data provides insights on potential data management similarities and differences. Such insight can be used going forward to better integrated data management practices.

In reviewing an organization's existing data management infrastructure, the examiner may also find data management practices that are not in line with an organization's data management—and business—priorities. For example, there is a

---

[22] It is important to differentiate between SORNs and architectural systems of record (SOR). The concept of SORN dates to the 1974 Privacy Act which mandates the publishing in the Federal Register of any IT or paper file system "that contains information on individuals and retrieves the information by a personal identifier." An architectural system of record, on the other hand, denotes an authoritative IT system in which data originates.

strong tendency for organizations today to incorporate big data analytics into their data management frameworks. It is important, when examining the organization's data management priorities, to evaluate to what extent such a grand and expensive undertaking is required. Certainly, if an organization is analyzing large-scale fraud patterns or health patterns, big data analytics makes a lot of sense. However, an organization will need to invest significantly in order to organize, store, and query new data sources and to effectively integrate the results. One example of this is the recent trend of law enforcement toward having more and more officers wear body cameras. Law enforcement agencies are finding that the amount of data these cameras generate is unexpectedly expensive to store and may be quite difficult to organize and query.[23]

6.3   Determining the Scope of the Data Strategy Initiative

As mentioned earlier, a data strategy can begin by focusing on a few data management domains, or even a single one, needed to solve a specific business issue. This might work well to solve a particularly thorny and urgent problem quickly. The key lies in solving the business problem at hand with an eye toward a more comprehensive data strategy. Thus, when addressing data quality, it makes sense to solve it in a way that expands the foundation for more robust data governance; when solving data interoperability, it is useful to incorporate data standards as broadly as practical; when embarking on big data and data analytics, it is important to think about how this new and large volume of data will be integrated with the existing data infrastructure.

Data strategies can and do focus on specific business issues. For example, an organization that wants to market more effectively to its customers (or provide better customer service) may have as its top priority a way to minimize customer duplicates (i.e., improved master data management). An agency that wants to better identify information needed in legal proceedings may focus on records management and eDiscovery. And an organization in which the data has been compromised has an immediate need to focus on data security.

Like any enterprise-level initiative, a data strategy is incremental in nature and must build on existing practices. In the previous sections, we discussed how to narrow a data strategy in accordance with the business strategy and how to align existing data management artifacts, processes, and tools with such a strategy. Often the scope of a data strategy so defined is still deemed too large in terms of cost or risk. In practice, there are additional ways to initially scope an organization's data strategy, both vertically and horizontally.

---

[23] Mearian, L., "As police move to adopt body cams, storage costs set to skyrocket," *Computerworld*, September 3, 2015, http://www.computerworld.com/article/2979627/cloud-storage/as-police-move-to-adopt-body-cams-storage-costs-set-to-skyrocket.html.

Vertical scoping entails managing the depth to which a data management domain is applied. For example, when tackling master data management, an organization might initially focus on key reference data. Such an approach would allow a team to implement master data management in a modest way, solving a useful and simple business need. After a successful outcome, the team may want to expand its efforts to the more complex management of customer or product data. Another way to scope vertically is by leveraging existing human capital. For example, a data governance initiative sometimes begins with an IT resource such as the data steward, later translating this function to a business resource. Frequently, organizations also scope their data management efforts horizontally. That is, they execute data management at a more local level than at the enterprise level, perhaps across multiple departments involved in the same line of business.

When narrowing the scope this way, it is important that the organization follow a disciplined approach to data management. One useful resource to help accomplish this is to reference a data management maturity model as a guideline. For example, consider the CMMI Data Management Maturity (DMM) Model.[24] This model details relative organizational maturity within several specific data management domains. The model also addresses maturity specific to a data management strategy. It presents the practitioner with the types of procedures and artifacts to be managed at various stages of maturity. In addition to highlighting artifacts and practices required for a given maturity level, data management maturity models typically also specify related data management domains. An organization's data strategy will differ based on its data management maturity level. Data management maturity models are described in more detail in Appendix A.

Another consideration for scoping data management might be focusing first on foundational data management domains that are fundamental to the overall effectiveness of data management. The Data Management Body of Knowledge (DMBOK) identifies data governance as one such underlying domain. By placing data governance in the center of their circular framework schematic and surrounding it with all the other data management domains, the DMBOK clearly highlights data governance's fundamental involvement in all data management areas. Another data management domain that many practitioners consider foundational is data architecture—the management and diagraming of where data is stored and how it flows across the enterprise. This domain, too, touches most other data management domains. Artifacts such as a business glossary, a data asset inventory, and data models are often among the first artifacts sought in data management. They are also often readily available to some extent, though they may be local in nature rather than at the enterprise level.

The CMMI Data Management Maturity Model highlights five data management practices that are foundational to data management. In addition to assessing and leveraging the strength of an organization's data management practice(s), CMMI states that "the model is also useful, in whole or in part, as a front-end activity for data infrastructure transformations, large analytics implementations, master data

---

[24] CMMI Institute, "Data Management Maturity (DMM) Model," Ver. 1.0, August 2014.

Table 6.1 CMMI's Data management maturity model categories

Data management category	Description[a]
Data management strategy	Create, communicate, justify, and fund a unifying vision for data management
Data quality	A business-driven strategy and approach to assess quality, detect defects, and cleanse data
Data operations	Systematic approach to address business drivers and processes, building knowledge for maximizing data assets
Platform architecture	A collaborative approach to architecting the target state with appropriate standards, controls, and toolsets
Data governance	Active organization-wide participation in key initiatives and critical decisions essential for the data assets

[a]Note: The CMMI DMM Model also includes a set of supporting services that support "adoption, execution, and improvement of data management processes, including measurement and analysis, process management/quality assurance, risk management, and configuration management

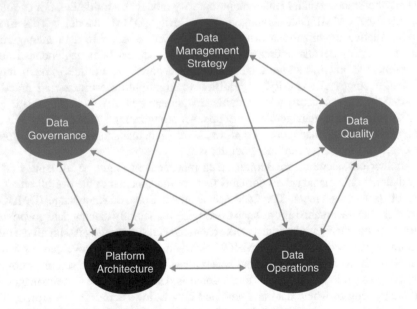

Fig. 6.1 CMMI's Data management maturity model categories

management solutions, and similar purposes."[25] These front-end data management categories are described in Table 6.1 and Fig. 6.1.

In a recent paper,[26] Peter Aiken points out that together the DMBOK and the CMMI DMM Model highlight the foundational capabilities on which to build advanced data

---

[25] CMMI Institute, *op. cit.*, p. 3.

[26] Aiken, P., "Succeeding at Data Management—BigCo Attempts to Leverage Data," *Journal of Data and Information Quality (JDIQ)*, Vol. 7, Is. 1-2, May 2016, http://dl.acm.org/citation.cfm?id=2893482.

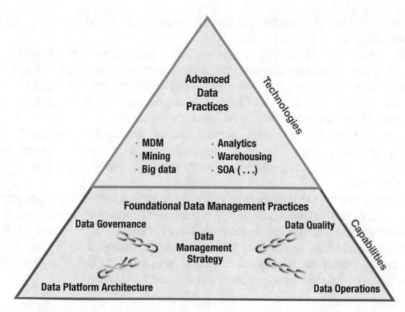

Fig. 6.2 Data management practices hierarchy

management practices. He explicitly depicts advanced data management domains that rest on foundational data management domains. The Data Management Practices Hierarchy diagram in Fig. 6.2 reflects the author's argument.

The author makes a couple of other points worth mentioning:

- Foundational data management practices rely on each other and are only as good as the weakest link. This reinforces the earlier point that to effectively deploy any data management domain, other domains are needed to some extent.
- For advanced data management domains, organizations have frequently relied on vendor-driven, technology-based approaches. However, without the underlying foundational domains, advanced technologies will underperform.

Not everyone will agree on exactly what constitutes foundational data management practices and what constitutes more advanced practices. For example, CMMI incorporates metadata management into data governance, one of its foundational data management practices, whereas others may explicitly define metadata management as a foundational data management domain. Other types of nuances also exist. Organizations may launch data management domains that are narrowly scoped but generally considered more advanced. For example, an organization may have a critical need to manage a universal list of locations. This type of modest master data effort can be executed in a foundational way and doesn't require technology. Of course, to be successful, it would need to incorporate some data governance (e.g., how are changes to the list managed over time), some data architecture (e.g., how is the list stored, updated, and shared), some metadata, and possibly components of other foundational domains.

Narrowing the data strategy in this way allows the organization to incrementally mature its data management practices. Although this type of scoping may seem obvious, it is important to recognize the difference between setting a narrow scope simply due to lack of resources or political will versus scoping in a coordinated, incremental way with data management in mind. The former approach is likely to yield many inconsistencies and duplications, resulting in frustration and re-work. The latter approach, though costlier up front, better avoids even more expensive data management inconsistencies and data mishaps down the road.

Most practitioners will agree that, generally speaking, certain data management practices are clearly more advanced and cannot be effectively accommodated without a strong data management foundation. For example, an organization would be taking on high risk by forging into big data analytics without a solid grasp of data governance, data architecture, metadata management, and data quality. To be effective, some fundamental data management practices must be executed.

6.4   Skills Needed for a Data Strategy

Crafting and executing a data strategy require business skills as well as data skills. As previous sections have shown, a data strategy must be developed in the context of meeting business objectives. Therefore, people intimately familiar with a given business and its industry are key to developing and executing a data strategy. In addition, data management experts are also key to both the design and execution of a data strategy. They are the people who understand the data management domains, how the existing data management infrastructure can be leveraged, and how to align it with business objectives.

Ideally, the people who design and implement a data strategy will have experience in both the business and data management. With the increasing interest in using large amounts of data to provide business insight, this is coming a bit more to fruition. Business-side executives' as well as analysts' interest in data has made them aware of data's potential to the business. This, in turn, has shifted some of the responsibility for data management to the business side from the IT side to which data management has historically (and often blindly) been relegated.

However, to effectively design and execute a data strategy requires not only business- and IT-side input, but input by people at all levels with experience in managing data across one or more of the domains discussed in this book. Organizations are usually staffed with people who understand and manage the business as well as technologists who manage a wide variety of an organization's technology infrastructure, ranging from networks to security. Such traditional staffing models do not account for data management professionals, attuned to managing data within the business and technology framework. This lack of data management professionals is evidenced by the growing trend in organizations to bring a Chief Data Officer (CDO) on board. The intent of the CDO is to lend a stronger voice to data as part of the organizational fabric.

Bringing a CDO on board can be a step in the right direction. It makes a statement that the organization intends to raise the importance of data as part of its business. However, Chief Data Officers can be more symbolic rather than effective if not provisioned with adequate authority and resources.[27] What is required are resources who understand data at both the executive as well as the operational levels. Having data management represented at the executive level ensures that a data strategy is designed properly and sufficient resources—both in terms of people and budget—are allocated. Data management resources at the operational level are also needed. These are the people who execute the data management domains integral to a data strategy, domains like data governance, data architecture, data security, and all the others. The exact skills required will differ based on the given business issue and relevant data management domains. These skills are covered in more detail in each of the sections on specific data management domains.

In the federal sector, the appointment of a Deputy Chief Technology Officer for Data Policy and Chief Data Scientist[28] highlights the growing importance being placed on data. Such appointments clearly indicate that the government recognizes data must be effectively harnessed and managed. In general, much of this focus is being placed on tapping an ever greater number of resources of information. Most of the focus on data, especially in business journals and by business-oriented firms, has been on reaping new insights from this growing body of available data. Effectively garnering and integrating this growing pool of data, however, is equally important and sometimes overlooked.

The previously mentioned example of increasing use by law enforcement of body cams as part of digital evidence management highlights potential challenges with managing large volumes of collected data. Law enforcement bodies throughout the country are embracing the wearing of body cameras as a tool to document discrepant accounts of confrontation between officers and the public. This is resulting in huge amounts of information—in this case, video—that come with both significant storage costs and the challenge of organizing the information in a way that that makes it easy to manage and retrieve.[29] Other types of digital evidence, such as internet searches and cellphone use, further exacerbate the digital evidence data management challenges. Along with that, potential policies and laws, such as those regarding search and seizure or jurisdiction related to digital evidence, are complicating how digital evidence can be used.[30] To effectively extrapolate value

---

[27] For a more detailed discussion of data oriented thinking and the rising role of the Chief Data Officer, see the Leading a Data Strategy chapter in Part II.

[28] See https://obamawhitehouse.archives.gov/blog/2015/02/18/white-house-names-dr-dj-patil-first-us-chief-data-scientist

[29] Mearian, L., *op. cit.*

[30] Goodison, E., Davis, R., & Jackson, B., "Digital Evidence and the U.S. Criminal Justice System," Rand Corporation, 2015.

from this kind of growing information pool requires that it be organized in a way that is accessible and integrated. In other words, it requires a data strategy or a coordinated approach to data management.

The skills required to design and execute a given data strategy differ based on the type of business and its priorities. The underlying data management principles, however, are the same. In terms of data management skills, both executives and operational staff who understand data management are needed. The more broadly data management skills are represented, the better the chances that data will be managed according to its value.

6.5 Change Management

We end this chapter with a short mention of change management because it is an integral part of executing an effective data strategy. Coordinating the management of data across an organization presents a fundamental shift in how the value of data is perceived within an organization and subsequent resources are managed. This most often requires change in environmental politics and culture. Attempting a significant change in an organization without also addressing culture change has been repeatedly shown to result in high failure rates.[31] Factors such as management commitment, broad-based and frequent communication, identifying the right skills, and a focus on training are important components of executing a successful data strategy.

Much has been written about how to apply these factors. Some of these aspects are covered in the section on data governance. Data governance presents a clear shift in approach, signals a dedicated focus on data management, distinctly identifies accountability for data, and improves communication through a known escalation path for data questions and issues. In fact, data governance is central to data management in that it touches on essentially every other data management function. In so doing, organizational change will be brought to a group that is newly—and seriously—engaging in any aspect of data management.

Organizational change management (OCM) as a practice is beyond the scope of this book. Designing and executing OCM practices such a communication plan and managing stakeholder transitions are important aspects of any large organizational shift, and they are key to performing an enterprise data strategy as well. This can be accomplished by building OCM resources into the design and execution of a data strategy. Incorporating change management practices will foster the transition from an organization in which departments compete for data, individuals scramble to wrangle and integrate data, and it is difficult to know how trustworthy a particular dataset is to one that uses data to help drive organizational value.

---

[31] See, for example, LaClair, J., & Rao, R., "Helping Employees Embrace Change," *The McKinsey Quarterly*, No. 4, 2002.

Chapter 7
Overview of Data Management Frameworks

As we have seen, a data strategy is the coordinated approach of executing multiple data management domains to help manage revenue, cost, compliance, and risk. This chapter presents an overview of two data management frameworks that embody these domains.[1] These frameworks describe the various domains and their relationships, and they serve as valuable resources for comprehending their components. They are useful additional references for understanding individual data management domains and, in the case of the CMMI DMM model, assessing the organization's maturity in a given area.

Developing a data strategy requires us to understand these domains and how they relate and overlap. It relies on the effective execution of one or more data management domains to meet business needs. Creating a data strategy leverages data management domains, but it is not purely a formula-based approach. Depending on our own organization (large vs. small, cutting-edge tech. vs. manufacturing, externally facing vs. internally oriented, commercial vs. public, etc.), both the business drivers and the degree to which an organization applies these data management domains toward a formal data strategy will vary. Step one is to understand the various data management domains.

The following sections highlight three data management frameworks each of which presents components and approaches that are valuable parts of data management. There are many similarities between the components of these frameworks. There are also some differences. For example, the DMBOK refers to data management areas as knowledge areas, and the CMMI DMM refers to them as categories, which are subdivided into process areas.

The frameworks differ somewhat in how they refer to respective areas of data management, as well as to the degree each framework addresses an area. For instance, each of the following frameworks denotes data quality and data governance at a high level. Other domains—such as data architecture, metadata management, data

---

[1] For a more complete list of data management frameworks, as well as additional framework details, see Data Management Frameworks in Appendix A.

© Springer International Publishing AG 2018
M. Fleckenstein, L. Fellows, *Modern Data Strategy*,
https://doi.org/10.1007/978-3-319-68993-7_7

requirements, data integration and interoperability, and others—are called out at a high level in some cases but presented in a more embedded or more dispersed way in others. Finally, some domains are not universally covered by both frameworks, including data strategy, privacy and security, and master data management.

Such differences extend to other data management frameworks and are an indication that an overall, best-practice approach to data management is still evolving. We present this overview to familiarize the reader more with the commonalities than the differences. There are many commonalities within these and other frameworks, even if they are categorized somewhat differently across frameworks. Often the differences manifest themselves in variations of approach at lower levels of detail. The reader may choose to adhere to a specific framework, while still adopting core principles that hold true across all or several frameworks. Additional information on these as well as other frameworks can be found in Appendix A.

7.1   DAMA DMBOK

One of the best-known data management frameworks is the Data Management Association's (DAMA's) Body of Knowledge (DMBOK), originally published in 2009 and undergoing an update as of 2016.[2] The DMBOK framework highlights data management domains, which the DMBOK terms "knowledge areas."

The DMBOK also uses a graphic, the knowledge area wheel, to depict these domains.[3] Knowledge areas are represented as slices of a data management pie, with the data governance knowledge area in its center. The central placement of data governance in the DMBOK framework portrays its relative importance, as seen by the DMBOK. Though there are relationships between many of the data management domains, the DMBOK framework shows how significant data governance is to data management. Table 7.1 lists descriptions for the DMBOK knowledge areas, showing some evolution from the original DMBOK in terms of how knowledge areas are classified.

7.2   CMMI DMM Model

In 2014, the CMMI Institute published its Data Management Maturity (DMM) model. As mentioned earlier, the DMM segments the various data management components into five high-level categories (data management strategy, data quality,

---

[2] DAMA International, "The DAMA Guide to the Data Management Body of Knowledge," Technics Publications, 2009. The framework for ver. 2 was published in March 2014 and is available at https://www.dama.org/sites/default/files/download/DAMA-DMBOK2-Framework-V2-20140317-FINAL.pdf; as of this writing a draft for the full publication of version 2 is available for public comment.

[3] See https://www.dama.org/content/body-knowledge.

Table 7.1 DMBOK knowledge areas[a]

DMBOK knowledge area	Description
Data governance	Planning, oversight, and control over management of data and the use of data and data-related resources. Though we understand that governance covers "processes," not "things," the common term for Data Management Governance is Data Governance, and so we will use this term
Data architecture	The overall structure of data and data-related resources as an integral part of the enterprise architecture
Data modeling and design	Analysis, design, building, testing, and maintenance (was Data Development in the DAMA-DMBOK 1st ed.)
Data storage and operations	Structured physical data assets storage deployment and management (was Data Operations in the DAMA-DMBOK 1st ed.)
Data security	Ensuring privacy, confidentiality, and appropriate access
Data integration and interoperability	Acquisition, extraction, transformation, movement, delivery, replication, federation, virtualization, and operational support (a knowledge area new in DMBOK2)
Documents and content	Storing, protecting, indexing, and enabling access to data found in unstructured sources (electronic files and physical records), and making this data available for integration and interoperability with structured (database) data
Reference and master data	Managing shared data to reduce redundancy and ensure better data quality through standardized definition and use of data values
Data warehousing and business intelligence	Managing analytical data processing and enabling access to decision support data for reporting and analysis
Metadata	Collecting, categorizing, maintaining, integrating, controlling, managing, and delivering metadata
Data quality	Defining, monitoring, and improving data quality and maintaining data integrity

[a]See https://www.dama.org/sites/default/files/download/DAMA-DMBOK2-Framework-V2-20140317-FINAL.pdf

data operations, platform and architecture, and data governance) and one additional supporting processes category. Each of the categories is further divided into three to five supporting process areas. For example, data quality is divided into the following process areas: data quality strategy, data profiling, data quality assessment, and data cleansing. Figure 7.1 shows the breakdown of the CMMI DMM model categories and process areas.[4]

For each process area, the DMM lists a purpose, provides introductory notes, and discusses topics such as goals, core questions, and related process areas. One key feature of this framework is its orientation toward assessing the organization's level

---

[4]Licensed copies of the CMMI DMM model and its details are available at https://dmm-model-individual.dpdcart.com/. An unlicensed overview of categories and process areas is publicly available in the Building Enterprise Data Management Elearning Course Companion Guide, at http://cmmiinstitute.com/sites/default/files/resource_asset/DMM%20Elearning%20Course%20Companion%20Guide.pdf.

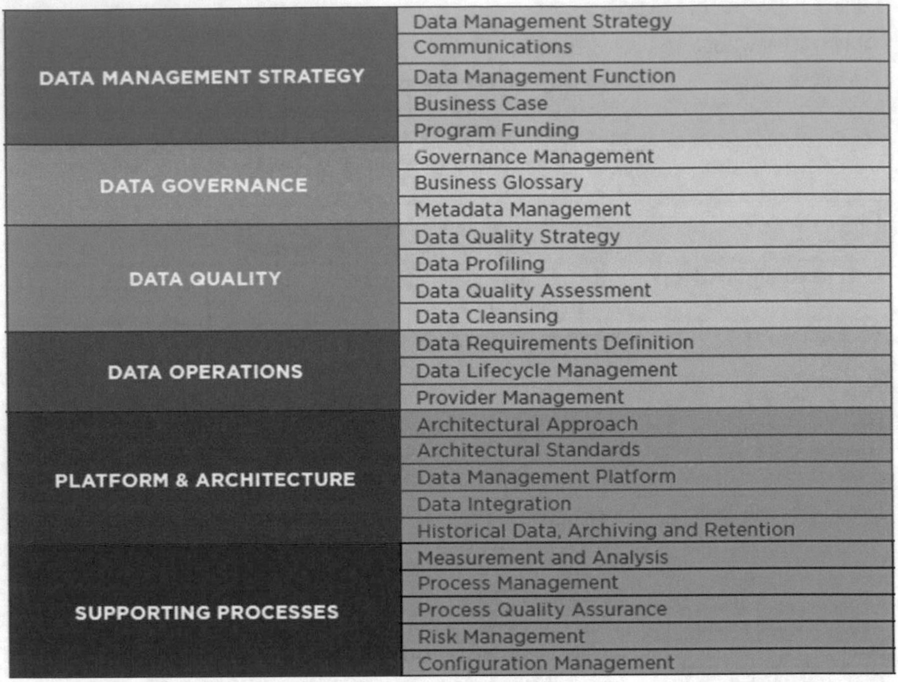

DATA MANAGEMENT STRATEGY	Data Management Strategy
	Communications
	Data Management Function
	Business Case
	Program Funding
DATA GOVERNANCE	Governance Management
	Business Glossary
	Metadata Management
DATA QUALITY	Data Quality Strategy
	Data Profiling
	Data Quality Assessment
	Data Cleansing
DATA OPERATIONS	Data Requirements Definition
	Data Lifecycle Management
	Provider Management
PLATFORM & ARCHITECTURE	Architectural Approach
	Architectural Standards
	Data Management Platform
	Data Integration
	Historical Data, Archiving and Retention
SUPPORTING PROCESSES	Measurement and Analysis
	Process Management
	Process Quality Assurance
	Risk Management
	Configuration Management

Fig. 7.1 CMMI DMM model categories and process areas

of maturity in a variety of data management areas. The DMM model applies five levels of maturity, characterized by increasing achievements: performed, managed, defined, measured, and optimized. More detailed information on the CMMI DMM model can be found in Appendix A.

7.3   Additional Frameworks

Many other frameworks serve as useful references for understanding the setdata management domains that play into a data strategy. We summarize many of these frameworks in Appendix A and point to more detailed information.

Some of these frameworks—such as the Zachman framework, The Open Group Architecture Framework (TOGAF), the Federal Enterprise Architecture (FEA) framework, and others—go beyond data management into enterprise architecture and cover some aspects of data management as a framework component. Others—such as the Data Governance Institute Data Governance Framework, National Archives and Records Administration's (NARA's) Records and Information Management (RIM) Maturity Model, or the National Information Exchange Model (NIEM)—focus on specific data management areas. Some frameworks are industry-specific and extend into details such as data models or data standards.

With the rising importance of data as part of our economy, more frameworks are constantly being developed. These frameworks overlap significantly, and they essentially cover data management, to a greater or lesser extent, in a very similar way. Together they present a set of data management areas that must be understood as part of an effective data strategy.

Part III
Data Management Domains

In this part, we cover some, but not all, data management domains. The previous part showed that domains vary somewhat between frameworks. More frameworks are presented in the appendices and both the overlap of key data management domains as well as differences in how they are expressed is evident. We consider the domains covered in this book to be key components of many data strategies.

In this part, we also turned to additional experts for certain chapters. Though the authors worked jointly with each expert to create the finished product, certain chapters in this part can be specifically attributed as follows:

Chapter	Author(s)
11. Data Quality	Mala Rajamani
12. Data Warehousing and Business Intelligence	Swami Natarajan
14. Data Privacy	Julie Snyder and Stuart Shapiro
15. Data Security	Julie Snyder and Stuart Shapiro
17. Records Management	Eliot Wilczek, Krista Ferrante, and Bob Toth

Chapter 8
Data Governance

8.1 What Is Data Governance?

The DMBOK places data governance at the center of its data management framework. So foundational to data management is data governance in the view of the DMBOK that without it, none of the other data management domains will succeed. The DMBOK defines data governance as: "the exercise of authority and control (planning, monitoring, and enforcement) over the management of data assets. The data governance function guides how all other data management functions are performed."[1]

The CMMI Data Management Maturity Model, though it does not explicitly place data governance in its visual center, defines it in equally important language with the following definition: "Develop the ownership, stewardship, and operational structure needed to ensure that corporate data is managed as a critical asset and implemented in an effective and sustainable manner."[2]

A final example we particularly like for its emphasis on business performance is: "Data governance is the discipline of administering data and information assets across an organization through formal oversight of the people, processes, technologies, and lines of business that influence data and information outcomes to drive business performance."[3] Although data management people often want to manage all data rigorously, the reality is that not all data is equal and data governance needs to prioritize what data and activities are of the most value to the enterprise, supporting business performance and managing risk.

---

[1] See DMBOK, Chap. 3 on Data Governance.

[2] See CMMI Data Management Maturity Model.

[3] Orr, J., *Data Governance for the Executive,* Senna Publishing, LLC, 2011.

© Springer International Publishing AG 2018
M. Fleckenstein, L. Fellows, *Modern Data Strategy*,
https://doi.org/10.1007/978-3-319-68993-7_8

These definitions highlight that data governance focuses on the rules and resources of how data management is executed. To whatever degree an organization wants to accomplish success within a particular data management domain—data quality, data architecture, master data management, or any of the other domains—data governance will be required to do so effectively.

Data governance is largely about collaboration, for example, connecting data producers and data consumers, and managing common or shared data for the benefit of the enterprise. It is also about "decisioning"—determining who makes decisions about data. This is not to suggest that decisions are made centrally, but rather to determine what level and specifically who can best make different types of data decisions to expedite the decision process. Sometimes if agreement at one level can't be reached, issues may be escalated and decisions made as a group. Though reaching agreement within a group takes longer, such decisions are more likely to stick and peer support or pressure can help align behavior across organizations to consider what's best for the enterprise as a whole.

A big part of data governance should be about helping people (business and technical) get their jobs done by providing them with resources to answer their questions, such as publishing the names of data stewards and authoritative sources and other metadata, and giving people a way to raise, and if necessary escalate, data issues that are hindering their ability to do their jobs. Data governance helps answer some basic data management questions. Some of these are listed in the Data Governance section in Appendix C.

Several books have been written on the components necessary for setting up and managing data governance.[4] Some variation in approach exists across these writings, but the fundamental components required to set up effective data governance are similar so we will not repeat them all here. In general, however, a data governance program includes the following components:

- Data Governance Hierarchy or Framework (described in the Who Is Data Governance section)
- Vision, Goals, and Priorities
- Data Management Principles
- Data Policies, Standards, and Guidelines
- Authoritative Sources and Other Resources for Staff
- Enterprise Data Processes
- Communications Infrastructure and Periodic Outreach Campaigns

---

[4] See, for example, Ladley, J., *Data Governance—How to Effectively Design, Deploy, and Sustain an Effective Data Governance Program,* Morgan Kaufmann, 2012.

Seiner, R. S.," Non-Invasive Data Governance—The Path Of Least Resistance And Greatest Success," Technics Publications, 2014.

Soares, S., "IBM Data Governance Unified Process," IBM Corporation, 2010.

8.1.1   *Vision, Goals, and Priorities*

Establishing scope is a prerequisite to defining an enterprise vision and goals for data management, and it involves determining the business units affected by data governance (or lack thereof) and the relevant stakeholders within those units. It also considers existing and forthcoming polices, strategies, and constraints. Finally, scope identifies the data that will be governed and data management domains required to govern this data.

The scope of a data governance program is often documented as part of a data governance charter and may evolve over time:

- If there's little enterprise buy-in for data governance, data governance might start with a specific business area and expand as buy-in improves.
- Some organizations might start with specific types of shared data, for example, a very limited set of key data for the initial phase of a master data management program, and later expand to all shared data.
- Many organizations start with traditional, structured data and later evolve to include unstructured content and records management.

If you're standing up enterprise data governance, however, defining the scope very narrowly could tie governance's hands and runs the risk that you won't be able to broaden it later. Defining the scope broadly and simply noting the initial areas of focus is a better alternative in most cases.

Authored in various combinations, a vision statement, goals, and priorities align a data governance program to the overall organizational mission and help focus both the program and corporate leadership on data management priorities. Recent publications on data governance[5] highlight the importance of aligning data governance with business needs.[6] This important recognition reflects both the need for business users to engage in data management and the actual trend in that direction. Business goals and strategies often already exist and can be cross-referenced with specific data management principles (discussed in the next section) and decomposed to data goals and priorities. Sometimes a vision and initial goals are captured as part of the process of defining data management principles. Aligning to business goals isn't a one-time activity, however, it should be revisited as the business goals change, often annually.

If a business goal is "to provide our customer with a one-stop on-line service portal," data management goals might include:

- "Formalize authoritative sources for customer data" or if you know you have issues in this area, the goal may be to "develop a customer master data capability."
- "Ensure key information for customers is shared across the enterprise timely, consistently, and correctly."[7]

---

[5] See, for example, Peyret, H., et al., "The Forrester Wave: Data Governance Tools, Q2, 2014," Forrester Research, Inc., June 24, 2014.

[6] This is opposed to a focus that incorrectly considers data governance to be a purely IT function.

[7] For additional examples of data management principles, see the Data Governance section in Appendix C.

As organizations mature, the vision, annual goals, and priorities may evolve into a more formal data strategy that is created in conjunction with data governance or at least validated through data governance as a way to ensure cross-organization buy-in.

8.1.2   Data Management Principles

Data management principles are foundational statements of organizational values. They are often aspirational and are used to convey an enterprise approach to data management. To be effective, data management principles must be treated as more than a checkbox. When asked if data is an asset, most people will agree. But if you ask what exactly that means, you'll get blank stares or a lot of different suggestions and possibly start fight. The definition of principles can be a means to begin changing behavior if approached as a process that includes reaching agreement on what principles (such as "data is an asset") mean, why it's important, and what, if any, are the implications to the organization for budget, staffing, time, processes, etc. Here is an example:

Principle: Data must be managed as an asset with real value to the organization. Rationale (What does the statement mean? Why is it important?)

Business decisions are based on accurate and timely information. As an agency asset, data and metadata have real, tangible value and should be carefully managed to ensure that the enterprise knows where data resides, understands its quality, knows who's accountable for it, and can access it when needed.

The true value of information is not realized when it remains in isolated pockets built to meet only local needs; shared, integrated information results in consistent and improved decisions. Shared Services and Systems such as an Enterprise Data Warehouse (EDW) or Master Data Management (MDM) solution can facilitate the business' access to consistent data. Note that some data will be localized and need not be managed on an enterprise level or shared. Identifying what should be shared is important because managing data at an enterprise level is expensive.

Implications (What are the challenges or even barriers to living by this principle?)

Data is owned by the enterprise, not by systems or individuals. The enterprise should recognize and formalize the responsibilities of roles, such as data stewards, with specific accountabilities for managing data. A *data governance framework* and guidelines must be developed to allow data stewards to coordinate with their peers and to communicate and escalate issues when needed. Data should be *governed cooperatively* to ensure that the interests of data stewards and users are represented and also that value to the enterprise is maximized.

The enterprise needs to understand the data it has and where it's stored (system and data asset catalog, dictionaries, models, etc.). The enterprise should designate *systems of record and other authoritative sources* as well as guidelines for making changes. The enterprise needs buy-in and commitment from both business areas and IT for this approach to achieve an effective enterprise data management environment that supports the business while managing risk and cost.

Having your data governance bodies define principles serves several purposes. It can be an effective way to educate your data governance members in a low-key way if they aren't knowledgeable in data. It's also a way to align your data governance members or at least understand who disagrees and why. And last, it's a way to begin to create a sense of ownership in your members and form a group dynamic for your governing bodies. Value comes from their shared understanding because until you reach agreement on concepts, you aren't going to have much success agreeing on policy. For instance, until you agree you need authoritative sources, you're not likely to reach agreement on the criteria for what makes a data store authoritative, let alone whether a specific data store is authoritative for customer address.

8.1.3   Data Policies, Standards, and Guidelines

Data management principles are a first step toward actionable governance and often drive the need for policies, standards, or guidelines.

The specific terms used and the degree of formality of data governance varies between organizations but tends to become more formal over time. An enterprise must decide for itself how formal its data governance should be, based on factors such as culture, priorities, and data maturity. For example:

- Some organizations might start with principles, informally agree on an aspiration data steward role toward which they will try to evolve and develop guidelines for such topics as involving stewards in defining data requirements, use of authoritative sources, modeling of data, data quality controls, etc. If you're starting from scratch, guidelines could be a good place to begin.
- A different organization, one that has a higher degree of maturity in their data management processes or a more formal culture like a branch of the military, might formalize their principles in a policy and address the same kinds of topics through directives, policies, or mandatory standards.

Figure 8.1 shows one possible evolution of a data management principle to one or more policies and then to standards. In this example, the principle of treating data as an organizational asset places accountability for data quality on data stewards. Accordingly, data standards state more specifically how data stewards must be involved to facilitate data quality. Additional examples of topics for consideration as principles, policies, and standards can be found in the Appendix C.

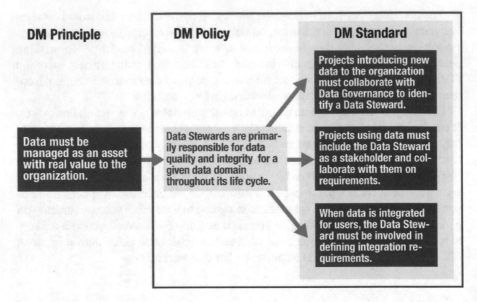

Fig. 8.1 Going from principle to policies and standards

8.1.4 Data Governance and Assurance

Assurance activities, sometimes also called enforcement or compliance, typically go hand in hand with data governance. Depending on the data management maturity and formality of the organization, how assurance is adopted varies, as shown in Fig. 8.2. The informal organization might start by simply measuring compliance, whereas the more formal organization might institute formal, procedural checks.

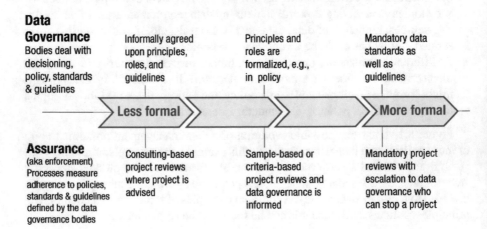

Fig. 8.2 Data governance and assurance spectrum

For example, in a more formal organization, assurance at the project level is sometimes delegated to data management or architecture groups and incorporated into
project lifecycle reviews, with data governance serving as the point of escalation.
For existing systems/processes, assurance might be incorporated into periodic risk
assessments, with data governance reviewing a sample and all data-related risks that
meet established criteria for likelihood and severity.

8.1.5   Authoritative Sources and Other Resources for Staff

Data governance should be about helping staff do their jobs. This includes providing a website or portal with such data governance information as:

- *A list of authoritative data sources,* maintained and published as a resource for
  both IT and business users across the organization. Data governance usually
  defines criteria for what constitutes "authoritative" and then collaborates with
  data architecture to identify candidates for each type of data because to evaluate
  and approve candidate authoritative sources often requires an understanding of
  the ecosystem.
- *Data governance members such as data stewards,* posted so that people know
  whom to call if they have an issue or just questions about data that they need to
  use.
- *A data governance email or phone line,* provided and monitored for those cases
  when people aren't sure whom to call or need to escalate an issue.
- *Other information and resources,* including links to metadata resources, a business glossary, business rules, data standards, or communication and management
  of data quality issues.
- *Existing assurance/compliance processes.*

8.1.6   Communications Infrastructure and Periodic Outreach Campaigns

To foster data governance requires a lot of effective communication. It includes
creating and adhering to data governance charters that specify how often data governance stakeholders meet and what their responsibilities are.[8] It requires routine
communications like agendas and meeting minutes and updates on cross-
organizational data quality issues. It also includes a communication infrastructure,
like a data governance website, mailbox, and help line, as well as branding of the
data governance organization through a communications program. It will also

---

[8] Data governance charters are discussed in more detail in the next section and examples are given
in Appendix C.

eventually include presenting metrics back to the business, possibly in the form of a dashboard. If either your executives or your employees don't know about your data governance program, you don't have data governance!

8.2   Who Is Data Governance?

Resources required for data governance are often already performing some data governance, albeit informally.[9] For example, employees with both deep knowledge of the business as well as related IT applications often take it upon themselves to ensure that only high-quality data is entered into the application. Such experts are prime candidates for data stewards in a more formal data governance framework.

Informal data stewards are limited in their ability to govern data because they lack a formal network with which to coordinate their efforts with other people working on data management. If, for example, a particular data steward is vigilant about the quality of data entered into one application, he or she has limited control over how that data is shared with and used by downstream systems. Additionally, with the lack of a formal data governance framework, it is difficult for informal data stewards to determine priorities. An informal data steward may have limited knowledge of which data issues are important to the enterprise, versus to his or her local department. What makes this even harder is that, most of the time, data stewards and other data management facilitators perform their tasks as a part-time effort of their overall responsibilities.

Formal data governance is a mechanism to better manage these situations. It explicitly engages people from all parts of the organization—from the business side and IT, and from executives to operational staff—with clearly stated roles and responsibilities. Data governance aligns data management priorities with business needs, as well as existing policies and procedures, and provides metrics and a maturity scale against which progress can be measured. It also provides a clearer escalation path for data issues and requests.

Data governance comprises (mostly) business and (some) IT executives, managers, and operational staff from across the enterprise who represent their organization's data producers and consumers. This should be a collaborative forum that understands its data in detail and also has the authority to make data decisions that stick. Participating organizations must agree to accept and support the decisions made because they are part of the decision-making process. Data governance is one of the ways in which an enterprise can promote and facilitate collaboration to achieve the culture change needed for a data strategy to be successful.

Data governance is typically structured in a hierarchical framework with an executive layer, a management layer, a data steward layer, and a data governance operations function to support and coordinate across these layers. A typical data governance framework and who participates at each level are described in more detail next.

---

[9] Ladley, J., *Data Governance—How to Effectively Design, Deploy, and Sustain an Effective Data Governance Program*, Morgan Kaufmann, 2012, p. 52.

8.2.1 Data Governance Framework

Numerous variations exist in industry depicting the layers of a data governance framework. A key characteristic of a functional data governance hierarchy is that the different levels of the hierarchy are aligned and in close communication. The straightforward framework in Fig. 8.3 has been successfully applied by MITRE Data Management.[10]

This model shows how all levels of an organization collaborate in data governance. These levels are described in more detail in the following sections.

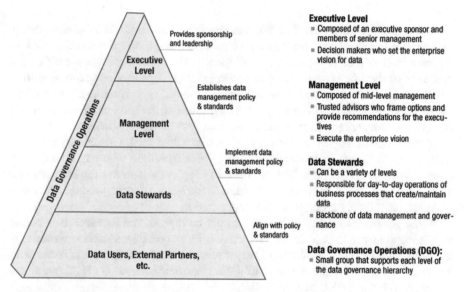

Fig. 8.3 Data governance framework

8.2.2 Data Governance Operations

In addition to (mostly) business representatives and (some) IT representatives at each level, it is a good idea to have a small number of individuals fully dedicated to the overall data governance initiative. This framework refers to those individuals as data governance operations (DGO). The DGO is the glue that ensures coordination across the levels of the data governance framework and the force that drives data governance forward. In addition to drafting material for the data governance discussion and providing meeting support for the executive- and management- level, the DGO may field data questions from data stewards and business users and track cross-organizational data issues. They may also research issues and facilitate the escalation of issues, when necessary.

---

[10] The author of this version of a data governance framework is Lorraine Fellows, principal systems engineer at The MITRE Corporation.

People in the data governance operations group understand data governance and act as the agents to facilitate data governance by closely working with each of the stakeholder groups. They help assess existing capability and organize the data governance approach. If an organization lacks the resources required for this group, the work of the data government operations group can be performed by external specialists and transitioned to organizational staff over time.

8.2.3   Executive Level

The executive level consists of decision makers (e.g., officers, administration directors or their deputies) who set the enterprise vision and tone for governing data as an asset in line with business concerns. Ideally, the executive level identifies the members of the management level to represent their organizations. The executive level also approves data management principles, policies, and standards as well as data-related strategies and roadmaps. It is the ultimate decision point for escalated issues, often involving risk, priorities, resource, and budget allocations.

In the commercial sector, the COO, CFO, or Chief Risk Officer might be the chair of this body, though there would likely be a facilitator who might be the VP under whom the DGO falls. The membership typically includes the executive of each line of business as well as others, such as the heads of legal, privacy, risk management, and so on, depending on the organization.

In the government sector, this level should be represented by executives below political appointees to provide as much continuity as possible. Members would certainly be SES-level and ideally head major mission areas within the enterprise who are major producers and consumers of data. Representation at this level optimizes that data governance decisions will stick.

It is not uncommon to create a charter at this level. At this level, a charter provides the executive a leadership framework for developing data management principles and policies that support and improve the operation of an organization's programs. It holds executives accountable for specific data governance responsibilities. An example of a charter for the executive level can be found under Data Governance Reference in Appendix C.

8.2.4   Management Level

The management level body executes the enterprise vision. It is also a trusted advisor to the executive level, for which it frames options and provides recommendations. From a strategic perspective, it is often this level that defines data management principles, policies, and standards for executive-level approval. The management-level body also collaborates with the executive level on data-related strategies and roadmap priorities. Because this level is aware of who in their organization is a good candidate for data steward, it often identifies existing data stewards. The management level might also determine the criteria for what constitutes an authoritative data source and coordinate with enterprise data architects to develop, maintain and publish a list of authoritative sources and guidance on when to use a system of record vs. an approved proxy such as a data warehouse. Depending on authority delegated by the executive level, the management level may decide escalated issues or just frame options and make recommendations to the executive level.

The management level might be chaired by the director of the DGO group and should include one or more business-side representatives from each major data producer or consumer in the enterprise. In the commercial sector, the membership might be anywhere from senior managers to senior directors or even VPs. In the government sector, the membership might be GS-14 or GS-15 level. People in the management level layer must be people that the executive level has confidence in or the hierarchy will break down. They should meet with their executive-level representative regularly. At a minimum they should meet as preparation for an executive level meeting to provide their perspective on what will be discussed and to give the executive level an update on relevant data issues.

A data governance charter at the management level is also common. A management-level charter is business-driven and facilitates communication between an organization's business units, makes recommendations to the executive level on data-related policies, standards, budget priorities, data quality, and escalated issues, and ensures the business needs are captured and considered and appropriately balanced with enterprise risk. An example of a charter for the management level can also be found under Data Governance Reference in Appendix C.

8.2.5   Data Stewards Level

If the DGO is the glue that ensures coordination across the data governance framework, data stewards are the backbone of data governance. Though the organizational level of data stewards may vary, data stewards typically manage day-to-day business processes that create data and supply it directly or indirectly to downstream business users. They maintain and publish associated metadata to provide transparency, work with known consumers to define data quality requirements/expectations, and maintain the quality of data for their respective data domain. They help to resolve data issues, conflicts, and inconsistencies within their authority and coordinate with their management level representatives. Data stewards may also participate to varying degrees in projects that create or leverage data from their domain.

Most organizations have people already performing aspects of data stewardship, even if informally. When starting out, the data governance framework needs agreement on the aspirational data steward roles and responsibilities. Subsequently, specific data stewards can be identified. It is not uncommon initially to find a mix of informal data stewards operating across both IT and business, or to have many data stewards for a particular data domain. Through more formal data governance and over time, the data stewards' jobs can be standardized, the data each steward manages can be better defined, and data stewardship can evolve to be represented primarily by the business, with support from IT.

8.3 Benefits of Data Governance

Data governance introduces some degree of formal process where informal, uncoordinated processes are likely in place. Additional formality adds some overhead, but, like formal processes in other business areas such as accounting, human resources, and procurement, it will result in significantly better outcomes and better user and customer experiences. Some of the objectives and benefits of data governance include:

- Defined authority and accountability for data. And collaboratively managed common data, at the enterprise level
- A clear escalation path for business users and data stewards to raise data issues in an efficient manner and get a timely and coordinated response
- Transparency into and improved understanding of data lineage, data quality, and data risk
- Collaboration on data issues between business areas and with IT

8.4 Implementing Data Governance

8.4.1 A Data Governance Framework

To begin, an initial approach to enterprise data governance should include establishing a data governance framework or perhaps enhancing an existing one. It is very likely that pieces of a data governance framework already exist. A partial capability, such as an executive level body, a management level body, or informal data stewards, can be a good starting point.

If a well-functioning and well-established executive level or management level exists, consider beginning with data management goals and principles. Such an approach takes time, but getting executive-level buy-in makes it more likely that the data strategy will persist even if one or two executives turn over.

If, on the other hand, strong but informal institutional data stewardship already exists, consider leveraging this. This approach can be tempting as a way to make progress more quickly, especially if specific data issues are known. However, this approach has inherent risk because it lacks buy-in at the executive level.

Exactly where an organization begins implementing a data governance framework depends in part on organizational culture and to what extent data governance is already present. In general, a purely top-down approach will likely be lengthy and costly before showing results, whereas a purely bottom-up approach will fail to engage executives sufficiently and can only go so far without executive support and engagement. It is not uncommon for an organization to begin with an approach targeted at the management level. This level can help identify the right stakeholders, both at the executive and data steward level, and also help prioritize specific data management issues. Such a two-pronged approach generates buy-in because it solves some specific data issues, and it creates the platform from which to help drive a high-level vision and principles.

8.4.2   Assessments

8.4.2.1   Current State Assessment

Even if it is a short, time-boxed effort, a current state assessment is a good first step to understanding the level of an organization's data maturity, how it compares to best practices, what pain points exist, and the current data environment in general. Such an assessment should look at existing artifacts and should include surveys and/or interviews with key stakeholders. A DGO can help drive such an assessment. It should look at all se areas:

- Known data-related pain points from both business and IT perspectives
- Existing data governance bodies and any other governance bodies that have some data role. This should include looking at existing data governance charters, memberships and participation, operational process, and accomplishments
- Data-related policies, standards, guidelines
- Data stewardship
- Depending on the organization's area of focus, data management practices in one or more of the following data management domains: data architecture and data modeling, data quality, metadata management, master data management, data warehousing, business intelligence, and analytics

8.4.2.2   Maturity Assessment

As part of the data governance initiative, the organization selects and commits to an industry-tested maturity model, such as the CMMI Data Management Maturity Model.[11] Additional assessment components are surveys that can be used both to assess overall data management maturity as well as gages of specific data issues.

Beware trying to use maturity level as a driver for data governance. Understanding the organizations maturity can be very useful within the data governance apparatus,

---

[11] CMMI Institute, "Data Management Maturity (DMM) Model, v. 1.0," CMMI Institute, 2014.

for example, within the DGO, when trying to gain an understanding of organizational pain points, planning how to move forward, and assessing overall progress. Maturity models don't sell well, however, especially in immature organizations, and those who try to promote maturity models and goals to "reach level x" risk coming across as academic. By focusing on resolving business issues, in an enterprise way, your data governance efforts likely will get more traction, and as you build out elements of an enterprise data management framework, the maturity of the organization will improve over time.

8.5   Data Governance Tools

To aid the data governance process, tools aimed at various aspects of data governance are beginning to emerge in the marketplace.[12] Because data governance is a broad domain that can and must be applied to any of the other data management domains, it is not surprising that different data governance tools take aim at data governance from different aspects. For example, some tools on the market emphasize governing data quality or metadata management or master data management, and so on. Each of these tools has developed data governance around a specific data management domain. Other data governance tools, which focus on data stewardship and collaboration to address a broader variety of data management issues, are also emerging.

All these tools serve primarily as a repository of data governance components, helping your data governance members better organize and coordinate their efforts. In some cases, the tools provide a workflow to support the data governance process. In all cases, these tools can, at best, help organize and support the work required to design and implement a data governance framework. The extent to which a given tool is helpful in addressing data governance depends on how well the organization has qualified (or is willing to qualify) its data governance effort.

---

[12] See, for example, Goetz, M., & Peyert, H., "Consider New Data Governance Software to Support Business-Led Efforts," Forrester Research, Inc., March 2014, or Peyert, H., & Goetz, M., "The Forrester Wave: Data Governance Tools, Q2 2014," Forrester Research, Inc., June 2014.

Chapter 9
Data Architecture

9.1 What Is Data Architecture?

Data architecture is a blueprint for how data is stored and flows across the enterprise over its life cycle. This sounds pretty simple. However, it is more intricate than it sounds. The focus of data architecture goes beyond individual systems to understand how data flows across systems; it goes beyond individual data stores to understand where the data is created, where it is maintained, how it is shared, and how it is changed across data stores. The focus of data architecture is also not on the hardware infrastructure, but rather on how the infrastructure network works to deliver trusted information.

All of these components—systems, data stores, infrastructure—must be taken into account as part of managing a data architecture, but they are not the drivers that should determine data architecture. Rather, they are components that come into play and work together to support how data is stored and flows.

Several different techniques are generally used to document data architecture. Some of the most common techniques include a business glossary, a data asset inventory, data standards, data models, and data lifecycle diagrams. None of these techniques by itself is sufficient to design, document, and manage data architecture. However, together they present an effective toolkit for managing data architecture.

9.1.1 Business Glossary

Because data architecture deals with how data flows and is stored across the organization, one thing that is fundamentally important is to agree on what data there is and what it means—at least for key organizational data.[1] This has implications for

---

[1] Views on where in a data management framework to place a business glossary vary. It is equally useful as part of other domains, such as metadata management, master data management, data governance, and others.

© Springer International Publishing AG 2018
M. Fleckenstein, L. Fellows, *Modern Data Strategy*,
https://doi.org/10.1007/978-3-319-68993-7_9

even the most trivial-seeming things. For example, an international organization may want to standardize the meaning of a "day" in order to report on daily totals consistently. A business glossary goes a long way toward solving this problem by documenting agreed upon terminology for key business vocabulary.

Only when the meaning of data is clear can the proper storage and flow of data be fully discerned. One technique that is quite effective in getting people to agree on data definitions is a business glossary, which can be defined as "a software application used to communicate and govern the organization's business concepts and terminology along with the associated definitions and relationships between those terms."[2] Simply put, a business glossary lists the terms that are important to an organization's business process and provides common, agreed upon definitions for those terms. A business glossary thereby promotes:

- An accurate understanding of terms
- The effective use of data
- A single definition for key business terms, which fosters communication and reduces confusion about what data means

Maintaining a business glossary is a data management technique that is also often leveraged in conjunction with data quality, data governance, and enterprise architecture. For example, consider the implication of whether a data item labeled "zip code" is a five-digit number or includes the four-digit extension. Business requirements for this may determine the necessary data quality, field-size, process flow, and so on. As such, a business glossary is a valuable technique that is useful across a variety business operations and data management domains. It can serve as a cornerstone on which to build a data architecture.[3]

9.1.2 Data Asset Inventory

It may be a little obvious, but a list—and subsequent detailing—of production databases and other data stores can be a useful place to start to understand your current data environment. You might be surprised by how many organizations are not sure how many data stores they have or cannot provide a list or do not know whom to contact for more information. It is possible to execute a system inventory query that returns information on the number of systems and connections to other systems. If an inventory of systems or applications exists, this is a good place to start. However, this type of inventory doesn't disclose much about how data is stored or flows. Also, such an inventory may not reflect relationships with other systems/applications. From a

---

[2] Fryman, L., "What Is a Business Glossary," BeyeNETWORK, September 13, 2012, http://www.b-eye-network.com/view/16371.

[3] A business glossary is a useful foundational artifact across many data management areas, such as data governance, metadata management, master data management, data quality, records management, and additional domains.

data management perspective, this type of inventory becomes more valuable as it starts to reflect data, even at a high level. For example, what data is stored in each data store? What data flows between data stores as well as between data stores and applications?

But be aware that the relationship between systems and data stores is not always one to one. Sometimes multiple systems use the same data store, for example. This is particularly true over time as systems are replaced or partly replaced, but the legacy database lives on because of some critical process that was not migrated. To gather this information, it is useful to speak with system owners and users as well as with database administrators. Data models, data-sharing agreements, and privacy impact statements, if they are available, may also contain useful material. As you research, it is often useful to create a list of questions and people to ask. Some questions may not be obvious at first. For example, is the disaster recovery tier known and could it be used to prioritize the collection of additional information? At the very least, a list provides a yardstick against which you can measure progress.

9.1.3   Data Standards

When developing a data architecture, it is sometimes also helpful to create or reference data standards. Detailed (or low-level) data standards might include standard terms and definitions (e.g., HL7, FIBO), standard code sets (e.g., country codes), or data exchange standards (e.g., NIEM, ANSI, ISO).[4] If operating in a space where industry data standards are well developed (e.g., healthcare), referencing these standards when developing a data architecture is imperative. If your environment is more general, a combination of industry standards and in-house standards works well.

Most organizations operate in this type of relatively general environment, and much of the data fabric already exists. Such an environment requires organizations to determine the data standards to which they want to adhere. Data standards go beyond the business glossary in that they may specify not only a definition, but also how a given data item is represented, a list of valid values, a field format, and so on. Both a business glossary and data asset inventory are useful resources when determining data standards. A business glossary highlights those terms most important to the business—those terms in need of a standard. A data asset inventory begins to highlight where those data items may be stored and how they may differ, thus leading the way to a standard.

Because differences in standards likely exist within the organization itself, a good place to start is focusing on data exchange standards. That is, no matter how

---

[4] Such standards are particularly important for sharing data with entities outside the organization. Data architecture can extend to sharing data with entities outside the organization. Many data exchange standards continue to be developed to foster such exchanges. See the Data Architecture References section in Appendix C for a brief discussion.

an organization has chosen to store its data, it should consider a standard for how this data is exchanged internally and with partners. It is important to note, though, that focusing only on data exchange standards has its limits. For example, it does not address whether the data being exchanged is of the desired quality or is authoritative.

Another area to consider standardizing is metadata. If your organization already has a metadata repository, it is useful to coordinate publishing relevant project information using existing metadata terms. Standardizing metadata, to the extent possible,[5] will aid searching for information going forward. This, in turn, helps document an organization's data architecture.

These types of detailed data standards are a good reference when developing, revising, or expanding a data architecture. They can also be useful to help resolve discrepancies in a business glossary. Besides the detailed types of data standards discussed so far, higher levels of data standards may also be reflected in the form of a policy or guidelines. They may be defined by data architecture or in conjunction with other areas of data management, such as data governance. Examples of data standards might include:

- Projects should have a logical data model, based on the enterprise model if one exists. A physical data model should be based on a logical model. (Data models are discussed next.)
- Projects should incorporate applicable data stewards as stakeholders to ensure that the correct data is used and that the use, quality, and limitations on the use and disclosure of data are understood.
- Projects should only get data from authoritative sources.
- If data is redundantly copied from another system, controls should be put in place to ensure that the source and target match.

9.1.4   Data Models

One of the most common techniques used to document data is the data model. Data models are sometimes overemphasized as the main component of data architecture. In fact, they are a useful part of data architecture—but only a part.[6]

Data models come in various shapes and sizes, each depicting data at different levels. Each of these data models reflects data and its relationship to other data.

---

[5] Vendor-based software tools such as extraction, transformation, and load (ETL) tools use proprietary metadata to track data. This presents some limits on the ability to standardize metadata. This type of metadata is typically technical in nature. An organization should still be able to standardize its business metadata to suit its needs.

[6] For a more detailed discussion of relational data modeling, see "The DAMA Guide to The Data Management Body of Knowledge (DAMA-DMBOK," Technics Publications, LLC, 2009. For a discussion on other types of data models, see the Data Analytics References section in Appendix C.

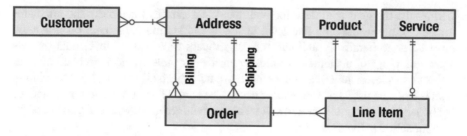

Fig. 9.1 Conceptual data model

At a conceptual level, subject areas[7] such as customer, order, and so on and their respective relationships to each other and to other subject areas are documented. A conceptual data model is meant to promote a common understanding of data in terms of high-level business entities and their relationships.[8]

The conceptual data model in Fig. 9.1 is an example of a high-level view of a customer order. It depicts an illustration of agreed upon terms by which an organization can refer to key categories such as customer and product. It also highlights the relationships between these categories. It shows that:

- A customer must have one or more addresses.
- An address may have zero to many customers.
- An order has both a billing and shipping address.
- An order has many line items, each of which is either a product or a service.[9]

Subject areas contained in a conceptual data model should be created based on business functionality. Subject areas can be broken down into categories, creating a multilayered hierarchy of related terms. For example, customer may encompass organization and individual. Sometimes categories can be further broken down into subcategories. For example, an organization may be a corporation, non-profit, governmental, and so on. In the end, conceptual data model subject areas, categories, and subcategories reflect high-level groupings of data well above the level of individual fields such as name, street address, city, state, and zip code.

Conceptual data models can be useful as a communication mechanism and, in an ideal world, form the foundation for lower level logical and physical data models.[10]

---

[7] High-level grouping terms vary. The DMBOK considers a subject area model the highest level model. Subject areas (as few as 10–12 total) are useful for developing an initial understanding environmental complexity, addressing questions such as how many systems have customer data? Categories (about 5–7 per subject area) are often useful to begin discussions of authoritative sources, data quality, and data stewardship domains.

[8] A business glossary can be a useful tool when defining subject areas.

[9] There are multiple notations used to denote relationships in data modeling. This diagram uses the Crow's Foot notation. One source for additional details on data modeling notation is https://en.wikipedia.org/wiki/Entity–relationship_model.

[10] In some cases, detailed logical and physical data models exist but conceptual models do not. Thus the terminology applied across multiple logical and physical data models may differ. For example, an event in one data model may be called an incident in a second data model. It is therefore sometimes useful to create a conceptual data model retroactively in order to synchronize terminology.

Ultimately, the goal is to describe and document entities (or tables) and attributes (or fields), but developing that level of detail and getting agreement on it usually must be done iteratively and can take significant time. Lower level data models show groupings of attributes or fields in entities or tables (e.g., individual address fields in an address table), and how tables relate to each other (e.g., how an address relates to a person). There are widely accepted standard notations and best practices for both how models are created and what symbols are used, which are enforced by data modeling software vendors.[11]

Physical data models use tables, fields, and relationships to document the design of how data is stored. Physical data models are relatively common and easily produced. Large database management systems, such as Oracle, DB2, and SQL Server all generate physical data models based on their database.

Logical data models, often used to graphically document low-level data requirements, must be separately developed. Logical data models are meant to be more understandable to the business community. The logical Address entity contains attributes easily understandable in English. In addition to having easily understandable terms, logical models usually provide additional context, such as entity and attribute definitions or information specifying to what category an attribute belongs. They can even include business rules and lists valid values. It is not difficult for business people to learn the modeling conventions. As such a logical data model is a good way to validate data requirements.

A key limitation of most physical and logical data models is that they are specific to a system. Systems are frequently built to address a specific business function and do not, at least initially and without enterprise-level guidance, take into account integration with other business functions and systems. In terms of data architecture, this limits the usefulness of most physical and logical data models because they do not address the broader need of showing how data flows across the enterprise. However, once the flow of data across systems is clear, these low-level, system-specific data models are an important tool to understanding, at the detail level, how data is stored in each system.

The exception to this is an enterprise-level data model, which is a logical data model covering standard definition of entities and attributes across the organization. An enterprise-level data model may be derived from a conceptual data model.[12] It is meant as a reference for new and updated system-level logical and physical data models to foster consistency. An enterprise model, if it exists, would constitute a useful part of data architecture. It is likely that, if an enterprise data model exists, an enterprise-level conceptual data model also exists.

Many organizations find themselves in the situation of having many legacy databases, some with data models and some without, each based on different terminology, resulting in apples-to-oranges business discussions and decisions made based on incorrect assumptions. If you don't already have agreed upon subject areas and

---

[11] These include IDEF1X, Crow's Foot, UML, and others.

[12] This is most likely if one or more conceptual level models already exist. It is also possible that an enterprise data model evolves from existing logical and physical data models.

data categories, it can be useful to reach agreement on these as a starting point. Then use interviews, surveys, or documentation to cross-reference the data categories and your data assets to help give you a picture of the enterprise data environment.

9.1.5   Data Lifecycle Diagrams

Business users, who need to understand where to find the trustworthy data they need, will find data models insufficient. A conceptual data model is useful for agreeing on the type of data that the business needs to capture, but it says little about where to find the right data. System-level physical and logical data models are excellent tools for detailing specifically where and how data is stored and how that data relates to other data, but these models do not typically convey how data flows beyond their specific system environment. A business will want to apply business context against data. One useful technique that can help address this challenge is the use of what we refer to as data lifecycle diagrams (DLD).[13] This type of diagram shows how data is stored and flows across the entire enterprise. For example, it might show how a given type of data, such as a claim, flows from end to end within an organization. A DLD is powerful because it is easily understandable by the business user, the IT developer, and executives because it graphically depicts how data flows across the organization.

One approach might be to create DLDs for each major data category not only to trace the flow of data through the environment, but to identify things such as potential systems of record (where the data is created or maintained), redundancy, latency, where data is being integrated and where there are unmet integration needs.

The exact scope of a data lifecycle diagram can vary in how it is defined. From a data architecture perspective, the most complete variation is one which reflects the entire environment for a given type of data, such as claims data, for example. Sometimes a slightly different view may be useful, such as limiting the scope of a DLD to a particular business use case or to a limited number of systems. Sometimes a DLD accomplishes both in the same diagram. While business use case views may not show all systems involved for a given type of data within the enterprise, they often show how data flows and is stored end-to-end specific to a business operation, and are therefore particularly well received by the business.

A DLD is typically done for both an "As-Is" and a "To-Be" version, showing both the current as well as the desired environment. In the sample genericized DLD in Fig. 9.2, he highlighted ovals explain these components.

- *Flow Start Indicator*: "Start" designators highlight data entry or the beginning of an independent process.
- *Data Flow*: These lines and labels show actual data flows (solid), queries (dashed), and human data exchanges (dotted).

---

[13] The term "data life cycle" in this context refers to the life cycle of data across a business use case rather than the life cycle of data from conception to purging.

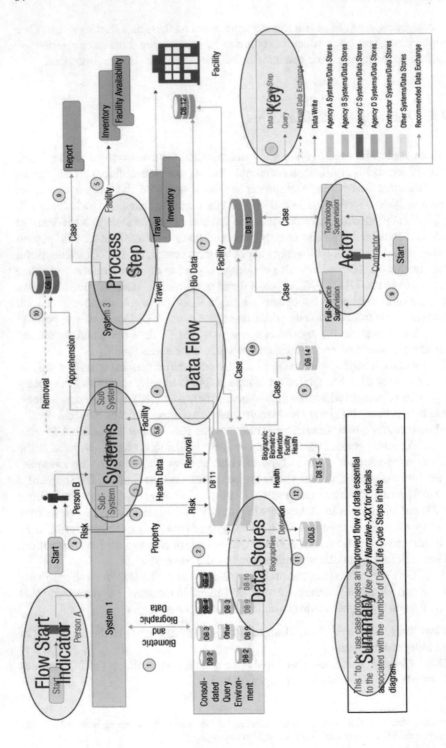

Fig. 9.2 Data lifecycle diagram

- *Data Source*: Drum shapes designate where data is stored.
- *System*: Square boxes indicate applications with user interfaces.
- *Process Step*: These small, yellow numbers refer back to the diagram narrative to highlight a specific step in a process.
- *Actor*: People icons depict individuals involved in data input or exchange.
- *Summary*: A short summary of the use case; a detailed description can be found in the accompanying diagram narrative.
- *Key*: Highlights information such as different colors to indicate system and data store ownership.

Data flows in the DLD are labeled to show what data is flowing. Typically, they are labeled with high-level data categories to start. They can be detailed with specific entities and attributes, where needed, over multiple iterations to highlight things like data redundancy and updates to the same data in more than one data store. The flow labels highlight where specific data flows, is entered and re-entered, and also is manually shared. A written narrative, about five pages long, accompanies each DLD and provides additional facts. For example, the narrative may spell out business rules that cannot be detailed on the diagram. As mentioned earlier, sections of the narrative relate directly back to diagram notations placed to emphasize a particular step.

More can be done with DLDs. For example, latency can be applied to each flow, highlighting how long it takes for data to get from point A to point B. Another overlay that can be applied to DLDs is a state transition overlay. Showing the same data (e.g., address) in all the places it exists (state) and where it is changed (transition) helps to resolve authoritative sources of data. Data flow diagrams can also be a useful technique to document or validate a data asset inventory. Because it is often helpful to augment documentation for a data inventory in graphical form, DLDs serve a useful technique for this.[14]

Techniques used for data architecture are still evolving, and which technique is the most appropriate depends significantly on what documentation is already available. We have found using DLDs and narratives to drive data architecture to be highly effective. DLDs can be developed in conjunction with existing data models, a business glossary, data standards, and data inventory, or DLDs can be used as a technique to help drive other components of data architecture. In our experience, DLDs have proven especially successful in driving data architecture because they are understandable by and useful for both business and technical users. On seeing a completed data flow diagram, it is not uncommon for users to express that they were only familiar with a part of a given data flow process. Furthermore, DLDs provide

---

[14] It is also possible to approach a data inventory by beginning with a system interface diagram and matrix. Together these two artifacts document one or more key organizational systems and their direct interfaces. This approach has the limitation that it is not business-process oriented and thus may be initially less understandable by the business user. However, it is a straightforward way to begin documenting where data is located and how it is shared, and the results can be leveraged when creating DLDs.

an excellent basis for educating new employees about data and systems, as well as communicating with transitory contractors.

9.2   Who Is Data Architecture?

Data architects guide how data is partitioned into systems, stored, shared, and integrated for use across the organization and sometimes outside it. They guide how data is standardized and organized within systems and data stores and for downstream needs, whether for transactional systems, for operational reporting, for analytics, or for any other downstream use. Technical experience may include data modeling, database management, system analysis, and software engineering. A data architect may have worked as a software engineer before specializing in an area such as warehousing or master data management and working their way into data architecture.

It is also immensely helpful if the data architects understand the business to address questions about how data is flows—and should flow—across the organization. Data architects often have backgrounds that span business and IT. Data architecture, like many of the other data management domains, should be driven by the business. This is because only the business understands what data is needed, how it is used, how important it is, what risks are associated with it, and how it relates to other data. It is also helpful if data architects understand how the organization reports on its business—what is measured and how, and how current the information has to be.

Data architects must communicate effectively. Data architecture requires significant collaboration between the business user and IT. For example, data architects must communicate effectively with system developers and database administrators to achieve effective data models. It is also helpful if data architects are senior enough in the organization to command attention because much about data architecture is driving a vision forward. They are usually fairly senior with good soft skills.

Where data architecture resides in the organization varies. Traditionally, data architecture resided within IT albeit often informally. Even more recently, information architecture is overwhelmingly owned by IT (40%) as opposed to business (11%).[15] With increased acceptance that data is a business concern, some data architecture functions have moved under Enterprise Information Management (EIM) groups, within business operations, or even under a CDO.

Sometimes all or part of data architecture is grouped with other types of architecture (business, software/application/system, technical/infrastructure) in an Enterprise Architecture (EA) group. This is intended to align the different aspects of architecture and foster communications between the different types of architects. EA is often within IT, where business architects and data architects may struggle for

---

[15] Leganza, G., "Changing Your Approach to Information Strategy? You're Not Alone," Forrester Research, Inc., October 2, 2014.

credibility. Unfortunately, some CIOs don't understand what the data architect role is, why it's needed, or why their system/application/solution architects can't do the same job. In theory, system/application/solution architects also could address data, but the reality is that these architects have different skillsets and different perspectives, and finding someone with both technology and data perspectives and strong experience in both is exceedingly rare. Moving EA to business operations can provide better credibility for business and data architects but may complicate relations with IT development teams.

As of this writing there is no formal certification for data architecture. There are, however, certifications for enterprise architecture.

With the focus on big data and analytics and on more and more tools that allow the business user to directly manipulate data, business users themselves are becoming important participants in driving data architecture. The better these users understand data terms, authoritative data sources, and data relationships, the easier it is to maintain a consistent data architecture.

It is not uncommon for larger organizations to employ multiple full-time data architects. Resources required also depend, to some extent, on the existence of other data management groups within the organization. For example, if data governance is already up and running, this group is likely to address some issues affecting data architecture. Typically, a single person does not have the complete set of skills to accommodate every aspect of data architecture. It is important for the data architect, therefore, to augment his or her skillset by working with other business and technical specialists. Ideally, the business should drive data architecture and work with IT to manage the software and hardware infrastructure—data stores, technical interfaces, and applications—required to meet business needs.

9.3   Benefits of Data Architecture

Data architecture provides an end-to-end overview of how key data is stored in and flows across an organization. It allows an organization to isolate examples of the various places specific data resides and how it moves, or should move. Benefits include:

- A fundamental understanding of what data exists in the organization and where it is stored
- Improved collaboration among data stakeholders through the use of common terms and definitions for data
- An understanding of authoritative and nonauthoritative data sources and an outline that can be leveraged to eliminate non-authoritative data sources, identify redundant data stores for possible consolidation or elimination, identify unmet integration needs, etc.
- A blueprint for communicating how data is stored and shared for a given business process

- Data lifecycle diagrams that are easily understood by everyone, including all levels of business users as well as technical staff

9.4   Data Architecture Framework

Depending on the data management framework that is leveraged, the approach used toward data architecture differs somewhat, though the aim is the same: to understand how data is stored and flows through the organization. The classic approach is to document process models and data models independently and then combine them to gain insight into how data is both stored and flows across the enterprise.[16]

For example, the DMBOK promotes "Value Chain Analysis,"[17] an approach that aligns data models with other process models as well as other data architecture components, such as technology platforms. Similarly, CMMI's Data Management Maturity Model discusses "Data Lifecycle Management,"[18] which highlights the need to understand where data is stored and how it flows for a given business process from conception to retirement.

Rather than combining process models and data models, the framework highlighted in this book embraces DLDs, which begin by depicting data storage and flow at a mid-level using category-level data flows. These diagrams can be successively iterated toward lower levels of data and, where needed, to a level low enough to align with logical and physical data models. In addition, we have highlighted several useful techniques that can be used in conjunction with data lifecycle diagrams, such as a business glossary, a data inventory, data models, and data standards.[19]

9.5   Implementing Data Architecture

Just about every organization already has some parts of a data architecture in place, for example:

---

[16] For example, TOGAF and DoDAF both employ separate techniques to document process models and logical/physical data models; process models are then aligned with data models to understand how data is used.

[17] DAMA, "The DAMA Guide to Data Management Body of Knowledge," 1st Ed., Technics Publications, LLC, 2009, Chap. 4.

[18] CMMI Institute, "Data Management Maturity (DMD) Model," Ver. 1.0, CMMI Institute, August 2014, Chapter "Data Lifecycle Management," pp. 105–110.

[19] There are many other techniques to help manage data architecture. For example, the CRUD (create, read, update, delete) matrix is a useful tool to manage potential conflicts for creating, updating, or deleting data. Such tools are useful for specific purposes rather than universally.

- Many organizations have a system inventory that could be used as a starting point to create a complementary data asset inventory.
- Data models at the physical and sometimes at the logical level are commonplace.
- You may have agreed upon subject areas and perhaps also data categories.
- System design or architecture documents sometimes summarize interface information.
- Frequently, business glossaries or conceptual data models exist at a more local level as a consequence of systems that were built to address a specific business function with limited budgets and regard for other systems. Even though they may be limited in scope and dated, these documents are often useful tools when developing a formal data architecture.
- As mentioned earlier, in the public sector it is quite useful to look for existing SORNs and PIAs.

A good place to begin is by seeking out and organizing this kind of existing data architecture documentation. Once you understand to what extent the data architecture has been documented and whether that documentation is primarily at the local level or also at the enterprise level, you can formulate an approach. An initial approach to data architecture can be further scoped by focusing on one or a few key organizational systems (and their interfacing systems). When focusing on key systems, a data asset inventory using a data interface diagram and matrix is a good place to start. As mentioned, this has the limitation of being more system-focused, but it yields an inventory of where data is stored and can be augmented with how data flows and is shared among key systems.

Alternatively, developing DLDs for these key datasets, key business processes, or key systems is another way to scope initial data architecture. This approach is more involved than creating a data inventory. Indeed, a data asset inventory can be quite useful when creating DLDs because the data inventory already provides a superset of data stores. Developing DLDs is a highly effective technique that captures the attention of both business and technical users. These diagrams and their associated short narratives are readily understandable by operational as well as executive personnel.

Development of a business glossary is another useful and foundational component of data architecture. A business glossary can be done as a stand-alone initiative or in conjunction with documenting data stores and flows. Though it is a useful technique, it is difficult to be formulaic about exactly when to develop a business glossary because the glossary by itself may not garner sufficient support from the business. Use it to help address data problems caused by term and definition differences. If such differences exist up front, a business glossary may help reconcile them. Alternatively, a business glossary can be defined in conjunction with other data architecture artifacts, such as a conceptual data model, a data inventory or DLDs, to foster the consistent use of data terms and definitions when developing these artifacts.

Data architecture is enabled when more formal pockets of data management already exist within the organization. For example, many organizations have an enterprise architecture function in place, though it may not be fully mature. This is likely a place within the organization that understands and cares about data, is maintaining some data architecture artifacts, and is working with others within the organization who want to understand and manage where data is stored and how it flows. Other potential pockets within the organization may manage aspects of data architecture. Enterprise data warehousing teams and data governance groups are two examples. Because these kinds of teams deal with integrating enterprise-level data on a regular basis, their levels of interest and documentation to support data architecture are likely to be significant.

Whether starting with a business glossary, data inventory, conceptual data model, DLDs, or another data architecture technique, it is important to understand that data architecture is not a project-level activity. To be useful to the business, data architecture needs to be continuously maintained. The business will turn to data architecture to answer questions such as:

- What is an inventory of our systems, applications, and data stores, and how do they interact?
- What is my authoritative source for information on a particular facility?
- How should new data that we have to store, due to new regulations or guidelines, be integrated and stored?
- Where is the right place to update information on a customer?
- Which data on several, conflicting enterprise reports is correct?
- What constitutes an event or an incident?
- What data does our organization share with or ingest from partners?

Answers to these kinds of questions change over time. Therefore, sufficient data management within a data architecture function must be ongoing.

9.6   Data Architecture Tools

The most common tools for documenting data architecture are data modeling tools. These tools can create physical and logical data models by connecting to a database. They also accommodate the association of physical and logical data models to conceptual data models by accommodating the capture of data categories. Data modeling tools are widely used at the system level.

Enterprise architecture suites are another set of available tools. These tools go beyond data architecture. They facilitate the integration of data architecture, business architecture, technical architecture, and IT planning and strategy. Consequentially, enterprise architecture tools accommodate the alignment of these architectures, for example, the alignment of process and data models. An investment in an enterprise architecture tool demands a large resource commitment in order to integrate these various models.

Some enterprise architecture tools also facilitate the capturing of a data asset inventory. However, these tools are costly and their functions go well beyond documenting data assets. On small data architecture efforts, the combination of a graphical tool and a spreadsheet tool will often do the trick, though these are time consuming to maintain.

Other tools that automate some of the documentation of where data is and how it is used are beginning to emerge. Sometimes referred to as information catalog tools, these tools employ the combination of a business glossary, text/data mining, and workflow design. They connect to traditional, structured environments as well as to big data, unstructured ones. They foster the organization of data sources and data into categories that help all levels of users, from business analyst to data scientist, determine the right data to use for a given type of report or analysis.

A good business glossary is fundamental to data architecture. There are tools on the market to facilitate a business glossary. These tools are often categorized as data governance tools and include the ability to manage a business glossary. These tools may be a good investment because data governance is so central to all data management, including data architecture. It is also possible to maintain a basic business glossary using a word processing tool.

Although there are tools that document and align data and process models, there are no tools specifically dedicated to maintaining data lifecycles as we have described them in this chapter. Here, too, a graphical tool along with a word processing tool will work.

Chapter 10
Master Data Management

10.1 What Is Master Data Management?

Master data management (MDM) focuses on ensuring that the data that is most important to the organization is well defined. Master data is singled out from other data because the organization considers it mission critical. Master data is typically a small dataset that is uniquely defined throughout the enterprise. Commonly cited master datasets are for customer and for product. But master data can be any entity sufficiently important to an organization that needs to be succinctly defined. As such, it can be a dataset of locations, employees, events, statuses, facilities, or any other entity that the organization deems critical to define in the same way.

The goal of master data management is to eliminate duplicates, share a consistent master dataset throughout the organization, and, in some cases, allow for collaborative updates to the master dataset. Eliminating duplicates is accomplished through probabilistic matching. Algorithms are fine-tuned to check for similarities in the desired data domain (e.g., customer). If two or more records closely match, business rules determine how these records are automatically combined—that is, which fields from which record are used to create the master. If there is a possible match, records are flagged for further inspection by a person who must resolve whether the records are the same or constitute two separate entities.

Once master data is defined and stored, it is available to the enterprise. Users can then use, inspect, and evaluate new additions to the master dataset. Depending on the data architecture employed, master data may reside in a central hub or in different locations that are centrally indexed. In either case, one or more authoritative systems, as well as a business process for managing updates, are determined. This combination of probabilistic matching and business rules to maintain the master dataset requires continual attention from the business with support from IT.

© Springer International Publishing AG 2018
M. Fleckenstein, L. Fellows, *Modern Data Strategy*,
https://doi.org/10.1007/978-3-319-68993-7_10

Master datasets are historically also small.[1] For customer, for example, it is important to have only a few key fields standardized universally, such as name and address. Other fields may be of varying interest and standard for more local use. Assuming, for example, that customer is an individual, as is often the case for public institutions, some information, such as health history or criminal background, may each be of interest to entirely different users of the data. Therefore, this information may not be part of the customer master dataset.[2] This allows local users to be very specific about the details of, in this case, health data or law-enforcement data that is important to them.

Master data management evolved from two main disciplines: customer data integration and product information management. This explains why so much of master data management is focused on customer and product. These types of master datasets can be quite complex. For example, for customer, points of contact often vary for different parts of an organization. Marketing, Operations, and Finance may each have different points of customer contact. Points of contact within Operations may further vary. So, in addition to having to maintain a de-duplicated, up-to-date master dataset, business users may have to manage the hierarchies relating different master data records.

However, effective master data management can begin with much less complex data, notably reference data. For example, an organization wanting to master its facilities so that they are referred to in the same way throughout can create and manage a master dataset of facilities and mandate its use. This would not only consolidate multiple potential facility lists within the enterprise; by definition, it would also create one or more authoritative sources for a facility master dataset and put in place a process to govern the facility master dataset. Beginning a master data initiative with a reference master dataset is a good litmus test for future increased master data scope.

10.2   Who Is Master Data Management?

Much of master data management is a process. The business must determine and manage the master dataset, author business rules on authoritative sources for master records for different circumstances, and manage duplicates that cannot otherwise

---

[1] It is worth noting that MDM is evolving through the use of automated discovery. In this case, algorithms help identify data that belongs to a given master data record. By crawling through large amounts of data, these algorithms are potentially able to assimilate much larger amounts of master data, allowing for significant expansion of the master dataset.

[2] Whether or not health history or criminal background information (or any other more specific information) is part of a master dataset is also highly dependent on the organization's overall business. If that business is health- or law-enforcement- related, the master dataset may include this type of information, especially as industry data standards for these and other areas emerge (see, for example, HL7 for health data standards and N-DEx for law-enforcement data exchange standards in Appendix C).

be resolved. However, MDM also requires a tool to perform probabilistic matching, automate business rules, and store the master dataset. The business must also work with IT to implement the automation process.

Initially, once a master data domain has been determined, it must be "mastered." If several datasets are competing for the domain, they must be matched, and if potential duplicates exist, these must be resolved—automatically, if possible; otherwise, through human intervention. If the dataset is small, for example, a set of reference data, it is possible to create a unified master manually, determine its authoritative sources, and put in place a governance process for both leveraging the master dataset as well as maintaining it. This can be done without a tool, but it does require the business to define the original datasets, how they should be consolidated, and the authoritative systems in which the master dataset resides. All this also requires the help of IT.

For large master datasets, such as customer, a tool is required for things such as probabilistic matching, applying automated business rules, maintaining hierarchies, and disseminating master data. The result is that large MDM implementations require a greater degree of participation by IT. This does not, however, absolve the business from engaging in MDM. In fact, MDM without a basic form of data governance, as described earlier cannot succeed.

10.3   Benefits of Master Data Management

Master data management helps the organization manage potential duplicates for data domains that are mission critical to the organization. This may include complex datasets like customer or product. It also includes mastering reference data. Benefits of MDM are:

- Reduction or elimination of duplicate records in mission critical datasets
- Availability of current, cleansed, consistent master data throughout the enterprise
- Automated probabilistic matching and application of business rules
- Known, managed authoritative sources for master data
- Potential collaborative management of the master dataset

10.4   Master Data Management Framework

MDM architecture is often described as one of three architectures: repository, registry, or hybrid.[3] A repository architecture means that master data is stored in a centralized data store. Hence the term "repository." The repository contains the

---

[3] Note that industry also uses other terms, e.g., Gartner uses the terms "centralized" vs. registry and "coexistence" vs. hybrid.

entire master dataset. A registry architecture implies that master data is not centrally stored, and that the registry stores pointers to where master data is stored. In either case, repository and registry are referred to as the hub because they serve the central role of keeping track of master data.

In a hybrid architecture—a combination repository and registry architecture—some portion of the master data is kept in a repository, usually those fields that are often and universally used. Other master dataset fields may be federated to data stores outside the hub, with a pointer in the hub to their location. Thus a hybrid architecture combines the repository and registry architecture styles.

Each of these architectures has its pros and cons, depending on the master data domain, the systems already in place, and the organization's need. If, for example, the organization decides to implement a repository architecture, it must decide whether updates to master data are made directly to the repository or via an existing application that interfaces with the hub. In the first case, users would be required to interact with two applications rather than one; they would update master data directly using an MDM hub user interface, then use their existing application for transaction processing. On the other hand, an existing application may itself interface with the hub, providing users with a single application that is integrated with the master data hub. In this case, the interface between the existing application and the master data hub is more complex.

If updates to the hub are made indirectly through applications, MDM architecture becomes even more complex if multiple applications are able to update the master dataset. In these situations, business rules must determine the priority one application has over another in making updates. As a simple, hypothetical example, if the customer address information conflicts in two authoritative applications, case status may be the determinant of which application prevails; the correct master address resides in the application with the more current case status because that is the most up-to-date information available.

Another consideration for a master data management framework is the frequency with which master data is updated and how updates are shared. For example, when an update is made to a master data record or the master dataset, it is possible to push those updates to consuming applications in near-real time, make the updates available through a publish and subscribe mechanism, or update consuming applications through a batch process. The method chosen depends on how urgent the business need is.

It is important to decide on an architecture and update frequency before implementing master data management. However, architecture and frequency can vary for each master data domain. The architecture for reference data, for example, is highly likely a repository style because the dataset is often a single field. Such small datasets typically do not have component parts, each of which might be managed in different locations. Similarly, frequency of update for reference data is likely to be publish and subscribe or batch because the urgency is not critical. The architecture for a complex data domain, such as customer, may be more federated and the timing more near-real time. In fact, it is not uncommon to have different

MDM architectures and update schemes operating in parallel, depending on the organization's need.[4]

By definition, MDM embodies some aspects of data quality. If data quality is poor, a suitable master record can never be created. One of the first tasks in master data management is to identify all the various (and potentially conflicting and duplicate) datasets that exist in the organization for the chosen master data domain. This domain must then be effectively de-duplicated, and that can only be done with reasonable data quality. If, for example, some address information exists in the comment field because the address field is not long enough to accommodate all address data, this data must be cleansed before it can be mastered.

Managing data cleansing, MDM architecture, probabilistic matching, hierarchy management, updates, and data sharing mandate a basic data governance structure. The right set of people must be identified to determine authoritative sources, cleanse data, author and automate business rules, resolve potential duplicates that cannot be automatically resolved, manage master data hierarchies, and collaborate on updates to the master dataset. Just as in a fully implemented data governance framework, this requires data stewards and decision makers, along with an escalation path to resolve potential conflicts. Master data management can be a good testing ground for a more formal, albeit fledgling, data governance framework.

10.5 Implementing Master Data Management

As mentioned earlier, one of the first tasks in master data management is to identify the super-set of data that will serve as the basis for master data residing in current applications and data stores. Regardless of the selected master data architecture, this super-set of future master data must be cleansed and de-duplicated, and then kept clean and free of duplicates.

Unless the initial master dataset is a reference dataset, a tool is required for both cleansing and deduplication. In the case of data cleansing, data is profiled to identify its robustness. In some cases, data can be cleansed automatically. For example, adding a missing zip code for an otherwise good address. In other cases, data may have to be manually inspected and cleansed.

In the case of de-duplication, whether the tool is proprietary or vendor-supplied, it employs one or more algorithms to de-duplicate data, or flag data for potential de-duplication. To be most effective, the tools' algorithms are adjusted to effectively identify duplicates in a specific organization. Numerous potentially matching records will require business user intervention for de-duplication. Business rules

---

[4] Gartner has defined a fourth type of architecture called a "consolidation" architecture, in which the MDM hub is used primarily to support MDM for data warehousing, and MDM is applied downstream from operational systems. Note that this fourth architecture type can still be a repository, registry, or hybrid design. For more details, see O'Kane, B., Palance, T., & Moran, P. M., "Magic Quadrant for Master Data Management Solutions," Gartner, January 19, 2017.

determine how matching records are de-duplicated and how the new master data is integrated with existing applications.

Equally important to deciding on a tool is putting in place a process to manage master data. This process borrows skills and tasks related not only to data cleansing, but also to data architecture and data governance. We already discussed how a simple data governance framework is critical to the success of MDM. Data governance is required initially to establish the master dataset, and it is required ongoing to monitor and resolve potential duplicates and to accommodate changes in the business process that need to be reflected in how master data is handled. There are more nuanced potential data governance considerations as well. For example, privacy may be a concern. If part of the master dataset is subject to restricted access, as in the case of health data, this becomes part of the governance process.

We also discussed some aspects of data architecture—MDM architecture, integration with transactional applications, frequency of updates, and collaborative updating. At a more detailed data architecture level, a data model for the master data must also be defined and implemented. This data model forms the basis by which master data will be universally disseminated. Note that this data model may extend to multiple repositories in the case of a hybrid architecture.

10.6   Master Data Management Tools

Undertaking a reference master data management initiative very likely does not require a tool, but undertaking more complex MDM initiatives does. Such a tool can be proprietary, but a good number of vendor tools exist, and they are evolving. In most cases, a probabilistic matching engine is a key feature of an MDM tool. A tool is also needed for automated business rules, data modeling, managing a master data hierarchy, and supporting the master data architecture. In addition, tools are increasingly incorporating data quality, workflow, and data stewardship components. Aside from pure MDM tools, CRM tools also perform some master data management.

Vendor tools are typically oriented toward a particular domain. The most common orientations are customer and product. These two specialties are so prominent that they have been evaluated as separate packaged solutions until recently.[5] Other domains in which tools specialize include financial services, healthcare, geospatial, parts, even reference data. Tools are trying hard to become multi-domain oriented, allowing users to leverage one platform to master several domains. This involves tuning matching algorithms, business rules, data models and architecture, and so on for each domain. It is often possible to implement customized domains with vendor tools initially targeted at one of the prominent domains, like customer.

---

[5] See, for example, Gartner's Magic Quadrant for each of Customer and Product MDM prior to 2017.

Tools typically support all master data architecture styles—repository, registry, and hybrid. Some tools support cloud integration, and some are becoming more integrated in their ability to include data from nontraditional sources, such as social media, through a search functionality. An entire industry is developing around integrating robust customer profiles from a plethora of both subscription-based and publicly available sources.[6] Other functionalities supported to differing degrees include data cleansing, data stewardship, and real-time MDM.

---

[6] These tools and services are not necessarily referred to as MDM. Forrester terms this set of tools and services "Data Management Platforms." Purchasers of this data include primarily marketers and advertisers. However, it is conceivable that this type of tool/service will find its way into other business functions, such as law enforcement, for example.

Chapter 11
Data Quality

11.1   What Is Data Quality?

Data quality refers to the level of quality of data available to the business user. Data quality has many definitions, but data is generally considered high quality if "they are fit for their intended uses in operations, decision making and planning."[1]

The concept of "fitness for intended use" is an important notion in the preceding definition. Users' expectations for data quality can often differ, even when discussing the same set of data used for the same purpose. Inherent to managing data quality are the challenges and complexity associated with different expectations and interpretations of data quality across the organization. As an example, data used in historical analysis, trending, and inference may not need to be as accurate in every instance as the data used to generate the organization's financial statements. The CFO may reasonably expect 100% accuracy for the data in the latter instance. Data quality may also be expressed in terms of its conformance to specifications and structure.

Defining quality from the perspective of fitness has implications to the investment made in building data quality. All data quality needs are not equal, and careful consideration should be given to both defining the need across its user base and investing to the appropriate level. As noted, the accuracy needs for financial reporting and associated investments may differ significantly from those for analytics.

Ensuring that business users have the quality of data needed to ensure the integrity of their business processes, whether the accurate inventorying of their products, reviewing their customer base or finances, or for the data used in their business analysis, is a core data management concern. The purpose of data quality *management* activities is to enable the availability of data that is "fit for use" for the business user.

---

[1] Redman, T. C., *Data Driven: Profiting from Your Most Important Business Asset,* Harvard Business Press, 2008, p. 56.

© Springer International Publishing AG 2018
M. Fleckenstein, L. Fellows, *Modern Data Strategy*,
https://doi.org/10.1007/978-3-319-68993-7_11

11.1.1   Data Quality Dimensions

Most people think of inaccurate or erroneous data in a data field when thinking of data quality. When viewed from the perspective of "fitness of purpose" in a business process, several kinds of issues with data can compromise its quality and use. The following data quality dimensions reveal a deeper level of complexity in the practices that contribute to them.

11.1.1.1   Accuracy

Accuracy refers to the correctness of a data value in comparison to a reference source. In many cases, however, the reference source may be many, uncertain, externally sourced, or in other ways debatable, or the data value may be dynamically computed. Establishing a certified, reference source of the data (system of record) is necessary to determine its accuracy.

Other aspects of accuracy are that the data represents the same precision as in the reference source, have a single consistent definition across instances, and adhere to a single defined set of values.

11.1.1.2   Completeness

Completeness refers to the completeness of the information set available to support a user's needs. Incompleteness could be due to missing datasets (such as reference data) or metadata that a business user needs in order to execute their tasks. Completeness (or lack thereof) then represents a data quality issue to the user.

For example, a loan underwriter requiring credit data from an external bureau in addition to the loan data provided by the borrower may find the data unfit for his or her purposes unless the external credit data was not available to them.

11.1.1.3   Consistency

Consistency refers to the consistent representation and interpretation of data across repositories, applications, tables, and fields and across internal and external sources—data elements must align in meaning and format across multiple instances and correlate to provide a single interpretation of the business model. Examples of inconsistencies would be the use of different account code values within different applications (inconsistent representation) representing the same account, differing "point-in-time" data from different sources (inconsistent interpretation), and so on.

Data inconsistency creates unreliable information because is difficult to determine which version of the information is correct. For example, it is difficult to make correct—and timely—decisions if those decisions are based on conflicting information.

11.1.1.4   Latency

A business user who needs today's data for a critical operational report has an issue if the available data is a week old. The "staleness" of the data presents a data quality problem from the user's perspective, making it unsuitable for his or her needs.

An aspect of this is the "currency" of the data in relation to the world that it models. Currency of data relates to the delay between the occurrence of an event and when it manifests itself as data. Depending on the need, delay in the representation of a real-life event may adversely impact the business process that needs it. Stock price, persisted a day after its change, would adversely impact market dynamics.

Another aspect, an oft-mentioned concern among business users, is the delay between the creation of data and when it is actually made available to the user, the "timeliness" of the data. Current data may be obtainable but not made available. As an example, data warehouses are typically loaded via batch processes providing data a day, or part thereof, after it is created. This reflects the necessary data quality for the business intelligence user looking to review historical data, but it does not meet the real-time needs of another business user.

Issues of latency are primarily addressed by technologies such as replication, real-time streaming, batch loads, and virtualization. Significant data quality (and technical) costs may be associated with reducing latency to near real time, so business users should carefully consider their needs before deciding the best approach.

11.1.1.5   Reasonableness

Reasonableness speaks to the overall credibility of a dataset, its quality in aggregate terms, and its accuracy to the domain it models. A loan officer may expect about 10% of the loans he or she owns to be delinquent in a particular business environment. Finding 50% loans delinquent in the dataset maybe a trigger for reviewing the quality of the data or other factors.

Measuring data quality in aggregate can be a reasonable approach and a balance from a cost perspective to measuring each individual element for its accuracy, consistency, etc.

Data quality issues may have different points of emphasis that matter to a consumer. Analytic users may emphasize the need for completeness in their dataset and the range of datasets they may be interested in; financial analysts may emphasize accuracy.

Many other perspectives and dimensions related to information quality are worth reviewing. Good data quality does not guarantee usefulness. Data quality should be looked at in conjunction with how relevant data is understood, documented, available, secure, and used by the business.[2] In this context, consider metrics such as Richard Wang's materials on *Information Quality in Context* and *Information*

---

[2] Leganza, G., "Drive Information Strategy Performance Management with Capability Models," Forrester Research, Inc., October 2, 2014.

Quality Measurement.[3] They include dimensions such as believability, value-added, relevancy, traceability, interpretability, and others.

In addition, new metrics will emerge that measure how well an information management solution supports a business process. Examples include reducing duplication of effort and shortening time-to-resolution for problems.[4]

Data management practices such as Master Data Management, Metadata Management, Data Architecture, and others can also be seen as driven by data quality as a primary motive. Managing data quality across the organization should also be a primary component in Data Governance practices and a central precept that drives its priorities.

Traditionally, there has been a tendency to rely primarily on IT practices and technologies to ensure data quality. The use of database technologies, data modeling constructs, the algorithmic and automated enforcement of business rules, and referential integrity were and will continue be a cornerstone to enabling data quality.

Database Management Systems (DBMS), particularly relational databases, constrain the content of data within them by enforcing various data quality constraints. For example:

- *A person must have a name and an SSN* can be enforced in the DBMS by requiring non-null values in columns storing these data points.
- *A mortgage has one or more borrowers* can be enforced in the DBMS using referential integrity.
- *U.S. postal codes should be constrained to the values for the 50 states* can be enforced in the DBMS using domain integrity.

The kind of database model used—Relational, NoSQL (graph, key-value…)—as well as specific DBMS implementations have implications for the level of constraints that can be enforced within the database, and correspondingly for data quality. However, although careful data modeling and databases can automate and enforce data quality, automated data quality will be only as good as the requirements, governance, and other supporting processes applied to it.

Data quality management is a much broader and encompassing capability that impacts and is embedded within most organizational processes—from the business users' articulation of their quality needs, the "shepherding" of data through its life cycle, and in the measuring/monitoring of data quality over an organization's and its data's lifetime.

Data is produced and consumed across different points of an organization's information value chain, not unlike the sub-processes along an assembly line that produce and consume sub-products/components. This may create an overly single-threaded analogy. Data in reality has more complex many-to-many relationships between production and consumption points. However, it is still a useful paradigm to use when thinking of the information value chain.

---

[3] Wang, R. Y., and Strong, D. M., "Beyond Accuracy: What Data Quality Means to Data Consumers," M. E. Sharpe, Spring 1996, http://mitiq.mit.edu/Documents/Publications/TDQMpub/14_Beyond_Accuracy.pdf.

[4] Leganza, G., "Information Strategies Move Center Stage," Forrester Research, Inc., May 20, 2013.

Data quality management begins from the point of birth of the data in the organization, whether ingested from external sources or created from within, to its travels through various data storage locations (internal and external) to its eventual "resting" place(s). Business and technical user collaboration is embedded in all aspects of this data "life," and the business users' engagement and active involvement in data quality management is central to achieving quality outcomes. Some of these key data quality activities are:

- *Data Profiling*: The data profiling technique is applied to a data source (database, file, etc.) to discover the characteristics and features of datasets. Profiling examines the data sources using statistical methods to establish summaries and a snapshot of the data structure, content, rules, and relationships. Such profiling helps baseline an understanding of the quality of data against expectations and its usability. Data profiling is foundational to establishing data quality metrics and building understanding and eventually confidence of the data among users.[5]
- *Data Quality Monitoring*: Organizations need a formalized way to set targets, measure conformance to those targets, and effectively communicate tangible data quality metrics to senior management and data owners. Standardized metrics provide everyone (executives, IT, and line-of-business managers) with a unified view of data and data quality and can also provide the basis for regulatory reporting where specific data quality reporting requirements exist. Data quality monitoring describes the ongoing practice of data profiling and reporting metrics to stakeholders, which provides a basis for defining improvement initiatives and improving trust of the data among the user community.
- *Data Cleansing*: Data cleansing, or data scrubbing, is the process of detecting and correcting (or removing) corrupt or inaccurate records from a record set, table, or database. It refers to identifying incomplete, incorrect, inaccurate, or irrelevant parts of the data and then replacing, modifying, or deleting the dirty or coarse data. Data cleansing may be performed interactively with data wrangling tools or as batch processing through scripting.[6] Best practices require that data be cleansed as close to the point of origin as possible in order to maintain consistency of the data across the environment. This may not always be practical, however.

11.1.2   Trusting Your Data

Interviews with business users on their single biggest data challenge/peeve leads invariably to some variation on the answer, "I don't trust my data." Further exploration reveals many underlying themes, such as not knowing the source and meaning of their data (see the next section and the Metadata chapter), not knowing which

---

[5] Sebastian-Coleman,L.,"Identifyingdataqualityissuesviadataprofiling,reasonability,"http://searchdata-management.techtarget.com/feature/Identifying-data-quality-issues-via-data-profiling-reasonability.
[6] See https://en.wikipedia.org/wiki/Data_cleansing.

source to use (see the Data Architecture chapter), and of not knowing the accuracy, latency, or some other aspect of the actual content.

All of the preceding concerns relate back to some type of data quality issue, that impede a business user from determining the data's fitness for use.

Data quality is top of mind for business and technology decision makers, but a lack of confidence in the data slows the business down, largely due to the time spent reconciling and verifying data against expectations.

Forrester's Q42014 Global Online Data Quality and Trust Survey[7] indicates that:

- "Confidence in the ability to use data to support business objectives is on shaky ground. Forty three percent of business and technology decision makers are somewhat confident and 25% are concerned about the quality of data."
- "Organizations waste time manually preparing and improving data. Nearly one third of data quality professionals spend more than 40% of their time vetting and validating data before their organization can use it for analysis and decision making."

Thomas Redman in a recent HBR article[8] notes: "Knowledge workers waste up to 50% of time hunting for data, identifying and correcting errors, and seeking confirmatory sources for data that they do not trust." So, what does having trustworthy sources of data look like? This question is worth considering as organizations attempt to mature their data practices. Organizations that can create a trusted data environment generally share the following characteristics.

- There is governance and ownership of the data—business domains assume responsibility for the data they produce and vested in ensuring suitable controls, and curation of their data across their organization.
- Metadata (related to the what, how, when, and where of data origin and location) is authoritatively defined and available to users, enabling governance and appropriate exploitation of data assets.
- The quality and business rules embedded in physical data stores align to business requirements.
- Data is generated and managed via automated processes and is predictable in terms of quality, performance, availability, and other business expectations.
- Data is properly secured and appropriately protected for privacy and access.
- Metrics related to the characteristics and quality of data are made available to users.
- Data changes are auditable and traceable.

Business users understand what their data is, know where it is sourced from, know the business rules imposed on it, and can verify its quality. Perhaps the most

---

[7] Goetz, M., Owens, L., & Jedinak, E., "Build Trusted Data with Data Quality," Forrester Research, Inc., February 26, 2015, https://www.forrester.com/report/Build+Trusted+Data+With+Data+Quality/-/E-RES83344.

[8] Redman, T., "Data's Credibility Problem," *Harvard Business Review*, December 2013, https://hbr.org/2013/12/datas-credibility-problem.

important characteristics are that there is accountability established for the data and confidence that there is an active business steward they can work with for the data they use.

11.1.3 Data Quality Challenges

Data quality issues are caused and perpetuated in an organization for several reasons, many of them rooted in organizational culture and process related issues, as well as poorly deployed automation and technology. Frequently, they point to the lack of a coherent data strategy and governance approach for data quality across the organization, one that builds data quality management into the business processes and is closely aligned to business priorities.

Data has tended to be treated as a by-product of the execution of business processes and managed from that perspective, with a series of ad hoc investments. This mindset needs to evolve to one that fully appreciates the opportunities and value that data provides. Foundational to addressing data quality needs that are driven by business needs and priorities is the development and governance of a data strategy that addresses these priorities with well-aligned data investments.

The following data quality issues reflect tactical challenges that occur due to the lack of a considered approach to managing data.

11.1.3.1 Inadequate Controls at the Point of Origin

For externally sourced data, this can be due to inadequate acquisition controls, poorly defined service level agreements (SLAs), and the lack of a governed process by which data is sourced into the organization. Business users can download data from the internet, can "explore" external sources, and can leverage the data in operational and analytic processes easily, given the enabling technologies available. Lack of business and technical controls in this process introduces data quality issues.

In the case of internal data, inadequate definition and/or application of business rules within transactional systems before originating content is a common reason. Errors introduced during manual data entry processes are also a common issue at the point of data origination.

Business areas that originate content (the Producers) tend to focus on their specific, local business process and the data needs surrounding it without considering broader organizational requirements. Concepts highlighted in the Data Governance chapter regarding stewardship and management of data as an enterprise asset are important to consider in the context of data creation. Poor and/or incompletely documented data quality requirements are a related issue.

11.1.3.2   Volume, Variety, Velocity

The modern-day organization is confronted with a rapid growth of the data ecosystem and the variety and volume of data available to it. The pace of data creation, the velocity, presents a related challenge of keeping apace in terms of identifying data quality issues at the speed the data is ingested.

Data is also increasingly stored in nonstandard structures, with the proliferation of NoSQL data formats driven by the growing storage of click-stream, social, machine, system log, and other data. The unpredictability in the structure and content of the data coming in exacerbates the problems of automating data quality checks.

11.1.3.3   Environment Complexity

Data is now stored and sourced across a highly distributed environment; distributed physically in locations such as the cloud, disparate technologies, and platforms; and distributed globally as well as across internal and external data sources.

Organizational boundaries increasingly blur when considering data, complicating data provenance and lineage, and questions of data quality.

The challenges associated with enabling coherence across dispersed systems, structures, origination systems, and prohibitive volumes significantly complicates data quality management.

11.1.3.4   Too Much Proliferation and Duplication

The technical ease of duplicating and sharing data, the low cost of storage, the ever-growing number of sets of data available for organizations to acquire, the "spreadmarts" proliferated on individual desktops, as well as our collective tendencies to duplicate and proliferate data also introduce data quality issues.

11.1.3.5   Poor Metadata, Unclear Definitions, and Multiple Interpretations

Organizations historically have not prioritized developing and documenting the data they create, acquire, and share, hence causing the issue of no common, consistent understanding of what their data means and should be used for. IT typically attempts to capture its understanding of the data in repositories to the best of their understanding. However, the metadata they capture tends to be technical and without business input.

Metadata represents the single, common interpretation of an organization's data assets and is critical to data quality. Knowing your data and the rules applied to it at the point of its origin as well as along the way prior to the point of consumption is critical to determining its "fitness for use."

Other causes for poor data quality range from use of manual and/or poorly controlled processes to cultural apathy and unawareness of data quality management practices. Some of these are identified in Table 11.1.[9]

These are all symptoms of issues that point to the need for:

- A data quality aware culture
- Business awareness and understanding of data quality management and how it circles back to their eventual "lack of trust" of data
- Business stewardship for data quality management and prioritization of investments to address it

11.2 Who Is Data Quality?

Data quality (and its management) is tightly woven into the data fabric of the organization and impacts everyone in the organization who works with that data, which is, for all intents and purposes, every person in the organization.

Key participants here are best thought in terms of data producers and consumers. In addition, IT also impacts the data quality process. Key IT roles that support data quality include data architects, data modelers, and database administrators (DBA).

Data producers, the "originators" of data, introduce the data into the organization's environment. Their role is very important to establishing high quality data at origin. Data governance often identifies the producer as the data steward or data owner primarily responsible for the quality of data established at the point of origin. Producers are responsible for the definition of the controls and business rules that constrain the data, that is, the "preventive" controls that determine the quality of data at inception.

Data consumers drive the reason for data quality. Consumers may be many and varied across the organization, needing the same data for different purposes depending on their particular business role, such as technical analysts, business analysts, or IT. It is important to understand that data quality expectations of different consumers will be different based on their needs and that this should drive architectural and governance approaches. A data scientist who is studying data for broad patterns may not have the same rigorous expectation of precision and quality of the data as the financial analyst who will be disclosing the organization's financial position.

---

[9] For additional details, see Talend, "Top 10 Root Causes of Data Quality Problems," Talend White Paper, http://docs.media.bitpipe.com/io_25x/io_25186/item_384743/Top%2010%20Root%20Causes%20 of%20Data%20Quality%20Problems-%20wp_en_dq_top_10_dq_problems.pdf and Sebastian-Coleman, L., "Identifying data quality issues via data profiling, reasonability", http://searchdata-management.techtarget.com/feature/Identifying-data-quality-issues-via-data-profiling-reasonability.

Table 11.1 Causes for poor data quality

Data quality cause	Description	Potential mitigations
Data conversion or integration from multiple sources	Data conversion typically occurs from some previously existing data source. The conversion process can create issues in the target data source due to missing business rules and misinterpretation causing losses "in translation." Issues also arise due to data conversions across two different data models such as from relational to a NoSQL model. These changes can impact the expected data quality of the dataset and give rise to unexpected data quality issues	Profile early and often—data may be fit for use in a source but not in the destination. Profiling helps evaluate data in the source and determine how it might fit in the destination Apply data quality tools when possible—data quality tools can be leveraged to apply standards in a uniform way, leading to more accurate sharing of data
Poorly defined, differing data quality requirements	The Marketing department may have different expectations of data quality than does Finance, which may then be applying different cleansing rules to a dataset, creating conflicting records as output. Such situations create issues for the end consumer who is then left with a "quality" issue and uncertainty about the data they are using	Data Governance is critical to addressing situations such as these. Setting up a cross-functional data governance team will ensure that people are in place to define a common data model and align on quality expectations
Non-conforming data references	Reconciling data across multiple differently defined and modeled reference datasets gives rise to data quality issues. Country codes defined by the two-character abbreviations versus a numerical code can present reconciliation challenges	Examine reports produced by different parts of the organization and/or profile data. Collaborate with data stewards to uncover nonconformance. Determine these kinds of differences and work with the business to reconcile them
Data aging	The challenge with aging data is determining at which point the information is no longer valid. Such decisions can be somewhat arbitrary and vary by usage. E.g., maintaining a former customer's address for more than 5 years is probably not useful if the customer has not been heard from in several years, despite marketing efforts. At the same time, maintaining customer address information for a homeowner's insurance claim may be necessary and even required by law. Business owners need to make such decisions, and the rules should be architected into the solution	Many MDM tools provide a platform for implementing survivorship rules for the same data from different sources Data governance (aligning on business rules and the decisions they drive as an organization) can help address this issue Apply the rules established for records management (see Records Management chapter) for retention to data in a similar manner. This way, outdated information is archived or destroyed and other information is kept to support business needs and meet compliance requirements
Poor database design	The data model used to represent information depicts content, relationships, and standardization. Incorrect relationships translate to incorrect representation of the domain depicted; loosely defined structures allow for inaccuracies in data. Also, the level of normalization in the model drives the amount of redundancy in the data model, which can cause data quality issues	Rigorous, thoughtful data model design that applies the use of standardized names and structures, while allowing sufficient flexibility to accommodate business needs

Data architects, modelers, and DBAs represent key IT roles to managing data quality. Data architects define and maintain the data environment blueprint, ensuring that it is laid out in accordance with needs and consumption patterns, managing redundancy, and deploying appropriate technology and controls to ensure that data fulfills user quality expectations as it moves through the environment.

Data modelers represent the domain and its content, the constraints, and the business rules that bound data and ensure alignment to its intent. Use of referential integrity, data types, "valid values," and relationships in a relational model are examples of data quality rules that are enforced systematically.

Database administrators oversee the care and feeding of the physical data stores, monitoring data for integrity issues and performance, and can provide input and guidance to managing data quality issues.

11.2.1   Data Quality Controls

Preventive controls are key to ensuring quality at transition and perhaps the most critical quality gate in the data quality cycle. This is achieved by controls within data origination systems, at manual data entry points, and via controls on data imported from external sources. Business users present a significant component to manage preventive controls.

The goal should be to ensure that the data has a clear definition, system of record, and managed duplication, and that it aligns to the business rules and constraints that represent the business it models. Frequently, data producers do not take sufficient care in addressing the quality requirements of consumers and tend to establish data that does not accurately represent the needs of the complete domain.

Other types of data quality controls can be *detective* or *corrective*. As the name indicates, detective controls are executed to ensure data quality after data has been created and may be executed across all parts of the data environment. Examples of detective controls include integrity checks after duplicating data, profiling with data quality tools, sampling, reporting, and other operational checks. Business and technical analysts, as well as IT, play a key role here.

Corrective controls are the processes executed to address data quality issues once they occur, pointing to issues in preventive or detective controls. These are typically procedural and should be fully auditable to ensure that modifications made to data after creation are clearly explained and understood. The recommended pattern to implementing corrective controls is to "correct" data at source and propagate the correction to all other points of consumption. Encountering incorrect data is inevitable, setting up the right processes to address this issue is critical to data quality management. Because corrective controls are a natural outcome of detective controls, producers and consumers, as well as IT, all play a role here.

11.3   Implementing Data Quality

This section discusses the processes and activities that an organization should establish in order to ensure that the quality of their data matures to align to user expectations.

As noted in prior sections, data quality management should be viewed as an ongoing function embedded into an organization deliberatively.

Data quality management broadly involves the following processes.

11.3.1   Defining Data Quality

Activities to define the data quality (DQ) expectations and needs of the organization are foundational to executing on an organization's data quality management priorities. These activities can be initiated by a variety of change management, governance, or compliance triggers in the organization. Most commonly, however, data quality requirements and business rules are expressed as part of a project life cycle. Stewards may also define the data quality needs for datasets they are responsible for outside of project and development processes.

Key considerations include:

- Projects and business users tend to be stovepiped in their data quality considerations; stewards should take care to consider the requirements of all stakeholders in the organization. A coordinated, collaborative data governance function can help enable the necessary holistic view of data quality and is an important supporting process.
- This activity also tends to be short changed due to project pressures—suitable rigor and documentation in defining data quality needs is important for clarity and aligning to a common understanding of organizational quality goals, in addition to being essential to DQ management.
- Educating users on data quality—its impact and importance as well as its dimensions through formal training, brown bags, and other mechanisms—helps build the necessary understanding that can evolve their articulation of quality needs and matures DQ management.
- Documenting and disseminating data quality requirements and business rules in an enterprise metadata capability enables a consistent understanding and transparency to the data quality expectations within the organization.

11.3.2   Deploying Data Quality

These are the processes that enforce DQ on physical data stores across the organization. Processes include the enforcement of DQ within data originating systems (data at source), at points of data acquisition from external sources, as data moves across stores, at points of consumption, in the archival and purging of data, and at other points in its life cycle.

This process is usually executed within system development life cycles as part of the development and deployment process, but it can also be enforced via manual processes and procedures.

Processes to deploy DQ are where the "rubber meets the road"—the quality of the data that users encounter will be based on the DQ enforcement deployed through these processes.

Key considerations include:

- DQ is best managed when rules are rigorously applied in data originating systems: at the point of creation. Implications from this are the need to clearly (and unambiguously) designate data originating systems (also called systems of record, or SOR) as well as to ensure that data is changed only at the SOR and distributed as read-only copies elsewhere.
- SLAs for externally sourced data should address DQ expectations and enforce them at the point of ingest.
- Though it is not always practical to enforce that data be changed only at source, making it auditable will provide transparency on changes and lets users know what they are getting.
- Automating DQ enforcement helps improve the predictability of outcomes, besides being more efficient.
- Ensuring documentation of DQ rules and its traceability to requirements applied across the organization is an important aspect to deployment.

11.3.3   Monitoring Data Quality

Monitoring and measuring data for quality provides an ongoing DQ health-check for the organization guiding understanding, awareness, and prioritization of DQ investments. This includes establishing processes to schedule data quality profiling, assess and analyze results, and report findings to concerned stakeholders.

DQ profiling can be initiated by a variety of triggers, based on organizational priorities, to address specific data quality issues or to build an assessment and awareness of data quality. Understanding data quality over time builds confidence among users (they know what they are getting) and helps drive funding for improvements in the areas impactful to organizational objectives.

Profiling can be approached from top-down and bottom-up perspectives. The bottom-up approach analyzes data within stores, providing statistics, summaries, and aggregates that are informative to stakeholders. Profiling like this can be driven in support of a variety of needs, both technical and business driven.

Another approach is to assess the health of data against domain rules and requirements provided by business SMEs (see the earlier Defining Data Quality section), the benefit being the ability to verify alignment of data quality to needs.

Metrics generated from profiling activities are typically published on a schedule that brings suitable attention to the health of the data organization and drives investments to address adversely impactful data quality issues to the business.

Organizations may choose to prioritize profiling of their critical data assets; data classification activities (described in the Data Classification section) may be considered to provide this guidance. DQ profiling vendors and tools could be considered for large-scale widespread deployments within an organization.

Key considerations include:

- Profiling is very important to informing other processes in this section—you cannot improve something that is not measured.
- Data quality has many dimensions to consider; careful consideration should be given to all of them in developing profiling characteristics. There is a tendency to think primarily in terms of accuracy.

11.3.4   Resolving Data Quality Issues

An organization requires processes to track, address, and resolve data quality issues as they are encountered in order to meet the data quality expectations of the organization.

Processes in this area can be triggered when regular business operations identify anomalous data or when embedded controls identify issues within processes such as when copying, moving, or transforming data. Embedded controls (particularly automated ones) are valuable in validating, identifying, and resolving issues in data in a timely and repeatable manner and preventing data degradation over time.

DQ issues management includes processes to identify, evaluate/analyze issues, execute corrective activities, and report on DQ issues to concerned stakeholders.

Key considerations include:

- Collecting data quality information issues over time and reporting to stakeholders on trends and metrics are important to building awareness of the state and progress of data quality issues.
- Embedding preventive controls within processes is very important to preempting slowdowns arising from data issues during mission critical operations.
- Activities to determine resolution should attempt to get at root causes by identifying the underlying or systemic issues that caused them, for example, issues in the business process, the systems that create the data, and issues with controls. Recurring data issues are costly to resolve, so due diligence upfront to resolve the source(s) of the problem is critical to building data quality into the organization.
- Ensure auditability of changes made in DQ issues management.
- Automating the issues resolution process with appropriate controls is recommended.

11.3.5 Measuring Data Quality

A business users' lack of trust of their data is rooted in data quality issues; "trust" and data quality are inextricably linked.

Lack of trust is closely associated with uncertainty about the quality of the data, such as its sourcing, content definition, or content accuracy. The issue is not only that the data source has quality issues, but that the issues that it may or may not have are unknown.

Knowing that the data in a store is, for example, about 40% accurate for key elements is a week old, is authoritative, or that some elements are inconsistent with the values as compared to another reference source improves the business users understanding of their data, and improves their ability to make informed choices about it. Eventually, this is key to establishing business users' trust of their data.

Establishing and maintaining data quality metrics are thus critical. The business user should invest in, on a prioritized basis, establishing data quality metrics for datasets and stores of interest, as well as in building data quality reporting processes for them. This provides visibility and awareness to the larger business user community and gets senior management attention. Exposing data quality measures is also a great way to build business cases for new capabilities, important to the data-driven approach that executives and decision makers emphasize.

In addition to traditional metrics in data quality, new metrics will emerge that measure how well an information management solution supports a business process. Examples include reducing duplication of effort and shortening time-to-resolution for problems.[10]

The next section identifies data quality measures that can be leveraged in a comprehensive data quality metrics program.

11.3.6 Data Classification

It is important to consider data classification in the context of data quality. As noted earlier, not all data is equal, as in it does not have equal data quality needs from the user's perspective. Given the limited investment dollars typically available for data management activities, it is worthwhile to consider classifying data from the perspective of business impact and to prioritize data quality investments based on that.

"Data classification is the process of sorting and categorizing data into various types, forms, or any other distinct class. Data classification enables the separation and classification of data according to dataset requirements for various business objectives."[11] This can be of particular importance for risk management, legal discovery, and compliance.

---

[10] Leganza, G., "Information Strategies Move Center Stage," Forrester Research, Inc., May 20, 2013.

[11] See Techopedia's definition at: https://www.techopedia.com/definition/13779/data-classification.

Engaging with the business to "classify" data for their critical business outcome perspectives can help drive thoughtful data quality investments and improve articulation of quality needs.

The term "critical data elements" is frequently used in this context. This is the identification of critical data elements as a data governance practice that helps organizations prioritize funding, directly aligned to improving revenue and product quality. Critical data often describes the parameters within which work must be performed. Critical data varies by industry, however, and it can be important to establishing data quality priorities.

11.3.7   Data Certification

The notion of data certification is considered in many organizations in the context of data quality as a formal control that validates and increases confidence in the data for consumers. Organizations should consider building out this control, particularly for their critical data or business processes (e.g., financial reporting). Certified data can be defined as "data that has been subjected to a structured quality process to ensure that it meets or exceeds the standards established by its intended consumers. Such standards are typically documented via service level agreements (SLA) and administered by an organized data governance structure."[12]

Figure 11.1 provides a high-level depiction of a potential certification process and its benefits.[13]

11.3.8   Data Quality—Trends and Challenges

The complexity and volume of data used by organizations are increasing exponentially, with a corresponding increase in data quality management challenges. Organizations are consuming more data from more sources as their needs increase in support of rapidly evolving business models, complex analytic needs, and increased digitization. They are going beyond the models of traditional structured data sourced from their internal transactional systems into traditional warehouse environments to using data in new and innovative ways.

Disruptive technologies such as Hadoop, In-memory databases, NoSQL, Warehouse appliance, and cloud technologies enable organizations to store and process large, varied, and nonstandard data structures. The strides made in computing

---

[12] Brunson, D., "Certified Data and the Certification Process for Financial Institutions," TechTarget, December 6, 2005. http://searchdatamanagement.techtarget.com/news/2240111233/ Certified-Data-and-the-Certification-Process-for-Financial-Institutions.

[13] See http://www.b-eye-network.com/images/content/4Big.jpg.

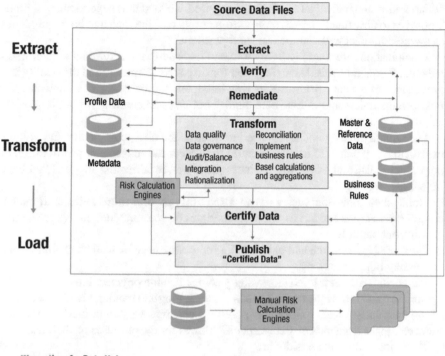

Fig. 11.1 Data certification process

power, storage technology, and infrastructure enable the storage of large volumes of data and increasingly complex analytic capabilities.

Organizations, thus, ingest data more rapidly, in ever-increasing volumes, of increasing variability and complexity, using a bewildering range of platforms and data management systems in support of increasingly complex business processes and data uses. The complexity in all these dimensions continue to trend up with the ever-growing needs of capabilities such as smart technology, the internet of things, social media analytics, digitization, machine learning, healthcare analytics, and so on.

All of these trends present new challenges to data quality management within organizations. Processes to verify, control, correct, and disseminate high-quality data are challenged to address the increasingly complex nature of the data landscape.

A CEB Study notes that "the boundaries across companies, functions and roles are becoming more fluid. As hierarchies give way to faster-moving matrices, greater collaboration and individual flexibility is required. This extends beyond the individual employee to how functions and units within companies interact, and how companies as a whole interact with competitors and partners."[14]

Organizations are sourcing from more external sources in additional to their internal data. Frequently, this data in ingested for discovery purposes, and the quality and provenance of the data that makes its way into internal processes are unknown and/or unknowable unless appropriate data quality policies and controls are put in place at acquisition points.

Data quality management will need to address the pace, complexity and volume of data at entry points of an organization to prevent the subsequent proliferation of poor quality data that jeopardize business processes, recalling the adage of "garbage in, garbage out."

Rapid data ingestion such as with streaming, require more agile, automated, control mechanisms and intervention technologies that can provide suitable preventive and upfront controls.

Balancing governance and agility is an increasing need as well as challenge and addressing both a necessity.

Given that data tends to be increasingly sourced within organizations to serve both exploratory and formal production needs, documenting and making visible the quality of the data using robust metadata capabilities becomes very important so business users can make decisions on data's specific fitness for the purposes of their use.

Some techniques to consider are:

- Expanding data governance and curation to include data discovery and exploratory needs.
- Automating information cataloging and discovery.
- Increasing automation of data management activities, workflow, and collaboration.
- Emphasizing centralized governance and policy definition, while executing in a distributed environment.

In addition to traditional metrics such as data quality, new metrics will emerge that measure how well an information management solution supports a business process. Examples include reducing duplication of effort and shortening time-to-resolution for problems.[15]

11.4   Data Quality Tools

Tools related to managing data quality in the environment are categorized in this section. Note that system automation technologies that ensure repeatable application of data quality in some way, if used appropriately, can be considered data

---

[14] See https://www.cebglobal.com/information-technology/digital-enterprise-2020/trend-spotter. html.

[15] Leganza, G., "Information Strategies Move Center Stage," Forrester Research, Inc., May 20, 2013.

quality "tools." For example, an application that validates a data element against business rules prior to persisting it or a DBMS that enforces integrity constraints both automate aspects of data quality management. That said, some categories of data quality tools are targeted specifically to the activities within data quality management.

The increasing complexity of the data environment has correspondingly increased data quality management needs and resulted in substantial growth in the data quality tools market.

Key functional features common to data quality products and tools include[16]:

- *Profiling and metrics*: The ability to profile and measure data quality against defined business, characteristics, and expectations using statistical techniques between and across datasets.
- *Standardization and cleansing*: Features include the ability to convert data to a consistent format and constrain to appropriate domain values based on predefined standards. Address normalization is an example.
- *Identity resolution*: Features are centered around relating, linking, merging, and consolidating entries across sets of data.
- *Monitoring*: The deployment of ongoing controls to ensure that data conforms to business rules of organization's data quality.
- *Issue resolution and workflow*: An interface and process that promote collaboration for the identification, quarantining, escalation, and resolution of data quality issues.
- *Cleaning and enhancement*: The enhancement of the value of data by appending related metadata attributes, including from external sources (e.g., consumer demographic attributes and geographic descriptors).

As noted earlier, many supporting capabilities within tools and products such as administration and operational capabilities also support data quality management. Of particular note is metadata management, discussed in detail in the Metadata chapter.

---

[16] Judah, S., & Friedman, T., "Magic Quadrant for Data Quality Tools." Gartner Research, Inc., November 18, 2015.

Chapter 12
Data Warehousing and Business Intelligence

12.1 What Are Data Warehousing and Business Intelligence?

Traditionally data warehouses were built to reflect "snapshots" of the enterprise-level operational environment over time. In other words, a certain amount of operational data was recorded at a particular point in time and stored in a data warehouse. Originally, such snapshots were typically taken monthly. Today, they are often taken multiple times per day. Data warehouses provide a history of the operational environment suitable for trend analysis. This allows analysts and business executives to plan for the future based on recent trends. Answers to such questions as how have revenue or costs evolved over time and the ability to "slice and dice" such data are typical functions asked of a data warehouse.

Often a data warehouse integrates data from multiple authoritative, operational data sources. This extends the ability of business users to perform analysis. For example, an insurance company will want to combine data from its underwriting and its claims systems to analyze how to price future policies. Combining data from multiple systems in a data warehouse is ideally done at the most granular level possible. This ultimately allows business users and executives to drill down into specific scenarios when presented with quarterly or annual performance summaries. However, such integration is limited to the lowest common denominator. For example, if one source system contains transactional sales data of an item and another system contains bulk purchasing data of the same item, analysis on profit between these two sources is limited to the bulk level at which the items were purchased.

© Springer International Publishing AG 2018
M. Fleckenstein, L. Fellows, *Modern Data Strategy*,
https://doi.org/10.1007/978-3-319-68993-7_12

12.1.1   Data Warehouse Architectural Components

Figure 12.1 shows some key architectural components of a traditional data warehouse.

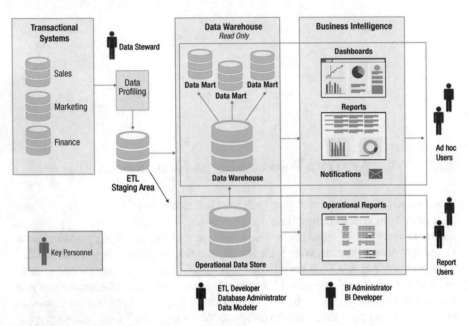

Fig. 12.1   Data warehousing architectural components

12.1.1.1   Staging Area

The staging area is designed to minimize the extract burden on source systems. Here, all data needed for loading the data warehouse is available in one place. It allows for the transformation/integration and any required data cleansing before the data is loaded into the data warehouse. Note that the staging area is a transient storage area that is strictly for developers and is not accessible to end users for reporting.

12.1.1.2   Extract Transform Load

The extract-transform-load (ETL) layer is one of the key components of a data warehouse. ETL is used for extracting the data snapshots from one or more source systems, cleansing and transforming/integrating the data, and loading the data into the data warehouse. Some ETL functions include the creation of surrogate keys, summarization/aggregation of data, and formatting data.

12.1.1.3   Operational Data Store

As the name suggests, the operational data store (ODS) is used to store operational data. It is also often used for operational reporting and eliminates the need to query the application databases. Querying the ODS provides the benefit of reducing overhead on the operational system and provides almost the same low latency as the operational system itself for querying. An additional benefit of the ODS is that, just like the data warehouse, it often contains data integrated from multiple sources. The ODS also differs from the data warehouse in that the data warehouse stores significant historical information, whereas the amount of historical information in an ODS is not much—perhaps a couple of months' worth of data.

12.1.1.4   Data Mart

Data marts are an extension of the data warehouse that contains a subset of data stored in the data warehouse. In addition to enterprise data from the data warehouse, data marts may contain local data. Data marts are subject specific and usually serve a specific business component, such as finance, marketing, or sales.

12.1.1.5   Business Intelligence

Traditional business intelligence (BI) is a reporting and analysis layer implemented on top of a data warehouse for historical reporting and trend analysis. Such a layer may extend to the ODS for operational reporting. Traditional BI tools provide a semantic layer that allows for the translation of data terms as they are stored in a database to terms that make sense to the business user. This extends to derived terms that may only exist in the BI layer. For example, the user may require a term such as "widget container cost," which is the result of a calculation of the number of widgets per container times the cost per widget. The BI layer offers the user both pre-defined reports as well as the ability to build ad hoc reports via a drag-and-drop interface.

Bill Inmon, recognized by many as the father of the data warehouse, defines the term "data warehouse" as a subject-oriented, nonvolatile, integrated, time-variant collection of data in support of management's decisions.[1] The data warehouse forms the foundation for business intelligence.

- *Subject-oriented*: A data warehouse can be used to analyze one or more specific subject areas. For example, the marketing department might want to formulate

---

[1] Inmon, W. H, Strauss, D., & Neushloss, N., *DW 2.0: The Architecture for the Next Generation of Data Warehousing,* Morgan Kaufmann, July 28, 2010.

strategies for marketing new products to help them make better decisions, by analyzing their data in conjunction with sales data.

- *Integrated*: Data warehouses must consolidate data from disparate sources into a consistent format that can be used for reporting and analysis. They must resolve problems such as naming conflicts and inconsistencies among units of measure.
- *Time-variant*: To discover trends in business, a data warehouse contains historical "snapshots" of data at a point in time. A data warehouse's focus on change over time is what is meant by the term time-variant.
- *Nonvolatile*: Nonvolatile means that, once entered into the warehouse, data should not change.

Other key characteristics of a data warehouse include:

- Updates are performed by the application processes only for refreshing the data on a periodic basis (hourly, daily, weekly, monthly). Updates may also be triggered by events. Each case is a snapshot at a particular time.
- The data warehouse data model is optimized for querying, whereas transaction processing systems are optimized for operations such as insert, update, and delete.
- Data warehouses are often expanded by using data marts. Data marts contain a subset of the data in a data warehouse, usually tailored to a certain area of the organization. Data marts may be augmented with local data that is important to that part of the organization.

Data warehouses and data marts provide centralized data repositories for reporting and analytics. Data warehouse architectures include a staging area for bringing in raw data from multiple data sources, which is then transformed into a report-friendly data model in the data warehouse.

When data warehouses first started out, data was loaded/updated on a periodic basis—first monthly, then weekly, then usually nightly. Over time, the frequency of uploads increased to daily and even multiple times per day. With the explosion of data from sources, such as social media and other structured and unstructured sources, data warehouse architectures face a challenge keeping up with the rapid changes in both business needs and technology. The need for real-time, or close to real-time, data means that the traditional approach of loading data using batch processing (whether daily or hourly) does not always meet user requirements. Business users do not want to wait weeks and months for their requests to be completed—they need information as soon as possible to make better business decisions.

This has led to the development of an analytic environment in which the traditional data warehouse is augmented with additional data stores that may include transactional systems, operational data stores (ODS), data lakes, and more. An ODS stores a copy of operational data, sometimes integrated from multiple sources, and is available in a near-real-time fashion. This way it is accessible without affecting the performance of the actual operational system. A data lake is a storage repository that holds a very large amount of data, often from diverse sources, in native format until needed.

Fig. 12.2 Analytic environment data highway

In some respects, a data lake can be compared to a staging area of a data warehouse, but there are key differences. Just like a staging area, a data lake is a conglomeration point for raw data from diverse sources. However, a staging area only stores new data needed for addition to the data warehouse and is a transient data store. In contrast, a data lake typically stores all possible data that might be needed for an undefined amount of analysis and reporting, allowing analysts to explore new data relationships. In addition, a data lake is usually built on commodity hardware and software such as Hadoop, whereas traditional staging areas typically reside in structured databases that require specialized servers.

Ralph Kimball, another thought leader in data warehousing, describes such an analytic environment as a "data highway" with multiple caches of increasing latency.[2] Here data stores are loosely coupled, each accommodating business needs in an appropriately timely fashion. For example, represented on the left side of Fig. 12.2, certain situations that are extremely time-sensitive, such as fraud detection or cyberattack detection, demand immediate access to raw data, but sacrifice organization and data quality. At the other end of the spectrum is the enterprise data warehouse (EDW) with highly structured snapshots of data, collected over time, and the ability to produce repeatable, consistent reports, albeit at significantly higher latency.

In Kimball's view, the aim in this environment should be to glean data from each cache as needed to solve business demands and to structure data as early as possible (given business demands), with the eventual goal to structure all necessary data so that it is available for long-term analysis. This structured data can then even be used to help contextualize an unstructured environment going forward.

Traditional data warehouse architectures use a "schema on write" (define your schema, then write your data to it, then read your data) approach with well-defined data models. More recent additions to the analytic environment, which can handle much more data and are propelled by the business users' desire for immediate information, use a "schema on read" (load your data first, then define your schema when reading the data) approach, using database technologies such as Hadoop and NoSQL. This means that data consumers have a bigger role to play in creating a sensible schema when extracting data, but they have the advantage of having all the data readily available in the data lake. There is no need to provision a new staging area or ODS every time there is a new analytical/reporting requirement.

In conjunction with the new analytic environment in which the data warehouse plays a key part, a new set of data preparation tools that provide business users with a mechanism to analyze data with minimal involvement from IT has also evolved.

---

[2] Kimball, R., "Newly Emerging Best Practices for Big Data," The Kimball Group, September 30, 2012.

These tools allow business users to tap and manipulate data directly, rather than waiting for IT to write customized reports for them. It goes without saying that the business user must be highly sensitive to where in the analytical environment he or she is operating. If operating with raw data, data quality and consistency are likely issues. On the other hand, operating in an EDW environment provides the user with robust, consistent data, often with the ability to drill down many layers, albeit at the cost of high latency.

As mentioned, business intelligence traditionally goes hand in hand with data warehousing. Traditional business intelligence (BI) platforms are typically implemented on top of a data warehouse or an ODS. These COTS products present data in terms understandable by the business. They consist of a combination of pre-defined reports (sometimes with complex computation logic) as well as ad hoc reports that users are allowed to create using a drag-and-drop interface. As the term "business intelligence" implies, these tools are aimed at providing insight to the business. They do this by looking at historical data and projecting trends.

The need for more current data, the adoption of the analytic environment, and the evolution of data preparation tools are blurring the line between business intelligence and analytics. Clearly, it is possible to gain valuable business insight not just from historical trend analysis in an EDW, but also through much more real-time data analysis. Traditional BI tools are evolving to include functions such as streaming analytics, interactive discovery, advanced visualization, and other capabilities.

12.2   Who Is Data Warehousing and Business Intelligence?

Traditionally, implementing data warehousing and business intelligence required business knowledge from analysts as well as a wide spectrum of technical skills such as data architects, data modelers, developers, database administrators, data stewards, ETL developers, BI tool experts, and report developers. All these skills are still required. Building a data warehouse is a serious undertaking that relies on high data quality, authoritative data sources, and well-thought-out data models. With the evolution of the data warehouse to an analytic environment, other skills may also be required. For example, depending on business need, skills such as statistics or linguistics may be required to drive discovery and data matching.

Data warehouses are frequently designed using dimensional data models. These models, though relational in nature, differ from traditional relational database models and are well suited for reporting. Therefore, data warehouse teams often comprise developers and data modelers who are familiar with both standard relational design as well as dimensional modeling.

The probability of a successful data warehouse initiative increases if there is better collaboration between business users and IT. Data warehouse initiatives have traditionally been driven by IT with limited involvement from the business/user community, even though these initiatives are sponsored by business users. With the increasing use of data preparation tools, involvement of the business community takes on a much greater role and the business bears additional responsibility for leveraging data in a reliable way. Lack of coordination between business and IT often results in not satisfying the needs of the user community and can lead initiatives to fail. This, in turn, leads users to build their own solutions, such as local databases or even spreadsheets, perpetuating the data management problem. As discussed in the Implementing a Data Strategy chapter, building a data warehouse is considered to be an advanced data management domain, relying on foundational domains such as data quality, data architecture, data governance, and a data strategy to be firmly in place.

12.3 Implementing Data Warehousing and Business Intelligence

Implementing a data warehouse is typically the result of inadequate reporting. It often stems from an inability to generate well-integrated, enterprise-level reports or from a lack of good insight into what the organizational position was in the past or even from conflicting reports in both terms and numbers across departments. Therefore, a very good place to begin implementing a data warehouse is with an analysis of current reporting. Such an analysis will yield report inconsistencies and limitations. And, in collaboration with talking to business analysts, it should yield unmet reporting requirements and thus serve as a good foundation for designing a data warehouse.

Through a reports analysis before embarking on the data warehouse journey, the business needs that the data warehouse will be addressing are highly likely to surface. The traditional approach to implementing a data warehouse is to use a waterfall methodology. That is, the business and IT jointly determine the requirements up front, and then the data warehouse is designed and developed in relative isolation before it is revealed again to the business. Often, the way it is revealed is via the BI layer. Report designs have been drafted and the basic data infrastructure for ad hoc reporting has been put in place. The problem with this approach is that it takes a long time—months or even years—to design and implement a data warehouse.

The development cycle for a data warehouse can be reduced by initially limiting both the number of data sources as well as the number of data fields. It should be possible to design a stable data model using a few data sources reflected in key reports.

There is a strong trend toward agile development in software design. Various methodologies have evolved, but they all essentially advocate multi-week rather than multi-month cycles of iterative design and development that embrace high collaboration among business and IT users. The data warehouse design and development process can certainly benefit from a more agile approach. Traditional long-term development efforts are expensive and do not always succeed. However, the agile approach must also be adapted to designing a data warehouse. Unlike building a web-based user interface that is typically easy to reconfigure, the basic data architecture of a data warehouse must be relatively stable once created. The business must understand what it is it wants to measure and in what terms. Making radical changes to the fundamental data warehouse design can be cost prohibitive.

A long-term design and development cycle is not best suited to today's analytic environment where users want access to real-time data from a variety of sources. An agile approach is more suited to an analytic environment that includes data in raw or minimally cleansed and integrated formats. Such an environment may be implemented using sandboxes where users are free to combine different raw data sources and perform discovery. Resulting analytics and reports can be refined, incorporating user inputs at an early stage in the development life cycle. Repeatable queries and a stable underlying data structure can then become more formalized as part of a traditional enterprise data warehouse. Of course, this still requires that the foundational design of the data warehouse be able to accommodate these new findings.

The ability to analyze much larger datasets and the business need to perform analysis in closer to real time are giving rise to new tools and technologies in both the data warehousing and BI spaces. The next section looks at both traditional tools as well as some of the emerging trends in data warehouse and business intelligence technologies, and the next chapter looks more closely at data analytics and how analytics can complement data warehousing and business intelligence.

12.4   Data Warehousing and Business Intelligence Tools

Traditional data warehouse and BI initiatives require a variety of tools, either as part of the data warehouse environment itself or as a precursor to implementing a successful data warehouse. Table 12.1 lists the key set of tools needed.

With the exception of business intelligence tools, traditional tools in the data warehousing and business intelligence space are geared primarily to technical users and can be challenging for business analysts to understand. With the evolution of the analytic environment, business analysts are seeing more tools that they can use without burdening IT, for example, data preparation tools.

Data preparation tools help ease the data integration burden. These tools can be seen as complementing existing enterprise data integration tools (in the same way that a tool like Tableau co-exists with enterprise reporting tools). Data preparation tools can be used for rapid prototyping and for projects using agile methodologies that need quick turnaround. Many of these tools have features such as:

- A spreadsheet-style interface for mapping data elements
- Machine learning to identify correlations and patterns
- Built-in connectors for structured and unstructured data sources
- A tool to analyze and provide a scorecard for the quality of data
- The ability to recommend transformation rules for cleansing the data
- An audit trail of the rules applied to the data, so that they can be reused. Steps and business rules captured in the data preparation tools can be reused as building blocks for future data quality processes.

Table 12.1 Data warehousing and business intelligence key tools

Tool	Description
Data modeling	Data modeling tools are used to represent the relationships between the entities and attributes of a system. They can be used to create the conceptual model, logical model, and physical model. They also provide capabilities such as generating the database objects and reverse engineering a model from an existing database
Data quality	Data quality tools help users analyze data (profile) and take the steps necessary to cleanse the data to conform to business rules and data standards
Data integration	Data integration tools are used to extract data from one or more data sources, apply business rules to transform the data, and load the data into the data warehouse
Business intelligence	Business integration tools provide the interface for users to view the data using reports and dashboards. BI tools allow users to create pre-defined and ad hoc reports, dashboards, and scorecards
Database platform	Traditionally, the database platform in a data warehouse meant a relational database or a variant of the relational database, e.g., columnar database. With the need to store unstructured data, database platforms such as NoSQL are gaining adoption as part of an "analytic environment."
Metadata management	Metadata management tools provide a mechanism to capture, store, and search metadata such as data lineage, definition, usage, business rules, and impact analysis. Metadata provides additional context to reports and dashboards

Preparing data for analysis (cleansing, standardizing, and integrating) still consumes a large chunk of resources (both time and people) and takes away from the time that could be spent on gleaning insights from the data. Many BI tools now provide the functionality to perform some data preparation tasks.

In most large organizations, a single enterprise BI tool most likely will not satisfy the requirements of all the varied use cases (batch reports, ad hoc reports, dashboards, discovery, analytics, data mining, etc.). However, the number of BI tools being deployed needs to be balanced. Using too many BI tools makes managing them more difficult in terms of software licenses, maintenance contracts, training, availability of skilled personnel, and upgrading/migrating to newer versions. A data preparation tool may be used in addition to an enterprise data integration tool that already exists. In such cases, policies and procedures need to be developed so that users have the appropriate tool and data sources to apply to the relevant use case.

It is important to note that having a tool won't magically solve all problems; a strong data management foundation is needed. A BI tool by itself is not a panacea—the underlying data needs to be trusted. As mentioned, a data warehouse relies on foundational data management practices.

No matter the technology, a solid foundational design, along with solid data management practices, is a prerequisite for a well-functioning data warehouse. If the data is poor, drawn from non-authoritative sources, ineffectively integrated, or not applicable to business needs, no technology can report it sufficiently. That said, technologies are constantly emerging to improve the data warehouse and analytic environment experience. For example, in addition to traditional data warehousing, Forrester Research lists the following data warehouse solution categories[3]:

- Database appliances provide an alternative to buying hardware and software needed for a data warehouse. Database appliances include the hardware and software necessary for standing up a data warehouse environment and are pre-configured with all the tools—database, connectors to multiple data sources, data integration tool. Data warehouse appliances optimize software and hardware integration. Some vendors offer data warehousing appliances that optimize servers, storage, memory, and software to deliver faster analytics and predictive analytics. They also automate the administration, tuning, and scaling of data warehouses. The advantages of such an appliance are that they are optimized and can be set up and running fairly quickly. The disadvantages of a database appliance are that they are expensive and run the risk of being locked down to a specific vendor.
- Similar to appliances, data warehouse as a service (DWaaS) provides a data warehouse environment, albeit in the cloud. These new public cloud offerings deliver low-cost alternatives to on-premises data warehouse solutions, automating provisioning, configuration, security, tuning, optimization, scalability, availability, and backup.

Additional data warehouse[4] and BI technologies[5] include:

- In-memory architectures to support real-time analytics. Until recently, using a large in-memory platform was not an option because memory was expensive. Today, enterprise data warehouse vendors are starting to offer more scalable platforms that use distributed memory in a clustered configuration, integrated with solid-state drives (SSDs) seamlessly to process large amounts of data quickly.
- Many data warehouse vendors now offer the ability to integrate their solutions with Hadoop to store, process, and transform large amounts of structured and unstructured data. These enterprises are already using an approach to extract data from various source systems, such as IoT devices and cloud and traditional platforms, and then load it into Hadoop to perform aggregation and transformation, and finally load it into the data warehouse to support formal business intelligence.
- Data virtualization integrates disparate data sources in real time or near-real time to support analytics, predictive analytics, customer personalization, and real-time integrated analytics. With data warehouse solutions, data virtualization offers the ability to transform, cleanse, and integrate various sources before loading into a data warehouse platform.

---

[3] Forrester Wave—Enterprise Data Warehouse, Q4 2015, December 7, 2015.

[4] *Ibid.*

[5] "Stay On Top of New BI Technologies to Lead Your Enterprise into The Not-Too-Distant Future," Forrester Research, Inc., March 1, 2016.

- Big data sources, particularly in Hadoop, are often just a bunch of files. Trying to document, catalog, understand, model, and integrate all that data using traditional approaches will pose challenges. Instead, new data discovery, cataloging, and modeling technologies automate all or some of the steps—or make suggestions—using fuzzy matching, metadata, and existing business rules.
- With suggestive BI, many BI platforms suggest the most effective data visualization to analyze a particular dataset, depending on rules like data value types and sparsity. In some cases, the application automatically suggests the best dashboard for a given metric and even the next step to take, such as drilling down from an aggregate view to product or customer details, based on how others in your organization—or in other organizations, in the case of cloud-based multitenant BI platforms—are analyzing similar data in comparable situations.

Chapter 13
Data Analytics

13.1   What Is Data Analytics?

Analytics combines the use of mathematics and statistics with computer software to derive business knowledge from data. Analytics can be segmented into four types—descriptive, diagnostic, predictive, and prescriptive—as described by Gartner.[1] Descriptive analytics focuses on describing something that has already happened, and suggesting its root causes. This involves the observation of historical data to distinguish the patterns or "descriptions of past events" in order to gain insight by implementing searchable databases. Descriptive analytics, which remains the lion's share, typically hinges on basic querying, reporting, and visualization of historical data. Descriptive analytics is typically what is executed by traditional business intelligence platforms.

Diagnostic analytics answers the question of "why" did an event occur. For example, "why" did a certain group of terrorists decide to attack a specific place on a specific date. Other examples include "why" a large storm occurred in a given geographic region or "why" an unexplained traffic congestion occurred during non-peak traffic hours. This type of analytics requires researching patterns and benefits from large amounts of data.

More complex predictive and prescriptive analytics can help companies anticipate business opportunities and public institutions better serve society. For example, reducing customer churn, improving transportation efficiency, performing individualized medicine, and planning emergency responses and evacuations can all be done by analyzing large volumes of past (and sometimes current) data, modeling possible alternatives, and then applying those models to future or real-time scenarios.

---

[1] See http://www.gartner.com/newsroom/id/2881218. Note that there is some variation in these categories, depending on the source. For example, not all sources encompass the category of "diagnostic analytics."

Predictive analytics mines datasets for patterns indicative of future situations and behaviors by using data to determine the probable future outcome of an event or the likelihood of a situation. For instance, observations from historical data suggest that a particular terrorist group is more likely to attack at populated areas during a specific time during the day and the motive of their attack could be religious.

Finally, prescriptive analytics subsumes the results of predictive analytics to suggest actions that will best take advantage of the predicted scenarios. It analyzes potential decisions, the interactions between decisions, the influences on decisions, and the bearing that they all have on an outcome to ultimately prescribe an optimal course of action in real time. For example, trucking delivery companies are using their fleet's GPS data and applying prescriptive analytics to determine optimal routes and shorten delivery windows.[2] Simply put, prescriptive analytics "seeks to determine the best solution or outcome among various choices."[3]

Business users increasingly want to analyze large amounts of different types of data, sometimes close to real time. Different types of data include media such as email, social media, word processing documents, PDF documents, web content, increasingly images, and even video—really, almost any format you can think of. Near-real time analysis of data has become vital for certain business purposes for which speed is of the essence. For instance, identifying fraud, predicting or dealing with network outages, and real-time supply chain management are examples where immediate action is often required. Other business scenarios will continue to be explored at more leisure, such as improvements in healthcare, predicting long-term weather patterns, or improvements in energy efficiency.

Parallel to the increasing variety of data and information available to us is a rapid growth in the amount of data available to benefit analytics. Although estimates and forecasts vary somewhat, all agree that data traffic and storage continue to explode. Using a data traffic example, Cisco states that by the end of 2016, global IP traffic will reach 1.1 ZB per year and will reach 2.3 ZB per year by 2020.[4] Looking at the amount of data storage, IDC states that from 2013 to 2020, the digital universe will grow by a factor of 10—from 4.4 trillion GB to 44 trillion GB. It more than doubles every 2 years.[5] A zettabyte (ZB) is equivalent to a billion terabytes (TB) or a trillion gigabytes (GB). So, in terms of zettabytes that is a predicted increase in data storage from 4.4 to 44 ZB between 2013 and 2020. Another way to look at this is that it

[2] See, for example, Anglin, A., "UPS: Optimizing Delivery Routes," Harvard Business School Digital Initiative, April 12, 2015. https://openforum.hbs.org/challenge/understand-digital-transformation-of-business/data/ups-optimizing-delivery-routes/comments.

[3] Search CIO, "Prescriptive Analytics". (May 2012) (http://searchcio.techtarget.com/definition/Prescriptive-analytics).

[4] See "Cisco Visual Networking Index (VNI)," Cisco Systems, June 2016, http://www.cisco.com/c/en/us/solutions/collateral/service-provider/visual-networking-index-vni/vni-hyperconnectivity-wp.html.

[5] See "Data Growth, Business Opportunities, and the IT Imperatives," EMC and IDC, April 2014, http://www.emc.com/leadership/digital-universe/2014iview/executive-summary.htm.

represents about 152 million years of high-definition video, based on a 2-h, 1.5 GB video! This massive amount of data needs to be stored cost effectively, and people want to analyze it.

So, the challenge is to analyze much more data (volume), presented in increasingly different formats (variety) closer and closer to real time (velocity). Until recently, many organizations have limited their adoption of analytics due to the processing and data storage demands of executing analytics against very large and diverse datasets. This reluctance is starting to change, as a result of a growing awareness that big data platforms and big data analytics tools can help solve thorny business problems, and with the increasing commoditization of tools and platforms. More information on analytics platforms such as Hadoop can be found in the Data Analytics References in Appendix C. In this book, we adhere to Ralph Kimball's point of view of an analytic environment as a "data highway", highlighted in the Data Warehousing and Business Intelligence chapter, with multiple caches of increasing latency and data quality where data stores are loosely coupled, each accommodating business needs in an appropriately timely fashion. On one end are raw data sources, immediately available. On the other end is the enterprise data warehouse with cleansed, time-series data available at greater latency. Depending on the business need, analysis may require real-time execution against raw data or demand more robust data preparation and execution against more trusted data in an enterprise data warehouse.

13.2   Who Is Data Analytics?

Data analytics—or data science, as it is sometimes called—is not a new science. Organizations and individuals have been analyzing data for decades to find new patterns and help predict outcomes. For example, actuaries analyze insurance policies and resulting claims to construct predictive models on policy pricing and claims coverage. Other industries, ranging from weather prediction to gambling, make use of available data to gain insight into patterns and peer into the future.

What is relatively new is the much quicker and broad-based access to such insights by business analysts, based on reams of data to foster routine decision making. In the past, analytical models had to be meticulously constructed based on a limited set of data. This took time. It took time to gather new data, and it took time to construct predictive models and integrate them into the decision-making process. Because the amount of data was a limited sample, outliers were carefully examined to determine their relevance or irrelevance. With the ability to analyze entire datasets rather than samples, analysts can quickly determine the statistical significance of outliers. However, to do so requires skills beyond statistical analysis.

Typically stated requirements for needed resources in data analytics are encapsulated in the term "data scientist." Data scientist requirements highlight a combination of skills that include statistics, computer programming and, ideally, industry knowledge in the sector against which the analytics are applied. Many degree and certificate programs in data science have been introduced at universities in recent years. At first, these programs were introduced at the graduate level. More recently, they are also being offered at the undergraduate level. These programs primarily focus on statistics and computer skills, such as machine learning, and are occasionally industry focused, such as in healthcare. Data science is in such high demand that, per McKinsey, the United States alone faces a shortage of 140,000–190,000 people with deep analytical skills.[6]

An aspect of data science on which industry is just starting to focus is the organization and operationalization of data. For example, it is noteworthy that significant time is often spent up front to cleanse and organize data in a way that makes it possible to analyze. As mentioned earlier, wrangling data so that it can be effectively analyzed can consume 50–80% of an analyst's time.[7] Similarly, it is becoming clear that operationalizing important analytical findings to make them trustworthy and repeatable requires data management. Just as with the smaller amounts of data residing in numerous, dispersed data "silos" within an organization, big data requires a managed approach. If multiple data scientists are analyzing various aspects of a large data pool and coming to different, and perhaps similar conclusions, which one is correct? What is the most authoritative data source from the point of view of the business? How can the finding be standardized and repeated in the future?

The expectation of data scientists is that they find, retrieve, and deliver insights from data. Wrangling data to deliver insights is a de facto up-front requirement because without it, data cannot be effectively analyzed. However, data wrangling is a data management skill that can be accomplished by data analysts who may not be data scientists but are well versed in areas such as data architecture and interoperability. Similarly, data management around the resulting findings is not an expectation that is placed on data scientists. Yet, both front-end data wrangling to position data for effective analysis and back-end organization to achieve cleansed, trusted data are key requirements of data analytics.

As such, a data management team that includes data scientists as well as other data management professionals is an ideal solution for effective data analytics. A few data management skills that have an impact on or can leverage effective analytics include:

- *Data quality*: The cleansing of data for proper analysis
- *Metadata management*: The standardization of terms and routine tagging of content to aid search and analysis as well as data provenance
- *Data architecture*: Identification of the flow of information across the enterprise and of authoritative data sources to prevent data silos and duplicate or discrepant analyses

---

[6] Manyika, J., Chui, M., Brown, B., Bughin, J., Dobbs, R., Roxburgh, C., & Byers, A. H., "Big data: The next frontier for innovation, competition, and productivity,", McKinsey Global Institute, June 2011.

[7] Lohr, S., "For Big Data Scientists, 'Janitor Work' Is Key Hurdle to Insight," *New York Times*, August 17, 2014.

- *Data warehousing and business intelligence*: The storage of cleansed, trusted data for consistent historical reporting

So far, we have focused on the skills that make up data science. Equally important is a discussion of the business case that makes data analytics successful within an organization. The idea that analytics can be successful without understanding the business case against which analytics is directed is misplaced. Furthermore, it is worth remembering that having the business case for analytics is completely in line with a data strategy, which must first and foremost be aligned to a business strategy.[8]

Too often, organizations with a desire to execute big data analytics acquire data science skills, purchase big data technology, and cast a wide net without specific business use cases that underlie the need for these analytics. This is costly, overlooks the value of legacy technology, and ultimately limits the value of analytics.[9] Analytics must ultimately be business driven. As a result, business analysts must also be part of the analytics team.

The exact organization of analytics teams within enterprises is still evolving. Sometimes a team of data scientists operates within IT, for example, to foster reporting. Other times, a similar team operates as part of a business function, for example, to evaluate efficiencies within that function. The ideal integration of one or more data analytics teams into the organizational fabric may differ depending on business drivers. Today these teams frequently work in an isolated "data analytics" environment (sometimes also referred to as a "sandbox") that is separate from the operational systems environment of the organization and uses diverse data sources in an ad hoc fashion. Successful organizations align this type of exploratory environment with both the underlying business drivers and data management infrastructure to ensure useful and usable data analytics.

13.3   Implementing Data Analytics

Many books, blogs, and articles have been written on setting up a data analytics environment. Some variation to approach exists across these writings, but the fundamentals of setting up an effective data analytics framework are similar. This section outlines the main components typically leveraged when setting up such an environment.

---

[8] This is further confirmed by Tom Davenport, Director of Research at the International Institute for Analytics, in his book *Big Data at Work*, in which he interviewed more than 50 companies that were using big data analytics. Based on his interviews, the greatest benefit of using analytics is that it is a key factor in better decision-making capabilities and better enabling key strategic initiatives. Nearly two thirds of respondents say that analytics play an important role in driving business strategy.

[9] Aggarwal, S., & Manual, N., "Big data analytics should be driven by business needs, not technology," McKinsey Global Institute, June 2016.

As mentioned earlier, data analytics begins with defining the business objectives. Because the goal of the data analytics is to improve decision making, the objectives should be transformed to the right question(s) that can be answered by data analytics. Questions should be measurable, clear, and concise. Identifying the business goals and metrics needed to assess those goals early in the project provides the analysis with direction and avoids meaningless analytics.

After a problem is framed, data collection begins. To manipulate data effectively, it is useful to have a sandbox or analytics environment where data is collected for analytical model development and where different modeling techniques are explored and fine-tuned. The infrastructure for this analytics environment can be myriad structured and unstructured data stores and today often includes a NoSQL infrastructure. This type of environment is sometimes referred to as a data lake, meaning that it includes raw data from numerous sources in numerous structured and unstructured formats.

Data collection includes identifying the right data sources and might involve numerous data representations, such as structured, semi-structured (e.g., XML) or unstructured data like images, video, and audio. Data sources might comprise a transactional environment, a reporting environment, or a data lake, which in itself is a large conglomeration of data sources. These data sources might be internal or external or both. Data may be available at no cost, such as data from public institutions, social media, or published over the internet. Alternatively, data sources may contain pre-consolidated, carefully cleansed data. With such a plethora of data sources available, the analytics team must carefully consider data sources and data provenance to determine which data makes the most sense in addressing the business problem.

The desire to collect as much data as possible must be balanced with an approximation of which data sources are useful to address a business issue. It is worth mentioning that often the value of internal data is high. Most internal data has been cleansed and transformed to suit the mission. It should not be overlooked simply because of the excitement of so much other available data.

Once data sources are identified, data quality must be improved sufficiently to accommodate analytics. If the data has multiple formats, it needs to be transformed into a single form for analysis. If data is collected from multiple sources, it may be necessary to integrate multiple tables or records to create new records or value sets. This is an iterative process that continues with successive rounds of data analyses, each yielding increasing understanding. Analysts (or teams of analysts) also correct spelling mistakes, handle missing data, and weed out nonsense information. Data cleansing is a critical step in the data value chain—even with the best analysis, junk data will generate wrong results and mislead the business. More than one company has been surprised to discover that a large percentage of customers live in Schenectady, N.Y., a rather small town with population of less than 70,000 people and a zip code of 12345. Schenectady is disproportionately represented in almost every customer profile database.

Because the volume of data is likely to be significant to be representative for valid statistical analysis, data cleansing should scale to the extent possible. This is particularly poignant with a continuous data value chain that demands that incoming data be cleansed immediately and at very high rates. This usually means automating the cleansing process. However, it doesn't mean humans are not involved.

Data preparation and cleansing encompass activities required to transform raw data into a usable dataset for training, testing, and validating the analysis. These actions can include data modeling, data transformation, and data integration. In addition to those activities, analytics data preparation might include the insertion of appropriate default values, the composition of derived data, or other gap-filling techniques such as estimating missing data through independent analytical modeling. These efforts typically involve experienced analysts with good data management skills.

After data is prepared, the data scientists can actually get to work. Data can now be manipulated in different ways, such as plotting it out and finding correlations or outliers. Depending on the problem at hand and the approach used to address that problem, different models may be built, tested, and validated. As the data is manipulated, the need to revise the original objective or collect more data may become evident. This type of approach is often cyclical, involving multiple rounds of evolution, and helps to refine the focus on achieving the project's goals and objectives.

Many useful insights and new relationships may result from this type of analysis against large and diverse datasets. Models and algorithms applied by data scientists against key data sources have become required to address certain business functions that demand immediate attention. Additionally, organizations are increasingly embedding big data analytics into their product offerings. By embedding sensors into their product and service offerings, they can optimize maintenance and delivery, respectively.[10]

Yet, the promise of analytics, especially big data analytics, must be carefully weighed against its potential benefit. As we have seen, implementing big data analytics is an expensive and time-consuming undertaking that requires:

- An exploratory analytics environment with specialized hardware and software infrastructure. An organization will need resources with the skills to prop up such an environment and maintain it.
- Data scientists who are skilled at statistical programming and machine learning techniques or expert in analytical tools. Data scientists, if not already familiar with the business, must also understand the business problem they are attempting to address.
- Data management that ensures the data gathered and consumed from diverse sources is the right data and that it is cleansed and prepared for analysis. Furthermore, the analytics environment must ultimately interface with the existing operational and reporting information infrastructure.

It is expensive and risky to rely solely on the analysis of raw data from diverse sources, many of which may be outside the control of the analysts. Ultimately an organization, if it deems new analytical findings sufficiently important, must find a

---

[10] See, for example, Davenport, T. H., "Analytics 3.0," *Harvard Business Review*, December 2013.

way to integrate its findings with its existing data infrastructure. How, for example, does an organization track fraud over time? How does it tie fraudulent behavior to a known customer or member in its database? The analytics environment in which analytics occur must connect to other operational and reporting systems in a meaningful way, with data flowing in potentially both directions.

13.4   Data Analytics Framework

Exactly how individual data stores interact is highly specific to an organizations technology infrastructure and business environment. However, at a conceptual level, the underlying components are similar. Figure 13.1 depicts a framework that highlights these components.

An inner circle comprises data stores. This environment includes transactional data stores used for routing business processing; reporting data stores used for the various types of reporting, including near-real-time, ad hoc, and historical reporting; and a data lake, the voluminous data store made up of many different, non-integrated data sources, essentially representing the basis for analytics as we have defined it. At a more detailed level, these data stores might include operational data stores, data marts, multiple exploratory analytic environments, or various types of data stores to suit a given need along the data highway. This inner circle also denotes

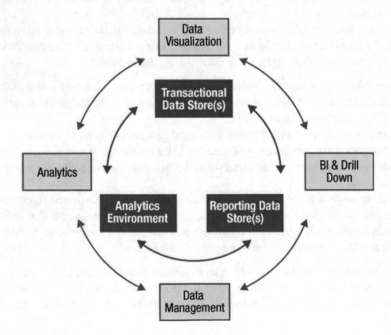

Fig. 13.1   Data analytics framework

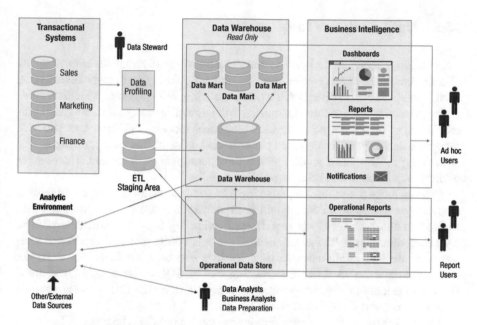

Fig. 13.2 Data analytics environment

the potential flow of data among these data stores. The flow of data from transactional to reporting data stores is well established. However, it is also possible that data might flow between each of these data sources and the analytics environment.

The outer circle reflects how these data sources are leveraged effectively when performing analytics. It shows that analytics is not an isolated activity. For example, we already know that effective data analytics requires data cleansing and preparation. However, it likely requires the application of additional data management skills, such as data architecture and data governance, to integrate the analytics or sandbox environment data with the remaining organizational data fabric. The outer circle also suggests an interplay or overlap between the processes used to manage data around analytics. For example, as we have already mentioned, there is a fuzzy line between analytics and business intelligence. Furthermore, each can use data visualization, and each can potentially have levels of drill down.

Extending the graphic from the previous chapter, which showed a typical data warehouse and business intelligence environment, to include an analytics environment might yield an environment similar to the one shown in Fig. 13.2. Here the analytic environment interacts with transactional data stores, the operational data store, and the traditional data warehouse. Data would typically flow from the more traditional sources into the analytic environment and be combined there with additional data from other sources. However, when consistent insights surface in the analytic environment, these might be added to the more traditional data stores as well.

13.5   Data Analytics Tools

Data analytics tools are designed to enable users to rapidly analyze large amounts of data, sometimes in real time or near real time. Depending on the type of analytics, such tools specialize in different functions, including infrastructure, statistical computing, visualization, machine learning, artificial intelligence, text mining, and others. Together they are used to develop analytical models, find new data patterns, recognize and respond to identified patterns, and enhance business performance by embedding the analytical models within the operational environment. The number of tools is quite large and keeps expanding rapidly.[11]

Data analytics tools must be able to ingest a wide variety of data types: structured data such as transactional data stored in relational databases; semi-structured data such as emails, web server, or mobile application log files; and unstructured data such as images, video, and social media. It is noteworthy that tool vendors of various sorts are integrating data analytics abilities into their products. For example, traditional database vendors are expanding into NoSQL databases, and traditional ETL and business intelligence vendors are incorporating the ability to extract data from a greater variety of data sources.

The market for analytics tools continues to evolve rapidly. The types of tools that are available vary in degree of maturity and, consequently, in capability and ease of use. Traditional vendors are eager to play in this arena and, consequently, are not only developing their own offerings, but expanding offerings through acquisitions, a pattern likely to continue. In addition, tools are becoming increasingly commoditized, requiring less exotic skills. Thus it may well be that your organization already has relatively easy access to some or all the hardware or software infrastructure necessary for big data analytics, as well as human resources who can more easily adapt to such environments because the skillsets required are somewhat similar to what they are accustomed. Along these same lines, a significant open source market has developed around big data and analytics.

Many of these vendors provide big data platforms and tools that support the different steps of analytics process—for example, data integration, data preparation, advanced analytics algorithms, data visualization, and other types of data management software. Depending on the projects' requirements, a set of criteria and functional requirements should be defined against which products should be evaluated prior to proceeding with a procurement decision.

---

[11] For one representation of the big data environment, including analytics tools, see http://matt-turck.com/wp-content/uploads/2016/03/Big-Data-Landscape-2016-v18-FINAL.png.

Chapter 14
Data Privacy

This chapter on data privacy focuses primarily on the public sector. Although data privacy is critical and evolving in both the private and public sectors, the perspectives, mandates, and drivers differ somewhat between these sectors. This is in contrast to many other areas of data management, which are addressed in similar ways in both the public and private sectors. That said, the chapter offers the lay-reader a respectable overview of data privacy.

14.1 What Is Data Privacy

Privacy writ large does not enjoy a consensus definition, and not for lack of trying. Philosophers, political scientists, sociologists, and lawyers, among others, have been exploring and arguing the nature of privacy for more than half a century and continue to do. One reason is that there are, in fact, multiple types of privacy, including data privacy. Even within data privacy, though, there is no comprehensive and universal conception of its essential nature.

As a result, notions of data privacy for operational purposes have historically focused on individual control over personal information, in effect leaving it to the individual to interpret what is or isn't acceptable from a privacy standpoint. This approach has been codified in the form of Fair Information Practice Principles (FIPPs), which establish process-based requirements for the treatment of personal information. FIPPs, as they are generically known, originated in a 1973 report, "Records, Computers, and the Rights of Citizens," for what was then the U.S. Department of Health, Education, and Welfare (HEW). The report, and the

© Springer International Publishing AG 2018
M. Fleckenstein, L. Fellows, *Modern Data Strategy*,
https://doi.org/10.1007/978-3-319-68993-7_14

commission that produced it, were prompted by concerns over the growth of data processing capabilities and the federal government's increasing exploitation of these. Since then, other versions of FIPPs have arisen, including, most notably, those contained in the Privacy Framework[1] of the Organization for Economic Cooperation and Development (OECD). Several federal departments, agencies, and programs, the Department of Homeland Security (DHS) in particular, have articulated their own versions of FIPPs. Although versions of FIPPs differ in various ways, they exhibit a high degree of commonality. As an illustrative example, the DHS FIPPs[2] are shown here:

- *Transparency*: DHS should be transparent and provide notice to the individual regarding its collection, use, dissemination, and maintenance of personally identifiable information (PII).
- *Individual Participation*: DHS should involve the individual in the process of using PII and, to the extent practicable, seek individual consent for the collection, use, dissemination, and maintenance of PII. DHS should also provide mechanisms for appropriate access, correction, and redress regarding DHS's use of PII.
- *Purpose Specification*: DHS should specifically articulate the authority that permits the collection of PII and specifically articulate the purpose or purposes for which the PII is intended to be used.
- *Data Minimization*: DHS should only collect PII that is directly relevant and necessary to accomplish the specified purpose(s) and only retain PII for as long as is necessary to fulfill the specified purpose(s).
- *Use Limitation*: DHS should use PII solely for the purpose(s) specified in the notice. Sharing PII outside the Department should be for a purpose compatible with the purpose for which the PII was collected.
- *Data Quality and Integrity*: DHS should, to the extent practicable, ensure that PII is accurate, relevant, timely, and complete.
- *Security*: DHS should protect PII (in all media) through appropriate security safeguards against risks such as loss, unauthorized access or use, destruction, modification, or unintended or inappropriate disclosure.
- *Accountability and Auditing*: DHS should be accountable for complying with these principles, providing training to all employees and contractors who use PII and auditing the actual use of PII to demonstrate compliance with these principles and all applicable privacy protection requirements.

Note that virtually all versions of FIPPs include a security principle, primarily to address confidentiality. Privacy and security can be considered orthogonal to each

---

[1] Organization for Economic Cooperation and Development (OECD), The OECD Privacy Framework, 2013.

[2] U.S. Department of Homeland Security, Privacy Policy Guidance Memorandum, Memorandum 2008-01, 2008. The OMB sets forth a U.S. governmentwide version of the FIPPs in its July 2016 updates to OMB Circular A-130. The OMB version includes the same notions as the DHS FIPPs and draws out other common notions, such as Authority and Access and Amendment.

other, with confidentiality as the point of intersection. Privacy aims to achieve the FIPPs, whereas security aims to achieve confidentiality, integrity, and availability (C-I-A). (See the Data Security chapter for a detailed discussion of security.) Neither is a subset of the other, but each supports the other. Privacy supports security by, among other things, making it more difficult to obtain personal information that can be leveraged in social engineering attacks.

The complementary nature of cyber security and data privacy, and the role played by FIPPs in the latter, were reinforced in 2013 when the National Institute of Standards and Technology (NIST) revised a fundamental component of its cyber security guidance (which federal agencies are required to follow) to include privacy. What had been *Recommended Security Controls for Federal Information Systems and Organizations* became, in revision 4, *Security and Privacy Controls for Federal Information Systems and Organizations*. In Special Publication 800-53r4, a FIPPs-based privacy control catalog (Appendix J) joined the security control catalog (Appendix F).

FIPPs frequently underlie privacy statutes and regulations, including those that apply to the U.S. federal government. Most notably, from a historical standpoint, the Privacy Act of 1974 (and since amended) was intended to implement the Code of Fair Information Practices put forward in the 1973 HEW report. The Privacy Act, focusing on "systems of records" of personal information (which can be paper-based as well as digital), is one of the principal privacy statutes that applies specifically to federal agencies. Although there are some exceptions to specific requirements of the Privacy Act, no agency is wholly exempt from it. Among other requirements, agencies (and contractors acting on their behalf) must specify to individuals whether providing their information is voluntary or mandatory, confine its use and retention to stated purposes, ensure the information is relevant and of sufficient quality for those purposes, and provide mechanisms through which individuals can access and correct their information. Many of these details for a given system are spelled out in the system of records notice (SORN) that must be published in the Federal Register before the system becomes operational. (Note that a Privacy Act system of records is distinct from an architectural system of record.) Special requirements apply to so-called matching programs in which personal information from multiple systems of records or from one or more system of records and nonfederal records undergo computerized comparison in support of federal benefits programs. These requirements include the establishment of computer matching agreements, due process protections for the individuals to whom the records pertain, and oversight by agency Data Integrity Boards.

Also key to the management of personal information in the federal government are the privacy provisions of the E-Government Act of 2002. These levy website privacy requirements, including the posting of privacy policies, and mandate that privacy impact assessments (PIAs) be conducted on collections of personal information. A PIA is essentially a privacy risk analysis that, ideally, should be integrated into system and business process development to support identification and mitigation of privacy risks. Implementation varies across departments and agencies, but all

PIA implementations must conform to high-level guidance[3] issued by the Office of Management and Budget (OMB).

OMB regularly issues mandatory privacy guidance in the form of circulars and memoranda. Some of these, such as Circular A-130, Managing Information as a Strategic Resource,[4] address both privacy and security. Previous memoranda have, for example, addressed implementation guidance for the privacy provisions of the E-Government Act (as noted earlier), privacy incident evaluation and response, and privacy governance. Embedded in several of these are definitions of personally identifiable information (PII), which is the term of art used by the U.S. government for personal information:

> The term "personally identifiable information" refers to information that can be used to distinguish or trace an individual's identity, either alone or when combined with other information that is linked or linkable to a specific individual.[5]

Other, more targeted requirements apply to specific aspects of agency activities. For example, the Confidential Information Protection and Statistical Efficiency Act (CIPSEA), Title V of the E-Government Act, establishes confidentiality protections on data collected by or on behalf of U.S. government agencies for statistical purposes. The Common Rule for the Protection of Human Subjects regulates federally funded human subjects research regardless of who actually performs the research. These two mandates hold particular relevance for data governance as they cover two potentially broad contexts in which PII may be collected and used.

In addition to government-specific requirements, agencies are also subject to statutes and regulations that apply to any entity handling particular types of PII. The Health Information Portability and Accountability Act (HIPAA) Privacy Rule (as well as the Security Rule), for example, applies to protected health information (PHI) handled by any "covered entity"—healthcare provider, healthcare clearinghouse, or healthcare plan—irrespective of whether it's a private or public sector entity. Similarly, the Children's Online Privacy Protection Act (COPPA) applies to any operator of online services, including websites, either directed at children under 13 or known to be used by such children.

14.2   Who Is Data Privacy

The privacy resources required to support an agency vary widely. The number of personnel, types of skills needed, methods of performing privacy activities, technologies in use by the organization, and budget directly depend on the organization's mission and the nature of PII maintained. For example, organizations that

---

[3] U.S. Office of Management and Budget (OMB), OMB Guidance for Implementing the Privacy Provisions of the E-Government Act of 2002, Memorandum M-03-22, 2003.

[4] U.S. Office of Management and Budget (OMB), Circular A-130, Managing Information as a Strategic Resource, 2016.

[5] *Ibid.*

only conduct basic sales transactions have a lower volume of sensitive PII data elements and likely a lower number of personal records overall than an organization that provides widely used benefits and services to a larger number of the U.S. population.

Data privacy is an influencer of data governance practices. Privacy inputs to how data is managed are driven by the need to implement the FIPPs. Privacy programs do not typically have an enterprise- or mission-wide view of the organization, or even a full understanding of the priorities associated with a given initiative, which means privacy programs must work in partnership with other parts of the organization to achieve success with effectively addressing privacy. Many organizations employ cross-functional information risk committees to address privacy, security, and intellectual property risk, and some are going a step further and establishing cross-functional enterprise risk teams. Arguably, enterprise data governance is the ultimate manifestation of this trend, supporting and requiring coordination across all functions that deal with data, including privacy. Indeed, a strong data governance program must integrate privacy considerations to ensure meaningful data governance practices.

The placement of data privacy activities varies. Some agencies execute their privacy responsibilities under a single program. In those cases, the privacy programs may be located within the Chief Information Officer Organization (CIO), sometimes under the Chief Information Security Officer (CISO), the Office of General Counsel, or within other functions that deal with information and records management. For agencies with statutorily mandated Chief Privacy Officers,[6] the privacy program may be an office directly under the head of the agency. For example, the Department of Homeland Security's (DHS) Privacy Office is part of the Office of the Secretary. See Fig. 14.1.

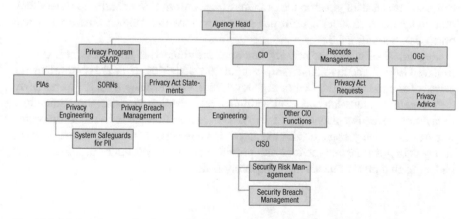

Fig. 14.1 Notional example of centralized privacy functions

---

[6] For example, the Homeland Security Act of 2002 mandated a privacy officer for the Department of Homeland Security and Consolidated Appropriations Act of 2005 mandated a privacy officer for the Department of Justice and other agencies subject to the act.

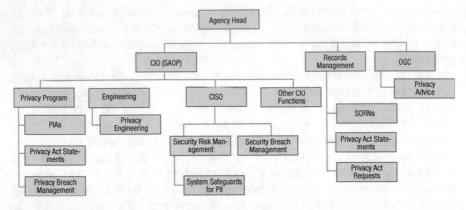

Fig. 14.2 Notional example of de-centralized privacy functions

Other agencies split responsibilities between multiple programs. For example, E-Government Act responsibilities may be owned by the CIO, Privacy Act responsibilities may be owned by the Records Management Office, and a separate privacy function may handle the remainder of privacy obligations. See Fig. 14.2.

Wherever privacy functions fall within an agency, even when they are consolidated under a single office, privacy relies on interfaces and partnerships with other agency functions to fully achieve its objectives. Examples of these partnerships include functions such as cybersecurity, records management and retention, data stewards, policy, acquisitions, human capital, legal, and Freedom of Information Act (FOIA). Privacy functions must also interact through external interfaces, which can also impact data governance practices (e.g., information sharing partners may require agencies to meet certain privacy obligations that impact data governance practices). See Fig. 14.3.

Regardless of where the privacy functions are situated in an agency, it is critical to have strong executive leadership support for activities. It is also important for privacy functions and the Senior Agency Official for Privacy (SAOP) to be fairly close together in location and level within the organization to assist communication. In addition, effective placement of the SAOP ensures that the individual filling this role can effectively engage with executive leaders across an agency in support of strong data governance practices and provides greater opportunity to influence the budget so that privacy needs are adequately addressed.

14.2.1   Privacy Components

Regardless of where privacy responsibilities are carried out in the organization, every executive branch agency is required to have a SAOP that is a senior official at the Deputy Assistant Secretary or equivalent level who serves in a central

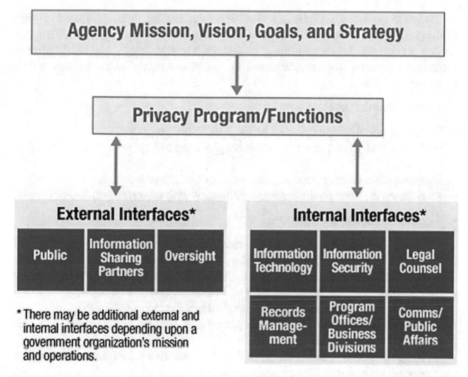

Fig. 14.3 Privacy organizational drivers and interfaces

leadership position at the agency, has visibility into relevant agency operations, and is positioned highly enough within the agency to regularly engage with other agency leadership, including the head of the agency.[7] The SAOP's role may be combined with other responsibilities, such as the CIO. OMB M-16-24 positions the SAOP's role as one primarily focused on risk management, accountability, and compliance with applicable data privacy laws, regulations, and policies. Responsibilities of this role include:

- Central policy-making role in the agency's development and evaluation of legislative, regulatory, and other policy proposals that implicate data privacy issues
- Overseeing, coordinating, and facilitating the agency's compliance efforts
- Developing agency policies and procedures
- Review privacy risks from the beginning and throughout the information life cycle.

---

[7] See U.S. Office of Management and Budget (OMB), Role and Designation of Senior Agency Officials for Privacy, Memorandum M-16-24, 2016.

The 2016 revisions to OMB A-130 reiterate the SAOP role as discussed in other OMB policy[8] and include additional privacy program responsibilities, which implies a more explicit set of responsibilities for SAOPs. The following examples of privacy program responsibilities are articulated in A-130 and may directly influence data governance decisions:

- General Requirements

  - Ensure coordination between privacy and other programs.
  - Ensure that privacy is addressed throughout the life cycle of each information system.
  - Incorporate privacy requirements into enterprise architecture.
  - Balance the need for information collection with the privacy risks.[9]

- Considerations for Managing PII

  - Maintain an inventory of agency information systems that involve PII, and regularly review and reduce its PII to the minimum necessary.
  - Eliminate unnecessary collection, maintenance, and use of social security numbers.
  - Follow approved records retention schedules for records with PII.
  - Limit the creation, collection, use, processing, storage, maintenance, dissemination, and disclosure of PII.
  - Require entities with which PII is shared to maintain the PII in an information system with a particular categorization level.
  - Impose conditions on the creation, collection, use, processing, storage, maintenance, dissemination, disclosure, and disposal of shared PII through agreements.[10]

- Budget and Acquisition

  - Include privacy requirements in IT solicitations.
  - Establish a process to evaluate privacy risks for IT investments.
  - Ensure that privacy risks are addressed and costs are included in IT capital investment plans and budgetary requests.
  - Ensure that investment plans meet the privacy requirements appropriate for the life cycle stage of the investment.[11]

- Contractors and Third Parties

  - Ensure that contracts and other agreements incorporate privacy requirements.
  - Oversee information systems operated by contractors.

---

[8]The SAOP role was originally discussed in OMB M-05-08, Designation of Senior Agency Officials for Privacy, 2005, which was later rescinded and replaced by M-16-24, Role and Designation of Senior Agency Officials for Privacy, 2016.

[9]OMB Circular A-130 (2016), Appendix II, 5.a.

[10]OMB Circular A-130 (2016), Appendix II, 5.b.

[11]OMB Circular A-130 (2016), Appendix II, 5.c.

- Implement policies on privacy oversight of contractors.
- Ensure implementation of privacy controls for contractor information systems.
- Maintain an inventory of contractor information systems.
- Ensure that incident response procedures are in place for contractor information systems.[12]

- Privacy Impact Assessments[13]
- Training and Accountability

  - Provide foundational and advanced privacy training.
  - Provide role-based privacy training to appropriate employees.
  - Hold personnel accountable for complying with privacy requirements and policies.
  - Establish rules of behavior for employees with access to PII and consequence for violating them.

- Incident Response

  - Maintain formal incident management and response policies and capabilities.
  - Establish roles and responsibilities to ensure oversight and coordination of incident response.
  - Report incidents in accordance with OMB guidance.
  - Provide reports on incidents as required.[14]

- Risk Management Framework

  - Review and approve the categorization of information systems that involve PII.
  - Implement a privacy control selection process.
  - Identify privacy control assessment methodologies and metrics.
  - Conduct assessments of privacy controls.
  - Review authorization packages for information systems that involve PII.
  - Encrypt moderate-impact and high-impact information.[15]

The SAOP may or may not be the same person as the Privacy Program Manager (PPM), who is responsible for executing the agency's day-to-day privacy program responsibilities. PPM titles may vary. Chief Privacy Officer is a commonly used title. Depending on whether the PPM is also responsible for other areas, they may have a title that reflects other responsibilities, such as Chief Privacy and FOIA Officer. Many of the responsibilities of privacy programs described earlier fall on the shoulders of the PPM as the operational lead for achieving privacy objectives for the agency.

---

[12] OMB Circular A-130 (2016), Appendix II, 5.d.

[13] OMB Circular A-130 (2016), Appendix II, 5.e.

[14] OMB Circular A-130 (2016), Appendix II, 5.h.

[15] OMB Circular A-130 (2016), Appendix II, 5.i.

PPMs are typically supported by one or more Privacy Analysts, depending on the size, mission, and budget of an agency. The specific roles and responsibilities for Privacy Analysts vary accordingly, with analysts taking on one or more of the privacy program responsibilities highlighted by OMB. In agencies with adequate resources to do so, Privacy Analysts may specialize only on one or two privacy program responsibilities, such as compliance documentation (e.g., PIAs and SORNs). Here again, the title for the Privacy Analyst role may vary widely within and among agencies. The situation in industry is equally variable.

14.3 Privacy Operations

Operationally, privacy programs tend to focus on compliance and risk management activities to implement the privacy components described in the previous section throughout the organization. There are both general interactions with a broad swath of the workforce that may come into contact with PII as well as targeted interactions with the parts of the organization that are directly responsible for making determinations about the PII collected, used, stored, shared, retained, or destroyed ("maintained").

The primary method of engaging the workforce regarding privacy requirements is through privacy education and awareness activities. Privacy education may include general privacy awareness training that most or all members of the workforce are required to take, ideally periodically (at least annually). Privacy awareness training typically covers topics such as:

- Why privacy is important to the organization's mission
- What privacy principles the organization has adopted
- How to recognize PII and properly safeguard it
- When and where to report privacy incidents
- Responsibility for supporting the organization's privacy principles and objectives

Additional role-specific privacy training is conducted to ensure that members of the workforce who work with sensitive PII, have special privileges, or otherwise require additional privacy training understand their responsibilities for handling PII. Examples of roles that often require, or at the very least benefit from, role-based privacy training include human resources professionals, systems designers and developers, database administrators, background investigations personnel, incident response personnel, and others with elevated privacy responsibilities.

Messages from privacy awareness training are reinforced through more frequent activities, such as email campaigns, posters in common areas of facilities, recognition of International Data Privacy Day, data clean-up events, and other activities. Privacy program websites are another widely used means of promoting continued awareness of privacy responsibilities and resources.

Embedding privacy practices into programs and systems is critical to ensuring that PII is managed appropriately. Though methodologies to ensure that privacy is embedded into organizational activities and systems are evolving, the areas that tend to garner the most support are those that are directly tied to compliance obligations, specifically:

- System of Records Notices
- Privacy Impact Assessments
- Implementation of the Risk Management Framework

The Privacy Act requires agencies to publish a System of Records Notice (SORN) in the Federal Register any time the agency will maintain information about individuals, regardless of the medium (e.g., paper file cabinet, computer system), and will retrieve that information by a data element that identifies an individual (e.g., case number, social security number). A SORN is: "the notice(s) published by an agency in the Federal Register upon the establishment and/or modification of a system of records describing the existence and character of the system. A SORN identifies the system of records, the purpose(s) of the system, the authority for maintenance of the records, the categories of records maintained in the system, the categories of individuals about whom records are maintained, the routine uses to which the records are subject, and additional details about the system as described in this Circular (A-108)."[16] SORNs also provide additional information such as how to request additional information about the System of Record as well as a copy of records maintained about individuals. Prior to collecting personal information that will go into a System of Records or changing an existing system of records, a complete, current SORN must be published in the Federal Register for a 30-day public comment period. OMB also receives a 10-day review period. Satisfying this review period requires building adequate time in the schedule to work through all the privacy decisions regarding how information will be managed, drafting the SORN in the organization's required template, and taking it through the organization's formal review and clearance process, allowing 40 days for the OMB and public comment reviews and adequate time to address any comments received from the public. That last step can require re-work to the system or procedures for handling PII if significant comments are received. All told, the procedures around publishing a SORN can take up to 6 months or more to complete.[17]

A PIA is "an analysis of how information is handled to ensure handling conforms to applicable legal, regulatory, and policy requirements regarding privacy; to determine the risks and effects of creating, collecting, using, processing, storing, maintaining, disseminating, disclosing, and disposing of information in identifiable

---

[16] OMB Circular A-108, Federal Agency Responsibilities for Review, Reporting, and Publication under the Privacy Act, 2016.

[17] It is important to differentiate between SORNs and architectural systems of record (SOR). The concept of SORN dates to the 1974 Privacy Act, which mandates the publishing in the Federal Register of any IT or paper file system "that contains information on individuals and retrieves the information by a personal identifier." An architectural system of record, on the other hand, denotes an authoritative IT system in which data originates.

form[18] in an electronic information system; and to examine and evaluate protections and alternate processes for handling information to mitigate potential privacy concerns. A PIA is both an analysis and a formal document detailing the process and the outcome of the analysis."[19] The PIA process is a risk management tool, and the PIA document provides both documentation that captures the organization's intent for managing privacy risk and a form of notice to the public about how the information is managed. Similar to SORNs, the PIA process should start the beginning phase of the systems engineering life cycle. The resulting PIA document should be reviewed and updated as design and development proceed to ensure that any new privacy risks that surface are also addressed. Also like SORNs, drafting PIA documents and working through the organization's formal review and clearance processes can take a nontrivial amount of time to complete. Unlike SORNs, however, PIAs do not require a formal public review and comment. (Also unlike SORNs, PIAs are often used by the private sector as well.) However, PIAs are made public and may still elicit attention from the privacy advocacy community and other members of the public that requires the organization's attention.

Both SORNs and PIAs require that program managers and system developers plan accordingly and start these processes in the beginning phase of the systems engineering life cycle. Additionally, they must ensure that programs adhere to statements made in these documents and that the systems supporting those programs behave as expected. Achieving this in complex socio-technical systems is increasingly challenging and has sparked the development of a discipline of privacy engineering. There is little consensus yet as to what constitutes privacy engineering, but efforts aimed at defining and evolving it, including one spearheaded by NIST, are accelerating.

An organization's implementation of the NIST Risk Management Framework (RMF) provides one pathway for ensuring that systems behave as expected from a security perspective. (The RMF operates at the tactical risk or information system level. This is the lowest tier in the three-tier NIST risk model, with the strategic risk or organization level at the top and missions and business processes in the middle.) The RMF is discussed in general terms in the Data Security chapter.

The control catalogs in NIST SP 800-53, Rev. 4, that are employed as part of the RMF process include a Privacy Control Catalog ("Appendix J") as well as the larger Security Control Catalog (Appendix F). These appendices specify technical, administrative, and operational privacy and security controls organized into families of related controls. Appendix J "provides a structured set of controls for protecting privacy and serves as a roadmap for organizations to use in identifying and implementing privacy controls concerning the entire life cycle of PII, whether in paper or electronic form."[20] In addition to Appendices J and F, NIST SP 800–53 provides a

---

[18]Although OMB uses the term "information in identifiable form" here, PII as defined in OMB M-07-16 and clarified in OMB M-10-23 are more widely used. OMB Circular A-130 further updated and streamlined the definition of PII in 2016 and will likely become the more widely used definition.

[19]OMB Circular A-130 (2016), Appendix II, 5.e.

[20]NIST SP 800-53, Rev. 4, Appendix J, page J-1.

number of program management controls in Appendix G that are also necessary to meet the security-related aspects of privacy.[21] Controls for a specific system typically are defined in the security and privacy plans for that system. Table 14.1 discusses how privacy fits into the RMF process.

14.4 Implementing Privacy

Data privacy implementation is best considered in terms of the information life cycle. This encompasses collection, creation and transformation, usage, disclosure, retention, and destruction of PII. Each stage brings its own issues and concerns, and privacy in any data governance program is only as strong as the weakest link in this chain. Strong privacy protections in one information lifecycle phase can be undermined by inadequate protections in another.

14.4.1 Collection

A key differentiator when collecting PII is whether the information is being collected directly from the individuals to whom the information pertains or is being collected from a third party. This is not an all or nothing proposition, and it may be the case that PII needs to be collected both directly and indirectly. Moreover, indirectly collected PII may come from multiple sources. The situation is further complicated by the steadily increasing amounts of data that individuals generate in the course of their activities but often are not expressly provided. Location data from cell phones, driving behavior from cars, and electricity consumption from homes are just some of the relatively new modes of data collection that potentially can be associated with specific individuals.

The direct/indirect distinction matters a great deal as the most accurate and up-to-date information tends to come from directly from individuals rather than third parties. This is why the Privacy Act requires that, to the greatest extent practicable, PII be collected directly from the individuals to whom it pertains when the information may result in adverse determinations. However, this dictate constitutes best practice in general because, irrespective of the potential consequences of errors, it tends to improve data quality.

---

[21] The overlay concept is described in NIST SP 800-53, Rev. 4, Appendix I. The Committee on National Security Systems (CNSS) has developed the Privacy Overlays, which are Attachment 6 to Appendix F of CNSS Instruction No. 1253. The Privacy Overlays provide a consistent approach for identifying whether information is PII, determining how sensitive that PII is, and using a predefined set of security and privacy controls as your starting point for protecting that information. Although it is only required for National Security Systems (NSS), it is based on requirements that are applicable to all government systems that maintain PII and is therefore also usable by any agency for any non-NSS.

Table 14.1 Privacy in the RMF

RMF step	Related privacy activities
Step 1: CATEGORIZE Information Systems	• Identify whether a system will or does maintain PII
	• Determine how sensitive the PII is and use the sensitivity of the PII as an input to determining the systems risk posture[a]
	• Categorize each information system as low, moderate, or high impact, according to the criteria in NIST standards and guidelines
	• The SAOP is responsible for reviewing and approving the categorization of information systems that create, collect, use, process, store, maintain, disseminate, disclose, or dispose of PII[b]
Step 2: SELECT Security Controls	• Select the applicable baseline (i.e., the initial subset of controls from the catalogs that are recommended for the system based on the outcome of Step 1)
	• Tailor (adjust) controls selected based on the unique needs of the system, including applying any applicable overlays (pre-defined tailored sets of controls) to ensure that all the required security and privacy controls are selected
	• For privacy controls, the SAOP is responsible for designating which controls will be treated as program management, common, information system-specific, and hybrid[c]
Step 3: IMPLEMENT Security Controls	• Implement all controls selected for the system, including privacy controls and privacy-supportive security controls
	• Document how controls are implemented in security plans and privacy plans (and ensure that the plans remain current over time)
Step 4: ASSESS Security Controls	• Assess all implemented controls, including privacy controls and privacy-supportive security controls to ensure that all the necessary controls were implemented effectively
	• The SAOP shall conduct an initial assessment of the privacy controls selected for an information system prior to operation, and shall assess the privacy controls periodically thereafter at a frequency sufficient to ensure compliance with applicable privacy requirements and to manage privacy risks[d]
Step 5: AUTHORIZE Information Systems	• Review all supporting artifacts, including those that provide privacy information, to make the "go/no go" risk acceptance determination to take the system operations
	• The SAOP provides inputs and recommendations that the Authorizing Official uses as input to the risk determination
Step 6: MONITOR Security Controls	• Monitor and assess implemented controls, including privacy controls and privacy-supportive security controls (at a frequency aligned with that of significant environmental changes)
	• Analyze the impacts of any changes to the security and privacy posture of the system
	• The SAOP is responsible for developing and maintain a privacy continuous monitoring (PCM) strategy and program

[a]Information systems may include other types of information beyond PII that are more or less sensitive. The sensitivity level of the PII is an input to the risk level of the system, but there is not a 1:1 mapping between the sensitivity of the PII and the risk level of the system
[b]OMB Circular A-130 (2016), Appendix II, 5.i
[c]OMB Circular A-130 (2016), Appendix II, 5.i
[d]OMB Circular NO. A-130, Appendix II, 5.i

When PII is indirectly collected, understanding and tracking the provenance of that information is critical because it provides a basis for assessing its fitness for purpose and for alerting the source to discovered errors. This includes the capacity to trace information back to the collection stage through the lifecycle stages that follow it. Maintaining traceability also supports root cause analysis when things go wrong.

One way of reducing the data quality issues that can arise from indirectly collecting PII from multiple sources is to operate on data in situ. This is the premise of virtual data warehouses in which information remains in the original systems and only the results of queries and other operations on that information are captured by the system in question. This helps ensure that every time the information is used, it is the most current and correct information available, as it can be updated and corrected on the originating system. Collection on an as-needed basis, moreover, can help minimize the amount of PII a system ingests.

If visibility across data sources is itself potentially problematic, some privacy enhancing technologies can enable operations to be performed across multiple data sources without revealing anything about the source data beyond what the result reveals. This is the objective of privacy-preserving data mining, which is based on the more general technique of secure multi-party computation. Although secure multi-party computation currently suffers from performance issues that are the subject of active research, there are tools that attempt to achieve similar effects through clever mechanics, but that lack the mathematical guarantees that secure multi-party computation affords.

Minimizing PII collected is a major privacy imperative. The Privacy Act (consistent with FIPPs) requires that only PII that is relevant and necessary to an authorized purpose be collected. Any collection of PII must be legally authorized, and individuals from whom PII is being directly collected must be informed of the authority under which they are being asked or required to provide PII. An applicable authority must underlie any indirect collection of PII as well.

There is no agreed way of reconciling PII minimization with big data analytics, but some thought must be given to controlling the scope of a system in terms of its purpose and the PII collected to achieve that purpose. Both the organization collecting the PII and the individuals to whom the PII pertains incur risk, even more so when the PII is sensitive. (As an example, the PII in a public directory of some sort would be considered much less sensitive, all else being equal, than a social security number or financial account number, because the unauthorized disclosure and use of these numbers pose much more risk to individuals. However, PII sensitivity can be highly contextual and therefore must be considered on a case-by-case basis.) Minimization, therefore, plays an important role in privacy risk management.

Both a legal requirement and a risk management benefit also apply to notice and consent, that is, informing individuals of practices related to the collection and use of PII, including what PII will be collected from other sources, and, if possible, obtaining their consent to that collection and those practices. Such consent may be implicit (opt out) or explicit (opt in). As with minimization, big data analytics can make this difficult to execute in a meaningful way, but some scoping and transparency mechanisms must be considered.

14.4.2   Creation/Transformation

System processes often manipulate information in ways that change it. This can be as simple as aggregation and as complex as inferring entirely new information. In doing so, it cannot be assumed that the sensitivity of the information remains the same. This is particularly true for PII, which tends to be highly contextual in the first place. Associating an address with a specific individual may seem innocuous enough, for example, but if the address is a shelter for abused spouses, that association may prove sensitive far beyond the sensitivity of each datum. Similarly, a sensitive attribute may be inferred from otherwise mundane information. This characterized the infamous Target case in which the retailer inferred that certain customers were pregnant based on the purchase of otherwise unremarkable items that it had determined were strongly correlated with the condition.[22]

This is a two-way street, though, and certain transformations can decrease rather than increase the sensitivity of PII. This is what several privacy enhancing technologies aim to accomplish, including de-identification or anonymization and differential privacy. De-identification aims to reduce the sensitivity of PII by manipulating it so as to significantly weaken the connection between the information and the specific persons to whom it pertains. It does this by altering or removing information that could directly or indirectly identify individuals and by reducing the information content of sensitive attributes, for example by replacing specific values with less specific categories of values. Differential privacy involves manipulating the responses to database queries to control potential inferences about specific individuals. This allows generalized knowledge, such as demographic patterns, for example, to be derived from datasets while hindering the ability to extract information regarding specific entries. Both techniques are applied to record-level information where records are associated with specific individuals. In contrast, statistical disclosure control, as applied, for example, to census data, aims to control potential inferences about individuals drawn from aggregate information. However, ultimately these and other techniques are applied to reduce information sensitivity.

When PII is manipulated to arrive at or support decisions about individuals, algorithmic bias is also a concern, especially in light of recent advances in machine learning. Unfair and, in some cases, illegal biases can be embedded in multiple ways in decision making and support systems based on machine learning. If the data used to train the system is itself biased, that bias will be reflected by the trained system. Even if the training data is not intrinsically biased, the system may end up incorporating impermissible biases because those biases correlate with some legitimate property that is relevant to the decision. Decision traceability can help combat algorithmic bias by revealing the reasoning steps leading to a given decision, and it is desirable in any case to support redress requests from individuals negatively affected by decisions in which the system played a role.

---

[22] Duhigg, C., "How Companies Learn Your Secrets," *New York Times*, February 16, 2012.

Finally, it's important to recognize that metadata (i.e., data about the data) can itself affect data sensitivity. A timestamp, for example, when associated with location information can place an individual at a specific place at a specific date and time. This information, depending on context, could render the information more sensitive than just location alone.

14.4.3 Usage/Processing

PII is collected and used for specific articulated purposes. Leveraging existing data in new ways to gain additional value from it, therefore, becomes problematic when that data is PII. Privacy notices and consents reflect specific uses of PII, and those uses are expected to be consistent with what was originally communicated. It can be tempting to expand the uses of any given collection of PII, and though privacy notices can be updated with new or additional purposes, consents must also be updated where applicable. Big data and machine learning are creating challenges to limiting mission creep, but examining practices on the ground reveals clear opportunities for exerting control over PII use. Big data analytics and machine learning are not unstructured, and otherwise inscrutable and control over PII use can be inserted into both design and operation.

Data is also expected to be of sufficient quality to properly support those uses, especially when those uses include decisions about individuals. For data privacy, quality is typically viewed in terms of accuracy (i.e., the data is correct), currency (i.e., the data is up to date), and completeness (i.e., all necessary data is present). Achieving this can require consistency checks on the data itself as well as interface controls that ensure the forms that data take match expectations (such as form fields aligned with data formats). When systems support decisions regarding the eligibility of individuals for some benefit or service, it is vital that the quality of the source information reflect the significance of the benefit and the potential impact of a denial. By the same token, if a potential result of a decision-making process is to assign someone a pejorative status (e.g., assignment to some kind of watch list), the quality of the data must align with the potential impact of the stigmatization.

Both in cases of denied eligibility and in cases of stigmatization, it is crucial that, unless contrary to the mission, both the organization and the system support access to and correction of PII and redress of erroneous decisions and their impacts. This means that not only must organizational processes exist, as per the Privacy Act, to enable individuals to examine the data held about them and to request its correction, but processes should also exist to enable decisions to be examined and corrected. Systems must include the functionality necessary to support these processes, including, as mentioned earlier, decision traceability. This can prove difficult in cases involving big data and/or machine learning, but the increasing use of both of these makes it imperative to find ways of incorporating these needs into their design.

14.4.4   Disclosure/Dissemination

Minimizing the disclosure of PII is just as important as minimizing the collection of PII. Outgoing PII is just as much a function of purpose as incoming PII, and therefore, disclosures should be consistent with the system's purposes and should only include the PII necessary for that purpose. Entire records should not be disclosed if only a subset of the information is required. Though it is often easier to just provide everything pertaining to a person rather than only what is necessary, this is not only contrary to good privacy practice, but it also subjects both organizations and individuals to unnecessary risk.

When minimizing disclosures, it is important to appreciate the distinction between identity disclosure and attribute disclosure. Identity disclosure is the disclosure of information that directly points to a specific individual. Attribute disclosure is the disclosure of information that, although it is not directly pointing to a specific individual, nevertheless pertains to a specific individual. This distinction is important because, depending on the context, attributes can be associated with an identifiable individual even if identity is not disclosed. This can happen when multiple attributes act as quasi-identifiers that enable linkage with another data source that contains identifying information. It can also happen if it is known that a certain individual's attributes are included in the disclosed data. If, on the basis of some attributes, a subset of records can be determined to include that person's record, and those records share the same value for some other attribute, that attribute for that specific person has been disclosed, even if their identity wasn't. For example, if all the medical records in such a set show HIV status as positive, that person's HIV status has been revealed, irrespective of which specific record is theirs. In other words, disclosures can end up disclosing more information about specific individuals than intended.

Even assuming appropriate minimization, the risks arising from disclosures of PII, including the risk of noncompliance with legal obligations and stated practices, must be addressed. A key mechanism for doing so is a data use agreement or a more general memorandum of agreement or understanding. Such documents explicitly commit the receiving organization to handling the information in specified ways, including required security measures and permissible uses. Such agreements can also include auditing provisions to enable the disclosing entity to ensure itself that the receiving entity is complying with the agreement.

Logging of selected actions or events can support these provisions. Logging is also necessary on the part of the disclosing entity. Keeping a record of what data has been disclosed to whom when and under what circumstances is not only good practice, it is required by the Privacy Act. Further, these logs will support the propagation of corrections to disclosed information as necessary, which is also required by the Privacy Act.

14.4.5   Retention/Storage

There is a tendency, exacerbated by the steadily shrinking cost of storage, to want to keep data, including PII, for long periods of time. The rationale for this desire is typically "just in case," however, "just in case" does not constitute a legitimate business purpose. As a result, organizations and individuals end up incurring risk in return for no clear benefit. Retention periods for PII should be carefully considered in light of the purposes for which the information is being used as well as related concerns such as legal requirements and general retention schedules (based on record types) promulgated by the National Archives and Records Administration (NARA). (Many private sector organizations, particularly large ones, establish their own retention schedules—reflected in their privacy policies with respect to PII—based on an analysis of business needs, legal requirements, and potential liability, among other considerations. The retention period associated with data must be tracked, preferably using automated mechanisms. Retention periods should also be periodically re-evaluated (which can be done as part of the PIA refresh process). If, for example, PII is being kept for 20 years, but no one has accessed a record more than 5 years old, the retention period may be excessive.

This process is further complicated if PII needs to be retained (e.g., due to statutory requirements or ongoing litigation) past the point at which a system is decommissioned. In these cases, it's vital to keep track of this "disembodied" data and to ensure that the data is destroyed when the retention period expires. Establishing what data is being retained, how, and where should be a formal part of the decommissioning process.

Retaining PII incurs costs beyond just the storage medium. Typically, access and correction processes must be available for that PII, and the functionality of the system must support these processes, enabling any PII pertaining to a specific individual to be located and modified. This can be more involved than it may appear because data may be distributed or replicated across multiple locations. This is further complicated by archival and backup mechanisms. Even in those cases, such as a virtual data warehouse, in which the data actually resides in a different system, it should be possible to facilitate access and correction requests regarding the data in the source systems.

14.4.6   Disposition/Destruction

The same circumstances that complicate managing PII retention also complicate managing PII destruction. PII may be distributed or replicated across multiple locations and may reside in archives and backups as well as in the operational components of the system. Particularly in the case of backups, it may take a certain amount of time for PII to be destroyed through routine backup cycles. This kind of time lag should be accounted for in stated retention periods and when tracking retention periods for specific data. In other words, the destruction process should actually begin prior to the expiration of the retention period so as to ensure that the data in all its manifestations has been expunged by the time the retention period actually expires.

If the system is being decommissioned, recording the disposition of the data, including PII, should be a formal part of the process. Note that the Privacy Act requires that notice be provided in the Federal Register when a system of records is decommissioned, just as notice must be provided when a system is stood up. It is advisable to set up a formal, documented process for decommissioning any system, but especially one containing PII.

14.5   Privacy Tools

A variety of commercial and open source tools exist that can support privacy. They range from tools supporting data collection and analysis for PIAs to infrastructure-level tools supporting privacy protections to sophisticated tools supporting various forms of anonymization. In a number of cases, these are multi-purpose tools in the sense that they can also be applied to types of information other than PII and/or in the sense that they include significant unrelated functionality.

As the principal mechanism for performing privacy risk analysis, PIAs are supported by several tools, including methods and templates. These methods, many of them promulgated by international data protection authorities, offer more structured approaches to identifying and evaluating privacy risks than the PIA processes and templates the federal government typically uses. (NIST has published a draft Privacy Risk Management Framework as well.) Although PIA templates are typically mandated by individual departments and agencies, some of these methods could still be leveraged within the PIA process to support analysis of privacy risks. There are also technological supports for PIAs in the form of computer-based tools. These tools tend to be customizable so they can implement whatever template an agency is using. Most include some kind of workflow management functionality, and some also include analysis capabilities, which can range from simple score calculation to actual risk identification.

The most popular infrastructure-level tool, by far, is the data loss prevention (DLP) suite. DLP suites typically consist of a network component, a server component, and an endpoint (workstation) component. All three components operate on the basis of information policies established from a central console. These policies address what kinds of operations are allowed for certain kinds of information and also specify how violations should be handled. Thus DLP allows organizations to, for example, prevent PII or particular types of PII from being transferred from workstations to external media, stored on particular servers, or sent beyond the network perimeter. Many organizations find DLP, though far from infallible, a valuable risk mitigation, not only for privacy risk but for risks involving other types of information, such as intellectual property. Another infrastructure-level tool gaining popularity is tokenization, in which sensitive PII (or other information) is replaced by tokens linked to the actual data values secured in a repository. When necessary, an actual data value can be retrieved on the basis of its token. When not needed, though, the actual values remain locked away while systems maintain and work with the tokens.

Other multi-purpose enterprise tools can support even more sophisticated measures, including anonymization (also referred to as de-identification, among other terms). Although there are several stand-alone anonymization tools, some enterprise data management platforms include anonymization capabilities (sometimes as an optional add-on). In either case, the tools support the transformation of PII so as to reduce its sensitivity. These tools support several different techniques, including masking and generalization. Most tools tend to focus on transforming either structured or unstructured data. In both cases, the tools' principal support is to automate transformations that must be carefully planned by experts with deep knowledge of the data and its context, both before and after transformation.

Chapter 15
Data Security

Data security is critical and evolving in both the private and public sectors. Although the perspectives, mandates, and drivers differ somewhat between these sectors, there are also commonalities in the areas addressed. This chapter focuses primarily on the public sector. This contrasts with other areas of data management, which are addressed in similar ways in both the public and private sectors. This chapter offers the lay-reader an overview of data security. For the purposes of this book, the term "data security" is used throughout to reference what is known in other communities as "information security" or "cybersecurity."

15.1   What Is Data Security?

Data security is one part of an organization's overall data strategy. In very general terms, it is about protecting information. Data security is often described simply as getting the right information to the right people at the right time.

Practices for protecting information have been around as long as data and information. Terminology and activities for data security have evolved over time alongside changes in technologies, and they continue to vary across industries and legal regimes. However, common concepts persist across the many laws, regulations, and practices regardless of geography and industry. Data security, in this case noted as "information security," is defined for federal government agencies in the U.S. Code as "protecting information and information systems from unauthorized access, use, disclosure, disruption, modification, or destruction in order to provide—.

(a) integrity, which means guarding against improper information modification or destruction, and includes ensuring information nonrepudiation and authenticity;
(b) confidentiality, which means preserving authorized restrictions on access and disclosure, including means for protecting personal privacy and proprietary information; and

© Springer International Publishing AG 2018
M. Fleckenstein, L. Fellows, *Modern Data Strategy*,
https://doi.org/10.1007/978-3-319-68993-7_15

(c) availability, which means ensuring timely and reliable access to and use of
    information."[1,2]

Confidentiality, integrity, and availability (abbreviated collectively as "C-I-A"),
are widely recognized and agreed upon security objectives that form the basis for a
robust body of supporting standards internationally.

U.S. federal agency security practices are governed by the E-Government Act of
2002 and the Federal Information Security Modernization Act of 2014 (FISMA),[3]
both of which focus on information systems. As stated in National Institute of
Standards and Technology (NIST) Special Publication (SP) 800-39, "Managing
Information Security Risk: Organization, Mission, and Information System View":

> The E-Government Act (P.L. 107-347) recognizes the importance of information security to
> the economic and national security interests of the United States. Title III of the
> E-Government Act, entitled the Federal Information Security Management Act (FISMA),
> emphasizes the need for organizations to develop, document, and implement an organization-
> wide program to provide security for the information systems that support its operations
> and assets.[4]

The following three organizations drive data security policy and standards for U.S.
government agencies:

- *Office of Management and Budget (OMB)*: OMB sets security policy for complying with E-Government Act and FISMA requirements. OMB policies range
  in detail and subject matter, from memos that target a particular initiative
  (e.g., annual FISMA reporting guidance) to broad-ranging guidance, such as
  Circular A-130, "Managing Information as a Strategic Resource."
- *The National Institute of Standards and Technology (NIST)*: NIST is a non-
  regulatory component of the Department of Commerce and is often tasked to
  develop standards and guidance that will aid agencies in implementing their data
  security requirements. Though most NIST documents are written for federal
  agencies, private sector entities are known to use them, especially when no other
  standards are available for their industry or when available standards may not
  fully meet their needs. In some instances, NIST works directly with the private

---

[1] This definition is provided at 44 U.S.C. Sec 3552. The definition used prior to that was found at
44 U.S.C. 3542. The more recent definition includes the original definition and adds definitions for
integrity, confidentiality, and availability.

[2] The term "cybersecurity" is used synonymously with "information security" within the government and "data security" in this chapter. National Security Directive (NSPD) 54/Homeland
Security Directive (HSPD) 23, *Cybersecurity Policy*, defines cybersecurity as: "Prevention of dam-
age to, protection of, and restoration of computers, electronic communications systems, electronic
communications services, wire communication, and electronic communication, including information contained therein, to ensure its availability, integrity, authentication, confidentiality, and
nonrepudiation." Networked technology is ubiquitous today, making the need for distinguishing
among data security, information security, and cybersecurity largely irrelevant.

[3] FISMA was previously known as the Federal Information Security Management Act of 2002 until
it was updated and retitled in 2014.

[4] NIST SP 800-39, March 2011, Footnote 1, pg. IV.

sector to write guidance for entities outside the federal government. For example, NIST led the development of a framework to reduce cyber risks to critical infrastructure (the "Cybersecurity Framework") in response to Executive Order 13636, "Improving Critical Infrastructure Cybersecurity."

- *The Committee on National Security Systems (CNSS)*: CNSS sets policy and provides guidance and other resources to protect National Security Systems (NSS). It is a collaborative forum of 21 U.S. Government Executive Branch Departments and Agencies and serves the Intelligence Community, Department of Defense, and the Civil Agencies. Though the CNSS is primarily government-focused, its policies can influence government contractors and the defense industrial base, and many are publicly available.

In the private sector, data security laws and regulations are focused on the various industry sectors, with the most stringent regulations in industries that tend to deal with highly sensitive personal information, such as the financial and healthcare sectors. One or more government agencies may have regulatory authority over those industries and develop supporting regulations and guidance. In the United States, both the Federal Trade Commission (FTC) and the Securities Exchange Commission (SEC) have cross-industry authorities that include data security. The FTC frequently investigates and sanctions entities for matters like unfair, deceptive, or fraudulent practices that impact consumers. Security problems are commonly noted as primary or secondary causes of the issues FTC investigates, and many of their sanctions require improving security practices. The SEC has oversight of the Sarbanes-Oxley Act of 2002 ("SOX"), which was enacted in reaction to financial accounting scandals. SOX includes provisions for accountability and independent certification of public company financial audits, and part of that certification includes conducting security reviews to assess the integrity and reliability of an entity's financial information.

In addition to broad data security laws, regulations, and standards, specialized areas such as privacy (see the Data Privacy chapter) influence security decisions. Conversely, sound security practices are critical to achieving some privacy requirements, for example, maintaining confidentiality of personal information through such activities as access controls and encryption. For example, privacy regulations such as the HIPAA Privacy Rule may require that the access control scheme include only unique system user IDs to access personal information (i.e., no shared accounts). As another example, organizations that handle credit card transactions must meet Payment Card Industry Data Security Standards (PCI-DSS).

15.2   Who Is Data Security

In its early days, data security as an organizational function often arose, not surprisingly, within information systems organizations. As a result, data security often fell under a Chief Information Officer (CIO) or equivalent. The Federal Information Security Management Act (FISMA) solidified this arrangement within the federal government. Thus information security within federal agencies tends to fall under the CIO. Data security programs typically are under the cognizance of a Chief Information Security Officer (CISO), who reports to the CIO.

Though historically understandable, this placement can have problems. The most obvious is that the CIO, who has a broad area of information management concerns on which to focus, may insulate executive leadership from data security perspectives and concerns. Along these same lines, if a cross-functional enterprise risk team or committee, an organizational component that is appearing more and more, is structured such that its participants are at a uniform organizational level, the CISO may be excluded from direct participation and must rely on the CIO to represent their views and convey their concerns. A less obvious issue is that security may be simply considered part of the information technology trade-space in which various "nonfunctional" requirements or "quality attributes" are traded off against functional or other nonfunctional requirements. Therefore, it can be preferable for security to be on an organizational par with the CIO.

This has become easier as the CISO role has proliferated. (The role of Chief Privacy Officer has performed a similar service for privacy, elevating it out of lower organizational tiers.) Rather than being seen as a nominally more specialized function under the CIO, the role of the CISO is increasingly perceived as existing on the same plane as the CIO, with responsibilities cutting across as well as up and down the entire enterprise.

The data security function typically includes several more or less standardized hierarchical roles as shown in Fig. 15.1. This starts with the CISO himself or herself, who is responsible for a broad range of both programmatic and technical activities. These include development and operation of relevant enterprise-wide policies, training, incident response mechanisms, physical and logical security controls, and risk management processes. A CISO is also expected to be familiar with various security standards—for example, the ISO/IEC 27000 Information Security Management Systems family, Control Objectives for Information and Related Technologies (COBIT), the Critical Security Controls (CSC), and NIST Special Publication 800-53— and to leverage them as necessary and appropriate.

An Information System Security Manager (ISSM) is effectively a CISO to an organizational component (e.g., a business unit or program), responsible for the implementation and operation of enterprise policies, processes, and mechanisms within that component. An ISSM may be called on to develop component-specific implementation procedures and capabilities that address the component's operational context and to create additional processes or mechanisms required by that context. In some cases, that context may demand exceptions or alternatives to the normal enterprise requirements. An ISSM may report to the component business owner and/or the CISO.

An Information System Security Officer (ISSO) is responsible for the security of a specific information system. In other words, an ISSO serves as the security point of contact for that system and ensures that applicable security requirements, both enterprise wide and specific to the organizational component, are implemented and maintained for the system and its applications. An ISSO typically reports to the system owner, which may or may not be the business owner for the organizational component.

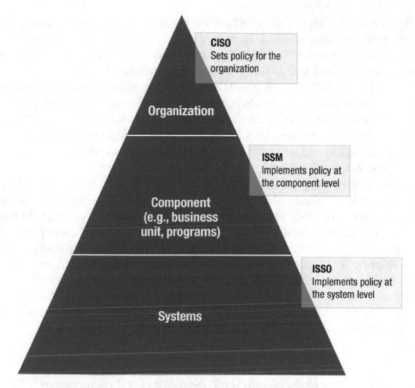

Fig. 15.1   Example of hierarchical data security roles

15.3   Implementing Data Security

Data security implementation can be based on a variety of mandates and guidelines. The U.S. government often relies on two:

1. The Framework for Improving Critical Infrastructure Cybersecurity[5] (known as the "Cybersecurity Framework") developed by NIST. NIST developed the Cybersecurity Framework in collaboration with the government and the private sector.
2. The NIST SP 800-37, *Guide for Applying the Risk Management Framework (RMF) to Federal Information Systems, A Security Life Cycle Approach*, provides RMF guidance. The intent of the RMF is to improve data security, strengthen risk management processes, and encourage reciprocity among federal agencies.[6]

Both the Cybersecurity Framework and RMF provide approaches that will help U.S. government organizations implement their data security programs and protect their information and information systems. The Cybersecurity Framework articulates security activities for programs. The Cybersecurity Framework was primarily

---

[5] https://www.nist.gov/cyberframework.

[6] NIST SP 800-37, Rev 1, Section 1.1, page 1.

written for critical infrastructure industries, but it provides helpful language and guidance that can also benefit U.S. government organizations with internal communication and, for those that may not yet have mature data security programs, help them determine where to start (or start enhancing what they have).

The RMF was written to support U.S. government agencies with risk management, and much of the body of supporting NIST publications specifically support data security risk management activities, both for programs and systems. This section provides a more in-depth look at the Cybersecurity Framework and the RMF, focusing on implementation, followed by a discussion of supporting standards and other factors that influence implementation.[7]

Although often compliance-driven in practice, data security is a risk-based practice. "How much" security a given dataset needs is driven by the individual data elements, what the data elements can be used to accomplish collectively, how sensitive the data is, how critical it is to a particular program or system, and potentially other factors. These considerations drive decisions when determining the appropriate administrative, technical, and physical safeguards that should be applied. Additionally, when considered in the context of enterprise risk and not just risk to a particular program or system, the implemented data security protections are evaluated against all risks to an enterprise, program, or system, and leadership must prioritize data security activities and resource allocation.

15.4   Using the Cybersecurity Framework to Implement Data Security

The Cybersecurity Framework discusses data security programs in clear, simple terms, making it consumable by almost anyone, including those with no prior knowledge of data security. It also distills hundreds of pages of security guidance and standards from multiple communities into a succinct package. This makes it a valuable communications tool for organizations that are in the beginning stages of developing a cybersecurity program as well as for data security programs as they communicate across their organizations with leadership, mission and business owners, and other stakeholders. It defines five key ongoing Functions for protecting assets, including information: Identify, Protect, Detect, Respond, and Recover.

The Cybersecurity Framework Functions organize basic cybersecurity activities at their highest level. They help an organization express its management of cybersecurity risk by organizing information, enabling risk management decisions, addressing threats, and improving by learning from previous activities. The functions also align with existing methodologies for incident management and help show the impact of investments in cybersecurity.[8] Organizing security and discussing it in this

---

[7] For additional detail on these frameworks, see the Data Security References section in Appendix B.

[8] Cybersecurity Framework, v1.0, p. 7.

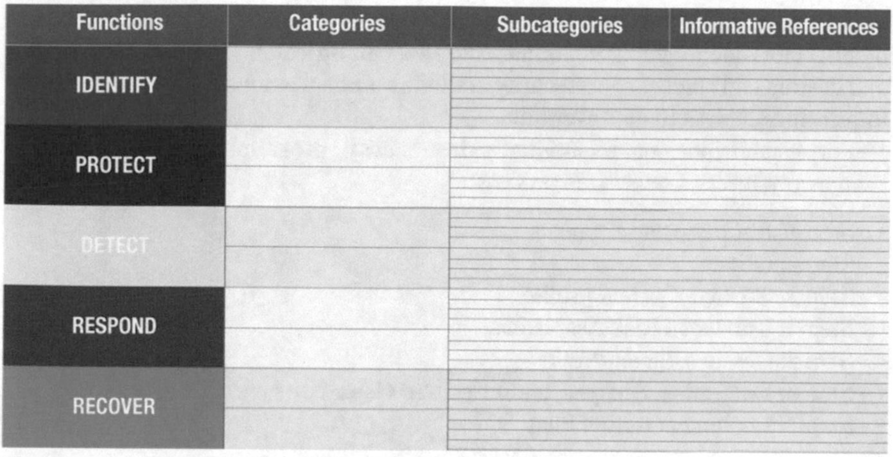

Functions	Categories	Subcategories	Informative References
IDENTIFY			
PROTECT			
DETECT			
RESPOND			
RECOVER			

Fig. 15.2 Cybersecurity Framework Core structure (Cybersecurity Framework, v1.0, Section 2.1, Figure 1)

way are generally easy for any audience to understand, regardless of cybersecurity experience.

Although presented linearly, the five Functions represent continuous activities. Each Function is divided into multiple Categories. Each Category ties cybersecurity outcomes to programmatic needs and particular activities, and is further divided into one or more Subcategories that represent results-oriented outcomes of technical and/or management activities.[9] Informative References include links to existing, widely applicable standards, such as ISO/IEC 27002, COBIT, and NIST SP 800-53. Figure 15.2 shows a notional example of how the elements of the Cybersecurity Framework Core structure fit together.

The Cybersecurity Framework also provides Implementation Tiers that "describe an increasing degree of rigor and sophistication in cybersecurity risk management practices and the extent to which cybersecurity risk management is informed by business needs and is integrated into an organization's overall risk management practices." Each Tier helps puts into context how an organization is postured in terms of risk management processes, integration of their risk management program, and external participation. Four Implementation Tiers are defined:

- Tier 1: Partial
- Tier 2: Risk Informed
- Tier 3: Repeatable
- Tier 4: Adaptive[10]

Framework Profiles provide views of the Framework Core through the lens of a particular organization or group of organizations, based on the influences of the

---

[9] Cybersecurity Framework, v1.0, Section 2.1.

[10] Cybersecurity Framework, v1.0, Section 2.2.

organization's mission objectives, regulatory requirements, industry goals, and other factors identified as important. Profiles can articulate both the current state and desired end state of cybersecurity activities. Organizations can then use Profiles to prioritize their activities over time.

For establishing or improving cybersecurity programs, the Cybersecurity Framework offers a seven-step process:

- Step 1: Prioritize and Scope
- Step 2: Orient
- Step 3: Create a Current Profile
- Step 4: Conduct a Risk Assessment
- Step 5: Create a Target Profile
- Step 6: Determine, Analyze, and Prioritize Gaps
- Step 7: Implement Action Plan

These seven steps can be repeated as necessary to improve over time.

15.4.1   Using the RMF to Implement Data Security

The RMF addresses concerns specific to the design, development, implementation, operation, and disposal of organizational information systems and the environments in which those systems operate.[11] The RMF provides the six steps shown in Fig. 15.3 in its security life cycle:

The RMF steps as presented in NIST SP 800-37 include:

- *Categorize* the information system and the information processed, stored, and transmitted by that system based on an impact analysis.[12]
- *Select* an initial set of baseline security controls for the information system based on the security categorization; tailoring and supplementing the security control baseline as needed based on an organizational assessment of risk and local conditions.[13]
- *Implement* the security controls and describe how the controls are employed within the information system and its environment of operation.
- *Assess* the security controls using appropriate assessment procedures to determine the extent to which the controls are implemented correctly, operating as intended, and producing the desired outcome with respect to meeting the security requirements for the system.
- *Authorize* information system operation based on a determination of the risk to organizational operations and assets, individuals, other organizations, and the

---

[11] NIST SP 800-39, *Managing Information Security Risk*, Section 3.1.

[12] FIPS 199 provides security categorization guidance for non-national security systems. CNSS Instruction 1253 provides similar guidance for national security systems.

[13] NIST Special Publication 800-53 provides security control selection guidance for non-national security systems. CNSS Instruction 1253 provides similar guidance for national security systems.

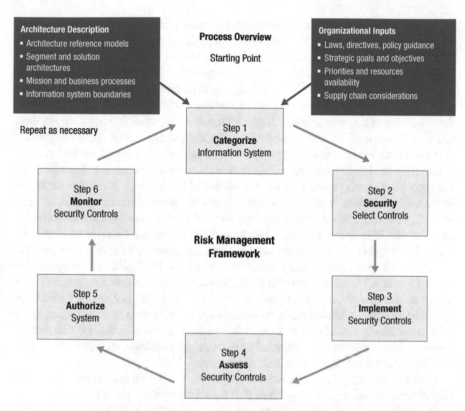

Fig. 15.3 Risk management framework (NIST SP 800-37, Rev1, *Guide for Applying the Risk Management Framework to Federal Information Systems, A Security Life Cycle Approach*, February 2010)

nation, resulting from the operation of the information system and the decision that this risk is acceptable.[14]

- *Monitor* the security controls in the information system on an ongoing basis, including assessing control effectiveness, documenting changes to the system or its environment of operation, conducting security impact analyses of the associated changes, and reporting the security state of the system to designated organizational officials.

The RMF accommodates both new information systems and existing information systems. New information systems assume starting at Step 1, where categorizing the information system—or put another way, understanding the risk posture of a planned system and the information it will handle—sets the foundation for the risk decisions made throughout the remaining steps. Existing information systems may revisit any step in the RMF, depending on where it is in its life cycle. When major changes are made, including changes to how information is handled, it is best to

---

[14] Note that authorization does not focus exclusively on security or privacy risks. Authorizing Officials are expected to evaluate all types of risks raised for an information system.

reevaluate risks under Step 1. However, for minor changes, it can be perfectly acceptable to only execute activities under Steps 2, 3, and 4. In recent years, Step 2, Select, and Step 6, Monitor, have received much attention.

For RMF Step 2, NIST and CNSS provide guidance for selecting security control baselines, which are subsets of available controls that are provided as a starting point of reasonable protections based on the risks associated with the system (i.e., the outcomes of the assessment at Step 1). Organizations then tailor, or adjust, these baselines however they see fit to address the unique aspects of their information system. Some communities began identifying sets of conditions or assumptions where they could augment these baselines with a more specific starting point, and the concept of overlays was devised. Revision 4 of NIST 80-53 offers this definition of overlays: "A specification of security controls, control enhancements, supplemental guidance, and other supporting information employed during the tailoring process, that is intended to complement (and further refine) security control baselines. The overlay specification may be more stringent or less stringent than the original security control baseline specification and can be applied to multiple information systems." Overlays provide a consistent approach to tailoring security control baselines in a given context, such as when working with personally identifiable information (PII) or when employing cross-domain solutions to move information from one security classification domain to another.[15] Even with the use of overlays, however, organizations may still need to make additional tailoring decisions to adequately protect specific systems and information.

Under RMF Step 6, organizations are now working to implement a concept called "continuous monitoring." NIST defines information ("data") security continuous monitoring as "Maintaining ongoing awareness of information security, vulnerabilities, and threats to support organizational risk management decisions," and goes on to clarify that the terms "continuous" and "ongoing" are not meant literally but rather that they "mean that security controls and organizational risks are assessed and analyzed at a frequency sufficient to support risk-based security decisions to adequately protect organization information."[16] Organizations have the flexibility under this definition to determine what works best for them.

15.4.2   Data System Security Control Standards

Standards are available for all aspects of data security information system management. For U.S. government organizations, the prevailing set of information system security control standards comes from NIST. As described by NIST, the

---

[15] See examples of overlays on the CNSS website http://www.cnss.gov. Through the site menus, navigate to Library → Instructions. Scroll down to CNSSI NO. 1253. Under that, you will see links multiple overlays listed as "CNSSI 1253F Attachment X," where X is a numbered attachment to Appendix F of 1253 with each overlay named underneath the attachment number.

[16] NIST SP 800-137, Information Security Continuous Monitoring (ISCM) for Federal Information Systems and Organizations.

purpose of SP 800-53 "is to provide guidelines for selecting and specifying security controls for organizations and information systems supporting the executive agencies of the federal government to meet the requirements of FIPS Publication 200, *Minimum Security Requirements for Federal Information and Information Systems.* The guidelines apply to all components[17] of an information system that process, store, or transmit federal information. The guidelines have been developed to achieve more secure information systems and effective risk management within the federal government by:

- Facilitating a more consistent, comparable, and repeatable approach for selecting and specifying security controls for information systems and organizations;
- Providing a stable, yet flexible catalog of security controls to meet current information protection needs and the demands of future protection needs based on changing threats, requirements, and technologies;
- Providing a recommendation for security controls for information systems categorized in accordance with FIPS Publication 199, *Standards for Security Categorization of Federal Information and Information Systems*;
- Creating a foundation for the development of assessment methods and procedures for determining security control effectiveness; and
- Improving communication among organizations by providing a common lexicon that supports discussion of risk management concepts."[18]

Many additional NIST standards are available to augment those described here.[19] As an example, some provide guidance for addressing specific technology-related topics, for example, cryptographic technologies, log management, cloud computing, and others address areas with unique mission or business impact such as supply chain risk management or protecting controlled unclassified information shared outside the federal government.

15.4.3   Linkages to Other Processes

Organizations use various approaches to managing the systems design and development or engineering life cycles—systems development life cycle (SDLC) or engineering life cycle (ELC)— and information management. SDLC or ELC activities include activities such as concept development, requirements engineering, system

---

[17] "Information system components include, for example, mainframes, workstations, servers (e.g., database, electronic mail, authentication, web, proxy, file, domain name), input/output devices (e.g., scanners, copiers, printers), network components (e.g., firewalls, routers, gateways, voice and data switches, process controllers, wireless access points, network appliances, sensors), operating systems, virtual machines, middleware, and applications." NIST SP 800-53, Rev. 4, Section 1.1.

[18] NIST SP 800-53, Rev. 4, Section 1.1.

[19] NIST maintains its publications at: http://csrc.nist.gov/publications/PubsSPs.html.

architecture, system design and development, system integration, test and evaluation, transition, operation, and maintenance. OMB Circular A-130 discusses the information management life cycle in terms of creation or collection, processing, dissemination, use, storage, and disposition, which includes destruction and deletion.[20] The data security implementation activities remain the same regardless of any specific approaches used for SDLC/ELC and the information life cycle.

15.4.4 Piecing Together Data Security Implementation Considerations

Though the Cybersecurity Framework and RMF are independent resources for implementing cybersecurity activities that evolved from separate needs, there are some commonalities in the types of activities performed using each framework. The diagram in Fig. 15.4 offers a way of thinking about how their system-level activities generally intersect for those organizations that are interested in using both frameworks. The diagram is organized using the Cybersecurity Framework due to the breadth and simplicity of its five Functions. The system-level activities in the RMF security lifecycle phases mostly intersect with Identify, Protect, and Detect.

Many information systems operate in a constantly changing environment, thus it is important to acknowledge that both the Cybersecurity Framework and RMF activities are often iterative in reality. Changes to the operating environment inevitably will require revisiting one or more cybersecurity activities. Operationally, aspects of the RMF Select and Implement steps may sometimes intersect with activities that are part

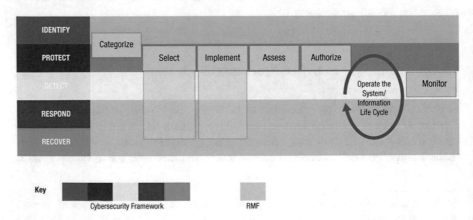

Fig. 15.4 High-level intersection of cybersecurity framework, system and information life cycles, and RMF activities

---

[20] OMB Circular A-130, 10.a.

of the Cybersecurity Framework's Detect, Respond, and Recover Functions. For example, insights from a detected incident and decisions made during the response and recovery processes may drive changes to selected controls (e.g., implementing a new control) and/or changes to how existing controls are implemented.

For more information regarding the relationship between the Cybersecurity and RMF from an organizational cybersecurity strategy perspective, see Appendix C, Data Security References, Data Security Frameworks.

15.5   Data Security Tools

Tools are available to cover most, if not all, areas of data security (for examples of security areas, see Table 18 in Appendix C). The space is too vast to characterize in detail for the purposes of this book. In general, data security tools continue to evolve to address new threats, reducing the need to develop security tools in-house. Many tools are focused on centralizing services that can be applied to multiple products and are capable of aggregating logs entries into actionable information. A robust body of market research through entities like Forrester Research and Gartner can provide insights into the various tool spaces.

Chapter 16
Metadata

"Organizations that don't know what information they have, or need, are unable to leverage information as an asset."[1] Metadata ensures data is visible, trusted, and usable. Metadata also facilitates data sharing. One might ask: Is data "shared" if it's exchanged or published without the necessary metadata to understand it? Data should be shared. This is a recognized data management principle. After all, the value of data is limited when it remains in isolated pockets built to meet local needs. Shared, integrated data results in consistent and improved decisions and customer service. There is general agreement that data is only "shared" if the metadata necessary to understand and use it effectively is also provided. This has implications for the importance of metadata management programs and also for data governance and for "open" datasets published by the government.

Similarly, good metadata will keep data from falling into the wrong hands. Although it is important for organizations to share data internally to foster consistent decision making, it is equally important for them to protect their data from competitors and to protect sensitive data in conformance with legal requirements. Good metadata helps organizations determine what data they should share and what data is sensitive or proprietary.

A 2016 survey by Dataversity found that nearly two-thirds of respondents felt "metadata is more important now than it was ten years ago." It found that traditional use cases, such as data governance, data quality improvement, data warehousing, and business intelligence are still the most common use cases for metadata. Master data management is another use case. However, the survey points out that new types of use cases are also driving home the importance of metadata. "The burgeoning importance of new technologies such as Big Data, the Internet of Things, Advanced

---

[1] De Simoni, G., "The Growth of the Metadata Management Tool Market is a Reality," Gartner, March 24, 2016.

Analytics, Data Lakes, Artificial Intelligence/Machine Learning, and Semantic Technologies are creating a landscape of more complexity, higher volumes of data, and an even greater need to govern and understand that data with more certainty."[2]

16.1   What Are Metadata and Metadata Management?

What exactly is metadata? The conventional definition is data about data, but there are better definitions. For example:

- "Metadata is information that describes various facets of an information asset to improve its usability throughout its life cycle."[3]
- "Metadata is a category of information that identifies, describes, explains, and provides content, context, structure, and classifications pertaining to an organization's data assets and enables effective retrieval, usage, and management of these assets."[4]

These definitions establish the purpose of "usability" and speak to the duration of the metadata as the "life cycle" of data. These definitions are inclusive, allowing that metadata is not just about structured data in databases or files but can include information about other types of unstructured or semi-structured information assets such as images, videos, emails, or documents.

The U.S. National Information Standards Organization and the Digital Library define the following three types of metadata[5]:

- *Descriptive metadata* (also sometimes referred to as business metadata) supports identification and discovery typically needed by the business. This includes basic identification information that would typically be recorded in a catalog entry, such as an identifier, a name or title, a subject or general description, or descriptive tags.
- *Structural metadata* (also sometimes referred to as technical metadata) defines components such as a data model, schema for a database, or interfaces, instantiated in the physical data layer.
- *Administrative metadata* (also sometimes referred to as operational metadata) relates to management of a resource. Who owns it? When and how was it was created? What type of asset is it? This category also includes security and rights

---

[2] Burbank, R., "Emerging Trends in Metadata Management: A Dataversity® 2016 Report on the Top Business & Technical Drivers for Metadata," Dataversity Education, LLC, 2016.

[3] Beyer, T., Lapkin, G., & De Simoni, G., "Gartner Clarifies the Definition of Metadata," Gartner, August 13, 2014.

[4] CMMI Institute, "Data Management Maturity (DMM) Model," Chapter on "Metadata Management," Ver. 1.0, August 2014.

[5] Beyer, T., Lapkin, G., & De Simoni, G., "Gartner Clarifies the Definition of Metadata," Gartner, August 13, 2014.

management metadata relating to intellectual property and metadata needed for archiving and preservation.

Historically, metadata approaches toward structured and unstructured information were quite separate and independent. The metadata approach to structured data focused on technical metadata, essentially defining a piece of data in the context of a record in a database table or a file. Data such as images, documents, and video were considered unstructured content, and the focus was to document descriptive metadata such as the title, author, publication date, and so on. However, with evolving technologies, the result is that the boundary between structured and unstructured data is becoming blurred. For example, with facial recognition, we can use an image to verify identity, just like a structured piece of data like social security number. Increasingly, business does not care about boundaries between structured and unstructured data; measures such as freshness and the source of data are of greater concern. More and more business problems will require examining structured and unstructured data jointly. This increases the importance of all types of metadata for information integration,[6] and the use of controlled vocabularies across the metadata spectrum through standardized taxonomies and ontologies.

16.1.1   Metadata Management

Metadata management is the "business discipline for managing the data about an organization's information assets [and it] encompasses the roles, responsibilities, processes, organization, and technology required to ensure that the metadata across the enterprise adds value to enterprise information."[7] Metadata management is often considered a foundational data management domain and a program needed not only to support data users in general but also other data management domains such as data governance, data architecture, MDM, data warehousing, analytics, and records management. In turn, these functions help to define requirements and priorities for metadata, and to define and validate metadata content.

16.1.2   Metadata vs. Data

Many organizations struggle with the distinction between data and metadata. The authors of the previously cited article "Gartner Clarifies the Definition of Metadata" discuss that "well-meaning but often misguided efforts to define metadata have

---

[6] Leganza, G., 'Information Strategies Move Center Stage," Forrester Research, Inc., May 20, 2013.

[7] De Simoni, G., "How Metadata Improves Business Opportunities and Threats," Gartner, August 13, 2014.

blurred the line between data and metadata" and then go on to definitively state that metadata is, in fact, data. We agree that metadata is data, and it must be managed accordingly. From the perspective of data management, the difference between data and metadata is not only blurry but largely irrelevant.

The same principles and patterns applied equally well to metadata. Here are a few examples:

- Metadata should have defined data stewards to be clear who is accountable and responsible for it.
- Metadata has systems of record where it is created and maintained, and it often has other authoritative sources. For example, a data model is a source of structural metadata about a database and might be published to the enterprise through a metadata repository. If an issue is found with the metadata, it ideally should be corrected in the system of record, and the corrections should flow downstream, just as best practice would have you correct business data.
- To realize its value, metadata needs to be shared for efficiency and productivity and to ensure consistency across the environment.
- Metadata often must be integrated with the same metadata from other sources to maximize its value to the enterprise. For example, to support a level of effort analysis, an analyst might leverage metadata to find related data models, process models, system catalogs, data quality results, and so on. Metadata is often extracted from sources such as data models and process models and combined into a metadata repository. As a central integrated hub of metadata, a metadata repository is analogous to an operational data store or data warehouse, but for metadata rather than operational data.
- Metadata itself should be classified or categorized as to its sensitivity, and in some cases, access to it should be restricted accordingly. Consider the case of an analyst at a financial services company who was researching a data quality issue. Using just the sample data from the issue report and the associated metadata, the analyst could determine the fundamentals of how various underwriting score-cards worked. That information was proprietary intellectual property. There wasn't much risk the analyst would run to a competitor with the information, but the data steward was aghast at how much the analyst was able to figure out from just the metadata and sample data. Based on discussion of this incident, the steward and the company's data management organization realized that some metadata is sensitive and should only be available to those who have a legitimate business need to know it.
- Quality requirements for key metadata should be defined and periodically assessed. For example, an organization might determine that data models and associated metadata will be required for internally built solutions (but not COTS because some COTS products do not provide this information). They might further decide that the data models for critical systems should be compared periodically to the database schema in production to measure accuracy of the metadata. After all, metadata is often used for level of effort analysis and if the metadata isn't an accurate reflection of the production system, the analysis results will be flawed.

Too many organizations spend too much time and effort in discussions of the distinction between data and metadata. Based on our experience, this is an artificial distinction and varies based on the perspective of the individuals involved in the discussion. Consider the following examples:

- To a business person, catalog information about systems and which systems act on what kind of data is "just" metadata, but someone in IT may view this as data that is critical to their job.
- Usage information showing who accesses data in a data lake is probably considered to be metadata by the person who is figuring out what information is most frequently accessed and therefore needs to be kept online versus archived or purged. That same information may be viewed as data by a security professional evaluating risks or researching incidents.
- The Creator and Contributor names (metadata) on a presentation or document could be employees who are also defined in an organization's HR system (data).
- Sentiment analysis of social media posts is considered metadata by some and derived data by others.

Our recommendation is to focus on what information the enterprise needs, how best to meet those needs, and how to capture and maintain what is needed, regardless of the labels that might apply to it: data vs. metadata, business data vs. technical data, reference data vs. master data. Continuing the earlier Creator/Contributor example, an HR system is presumably already the authoritative data source for employee data, but it could also be used to populate an author selection list used to more consistently collect metadata in a document management system. Employee is therefore both business data and metadata depending on context.

16.2 Who Is Metadata Management?

Like data governance, metadata management is everyone's business. Metadata management is sometimes confused with just the administration of a metadata repository or metadata toolset, but it should really involve many roles across both business and IT functions because "metadata is pervasive in the enterprise."[8]

- Data governance often establishes policy and requirements around metadata.
- With a broad mix of business as well as IT representatives, data governance should be able to capture requirements to cover the needs of the top four metadata users (in descending order): business users, data architects/data modelers, BI reporting teams, and developers.[9]

---

[8] De Simoni, G., "How Metadata Improves Business Opportunities and Threats," Gartner, August 13, 2014.

[9] Burbank, R., "Emerging Trends in Metadata Management: A Dataversity®2016 Report on the Top Business & Technical Drivers for Metadata," Dataversity Education, LLC, 2016.

- Document authors, process owners, data stewards, and business system owners often create or at least validate metadata content and help to maintain it. After all, the business is often the ultimate source for the definition of terms, valid values and other business rules, data categorizations, and legal or contractual restrictions on the use and disclosure of data.
- System maintainers in IT, and project staff such as data modelers and architects, add content and maintain metadata in data models or other architecture artifacts or tools that should be routinely extracted and loaded into a metadata repository.
- Users should report DQ problems, which may be captured as or linked through metadata.

Where the administration of a metadata repository resides in an organization varies, and there is no right solution. Options include within a data management organization, or a data governance organization with matrixed IT support, or in a tools group within IT, or a mix of these. Support tasks include the loading and integrating of metadata, support for data and metadata quality resolution, creation of query and reporting services (e.g., for projects, level-of-effort analyses, or support for efforts to incrementally standardize data definitions and taxonomies). As the organization matures, metadata management responsibilities might also include support for e-Discovery and the creation of services for federated search capabilities.

16.3   Benefits of Metadata Management

Data management principles often include that data be visible, accessible, usable, and trusted. Metadata helps with three of these four principles. Benefits of metadata and metadata management include:

- Metadata provides visibility to what data the organization has at the enterprise level, supporting discovery through document tagging and published system and data asset catalogs with mappings to a conceptual model or data categories. At the local level, metadata provides context for and insight into a document or image or the contents of a data store, for example, through publishing data models or schemas, dictionaries, lineage, and perhaps mappings to an enterprise logical model. This information in turn enables data governance and stewardship activities such as data lifecycle analysis and identification of candidate authoritative sources, implementation of master data management, level of effort analysis for proposed changes, as well as architecture analysis of the current enterprise data environment and evolution priorities to get to the target environment.
- Metadata improves usability and interoperability of data. It improves the productivity of stewards and knowledge workers, as well as architects and IT project staff, by providing them with information to understand the data they need and information to accurately compare data from different sources. "Metadata unlocks

the value of data … Metadata makes information valuable by allowing people to put that information to use."[10] "When metadata is well managed, the information assets are more useful and valuable; badly managed metadata can make information assets less useful and valuable—creating increased costs and risks related to those assets."[11] Toward the end of data's life cycle, metadata is also crucial to archiving—an archive must include the associated metadata to ensure that the information in the archive is recoverable at a later date!

- Metadata also improves trust in data simply by providing transparency into definitions, business rules, data quality, and provenance or lineage. Even if the quality of data isn't perfect, someone who can see what they're dealing with is more likely to be willing to reuse existing data and be able do so successfully, rather than having each area create their own duplicative data stores, run redundant edits, or leverage slightly different integration rules that increase enterprise confusion and the need for costly business reconciliations.

Examples of drivers for a metadata business case include:

- Improved productivity of data stewards, knowledge workers, and staff in general
- Faster, more complete, and accurate level of effort analysis for proposed changes, especially important in fast-changing industries
- The ability to find information/records to support legal requirements or FOIA, e.g., content of any type (records in a database, photos, emails, etc.) related to an individual, case or event
- The ability to respond to an internal or external audit

Ultimately metadata helps improve the quality of business decisions by making it easier for people to find the right data on which to base the decision, by providing clear definitions, business rules, and authoritative sources, as well as communicating categorizations and restrictions that might impact how the data can be used or disclosed. "A general lack of metadata management introduces the risk of data ignorance, and an overabundance of poorly managed metadata introduces the risk of data confusion."[12]

---

[10] Beyer, T., Lapkin, G., & De Simoni, G., "Gartner Clarifies the Definition of Metadata," Gartner, August 13 2014.

[11] De Simoni, G., "How Metadata Improves Business Opportunities and Threats," Gartner, August 13, 2014.

[12] De Simoni, G., "How Metadata Improves Business Opportunities and Threats," Gartner, August 13, 2014.

16.4   Metadata Frameworks

Numerous standards and vocabularies in the metadata space are intended to promote consistency and interoperability of metadata. Examples are listed in Appendix C, together with links to additional information. Figure 16.1 shows the different types of standards.

- The examples in blue are for cataloging digital artifacts or datasets. Dublin Core[13] is foundational, and DCAT builds on Dublin Core. The Common Warehouse Metamodel (CWM) defines a warehouse metamodel.
- The green examples relate to ontologies and establishing common vocabularies for specific subjects such as assets, organization, and people. OWL[14] is foundational.
- The yellow examples relate to ISO standards for metadata registries or repositories. For example, ISO 11179 defines foundational concepts such as classes and attributes, and the Common Warehouse Metamodel (CWM) defines a warehouse metamodel.
- Shown in purple, exchange standards such as NIEM and HL7 aren't metadata standards per se, but as we have seen, sometimes data for one person is metadata for another. So, exchange standards are related and can also be used for metadata definition when applicable.

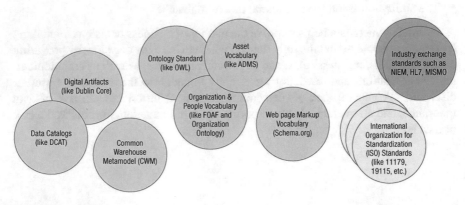

Fig. 16.1   Selected metadata-related standards

---

[13] The Dublin Core Metadata Initiative, or "DCMI," is an open organization supporting innovation in metadata design and best practices across the metadata ecology. For more information, see http://dublincore.org/documents/dcmi-terms/.

[14] The W3C Web Ontology Language (OWL) is a Semantic Web language designed to represent rich and complex knowledge about things, groups of things, and relations between things. For more information, see https://www.w3.org/2001/sw/wiki/OWL.

16.5   Implementing Metadata

In most organizations, individual groups (business users, data management or a narrower data modeling group, data architecture, records management, web-content management, etc.) often begin by collecting and publishing metadata through grassroots efforts. Though progress can be made in this way, inevitably the organization reaches a point at which it is almost impossible to move forward and mature without a viable enterprise data management (EDM) team and executive sponsorship.

Each organization should consider its business model and current business goals as an input to establishing metadata priorities. Often metadata already exists within organizations. Some of this metadata is technical and hidden in tools and data stores. Other metadata is likely descriptive metadata that helps users locally to better find and manage information important to them. Answers to the following questions will help to shape the priorities for building out or validating enterprise metadata.

- Is the enterprise working on a data warehouse or MDM initiative, and if so for what kinds of data?
- Where are reports working? Where are they failing?
- What, if any, analytics initiatives exist?
- Is the organization struggling to integrate digital documents, images and videos, or social media in business processes for customer management?
- Does the organization want to improve its records management?

If metadata management initiatives start with a focus on structured data, organizations have many potential sources for metadata that are often decentralized and not readily accessible to the employees, even sometimes locked into specialized tools that the average person doesn't have. Examples of sources include:

- Existing lists of business terms and acronyms as input to a Business Glossary
- System architecture documents or system architecture information in architecture tools
- A Business Reference Model and process models
- Data models and embedded dictionaries
- Database catalogs, file structures, and even copy books for mainframe data files
- Business users, data modelers, or a community of interest or practice for modeling may have already defined subject areas. They may have even defined data categories (a level between subject areas and entities) and may already have mapped databases or models to subject areas or data categories.
- ETL code with embedded data lineage mappings and transformation logic
- Data quality tools and resulting data quality statistics
- BI reports/tools with semantic layers
- Document or content management tools
- A policy or a privacy office might define specific data that is PII or PHI
- Policy or Legal might have defined levels of data sensitivity and examples of types of data that fall into each sensitivity level

An initial focus is often simply to provide a higher degree of transparency into the organization's current ecosystem by centrally documenting existing metadata and integrating it sufficiently to foster understanding. If the initial focus is on structured metadata, the following steps are fairly typical and align with other sections of this book, including the data governance and data architecture sections:

- Work with IT and data architecture to create and centrally publish an inventory of systems and data assets, as well as known business and technical points of contact (POCs). Key points to consider:
  - Validate the catalog through business users or data governance, if it exists.
  - Access to the inventory should generally be broadly available to business and IT staff. Some restrictions may be needed based on the content of the inventory.
  - Think about how the information will be maintained. A periodic survey or census is one way to ensure that the information is regularly updated, but incorporating checks into change management processes such as a systems development life cycle is a better way to keep information current. Will your program sponsor and other executives support this?
- Work with business system owners, IT system maintainers, and roles such as data governance, data architects, or data modelers, if they exist, to understand and document what data categories have already been created, used, and stored by respective systems. Centrally publish this information as an extension of the metadata inventory.

  A survey or census is one way to quickly gather a large set of information, particularly if you have visible executive support. Keep in mind that data uses may differ and multiple perspectives may need be documented.

  Understanding what data systems create, use, and store—even at a high level like subject areas and data categories—is useful to data architects and data stewards in understanding the data environment. It is often the starting point to create a data lifecycle diagram that will show graphically the degree of redundancy and complexity present in the current data environment. The information is a critical input to identifying authoritative data sources and migration priorities.
- If subject areas and data categories do not yet exist, work with business users, data architecture, and data governance to define them.
- Work with data governance, if it exists, and roles such as business process owners to map business functions and processes to data categories and add this to your metadata repository. This solidifies data lifecycle diagrams. This also helps data stewards by identifying stakeholders with whom they should collaborate to understand data requirements and to assess whether data quality meets existing and forecasted needs.
- Prioritize data assets to obtain or create data architecture diagrams such as lifecycle diagrams, data models, perhaps based on current initiative needs or just based on which data assets have the most users or are used by the most groups within the enterprise. If models do not exist and must be developed, extracting

schemas from database catalogs and publishing this information might be a first step. As more robust models are developed, the dictionary information, valid values, and other content typically maintained in such models can be prioritized for inclusion in the metadata repository. Work with business system owners to determine if any of this structural metadata might need to be restricted.

When the organization understands what is local in a given system or repository and where in the enterprise similar data exists, the organization (often through the efforts of data stewards) can begin to iteratively standardize metadata (semantics and classifications, formalizing a business glossary, attribute definitions, and taxonomies) used in structured data and metadata associated with documents, images, videos, and so on. This kind of standardization is typically an ongoing, multi-year activity driven by data governance.

If an organization wants to improve metadata associated with unstructured information such as documents and email, it may begin with inventorying descriptive metadata. Metadata, including descriptive metadata and administrative metadata, associated with unstructured data is, to some extent, often already embedded in the information asset itself (e.g., author of a document, or its creation date) and, as with structured data, tools that manage unstructured information will store a certain amount of technical metadata.

In addition, the organization may find it helpful to have a "data map," or architecture of its unstructured data assets. For this, it will likely be able to leverage a good portion of the same metadata identified for structured data. In other words, the terms used to identify data will be the same across the structured and unstructured data landscape. This is the case because the organization's business is the same, whether applied to structured or unstructured information. Key subject areas, data categories, and even data fields will be important in identifying and integrating information across the board.

That said, the amount of metadata can be overwhelming, and an organization should prioritize where it wants to focus its metadata efforts. It is certainly a good, fundamental practice to document data location and flow as described earlier for structured data. However, it may be equally or more important for an organization that is focused on customer service to focus on its ability to find important documents, thus shifting its metadata focus on the consistent tagging of its unstructured data. Consider again the example of police body cams. Such video is piling up in data stores. The ability to quickly find the right video depends significantly on the right metadata.

As the metadata management roles become more formalized, a central metadata repository is established, and differences in terms are resolved, more complex metadata, such as business rules and data interdependencies can be captured. Organizations—particularly those that are heavily regulated and subjected to external or internal audits—might undertake data lineage as a next step. Note that organizations will need metadata management tools to effectively address data lineage on any significant scale. Unlike catalog information, which is often collected and maintained manually, advanced metadata like lineage calls for automated capture as much as possible; many major ETL tools capture lineage information and can integrate with metadata repositories or at least export metadata for integration. Additionally, having a tool to visualize an advanced concept such as data lineage is helpful. Visualizing lineage makes it more useful for multiple purposes, from researching data quality issues to meeting audit or regulatory requirements. The ability to create—or better yet, generate—a graphical representation of lineage either forward from the system of record or backward, for example, from an analytic environment is a key metadata capability.

As organizations expand into wider varieties of data as well as new sources, classifying and understanding new information rapidly begins to exceeds what staff can effectively deal with. If your organization is expanding its use of data to include commercial datasets or using data lakes to evaluate large volumes of new content for value, you may want to look at emerging technologies. The future direction of metadata lies in automated discovery and classification tools to keep up with rising volumes of data. Keep in mind, however, that not all data is valuable; "on average, roughly one third of enterprise content is redundant, outdated, or trivial (ROT) and can be safely excluded from a metadata program."[15] Having a baseline metadata repository in place against which automated processes can execute is a typical up-front requirement for automated discovery and classification.

According to Gartner, data lakes will fail to deliver effective benefits in 9 out of 10 initiatives.[16] Gartner goes on to state that "data lakes provide an environment without the assurances and benefits common to traditional warehouses"; without "'just enough' information governance" and "either very skilled users or effective metadata management," you may not be able to "operationalize" your data lake. In other words, it may become a data swamp, a derisive term often used for an unmanaged data lake or sandbox environment.

It's important to remember that metadata is a program, not a project. Metadata requires lifetime care and feeding. It's not enough to periodically obtain current metadata and publish it. Business change processes, data steward processes, and IT software development life cycles should be enhanced to ensure that metadata is systematically kept up to date as a matter of routine. That requires executive sponsorship, collaboration across areas, and EDM resources and infrastructure. Close collaboration with a data governance group can be a great way to publicize the importance of metadata and to define or validate metadata requirements and priorities. Data governance members, if engaged, can help in obtaining and maintaining critical metadata from their respective business areas. Managing expectations of a metadata program is very important because, as Gartner notes, it can "take two years or longer to capture 'enough metadata' to be viewed as adding sufficient value to warrant the additional effort dictated by [enterprise metadata management] EMM."[17]

[15] Stewart, D., "Automatic Classification and Tagging Make Metadata Manageable for ECM and Search," Gartner, August 5, 2015.

[16] De Simoni, G., "Metadata Is the Fish Finder in Data Lakes," Gartner, October 5, 2015.

[17] De Simoni, G., "Overcoming the Challenges to Implementing Enterprise Metadata Management Across the Organization," Gartner, Refreshed August 27, 2014. Published August 14, 2012.

16.6   Metadata Management Tools

Many data management tools today, beyond metadata repositories, include metadata; examples include data modeling tools, ETL tools, data quality tools, and BI tools. Major vendors often sell these kinds of tools as a suite or set, that are, to varying degrees, integrated to include functions such as ETL, data quality, and MDM, all the while documenting technical and administrative metadata. Document or content management systems and record management systems are different products, but they also capture significant metadata that needs to be standardized and should ultimately leverage some of the same taxonomies for classification.

Gartner predicts that "while the market is still small, the need for organizations to treat information as an asset will make metadata management strategic and will drive significant growth for metadata management tools."[18] In "The Growth of the Metadata Management Tool Market Is a Reality," Gartner identifies the following minimum capabilities they now look for in their Magic Quadrant analysis of metadata management tools. They also list new capabilities they're seeing:

- Minimum capabilities

  - Metadata repository that supports management of metadata, publishing, and search capabilities
  - Business Glossary to communicate business terms
  - Data Lineage tracing data movement from its origin throughout the enterprise as it's shared and integrated for downstream processes and analytics
  - An impact analysis that conveys extensive details regarding the dependencies of information or the impact of a change within a data source
  - Rule Management relating to creation and editing of business attributes
  - Metadata ingestion and translation from a variety of sources, including architecture and data modeling tool, ETL tools, BI tools, DBMS catalogs, and a variety of source formats such as MS Word and Excel, and XML files

- Examples of new capabilities

  - Ability to address additional data types (like unstructured or semi-structured data) and to capture and enrich metadata when it's loaded, for example, into data lakes for evaluation
  - A combination of machine learning metadata and crowdsourcing metadata
  - Support for multivendor environments for data lineage
  - Semantic modeling combined with the flexibility of schema-less, graph-based data representation

Based on a 2016 Dataversity survey, most organizations do not begin with such a complicated toolset to manage metadata. "Fifty three percent of organizations are using tool-specific Metadata solutions in their organizations, while 50% are using

---

[18] De Simoni, G., "The Growth of the Metadata Management Tool Market is a Reality," Gartner, March 24, 2016.

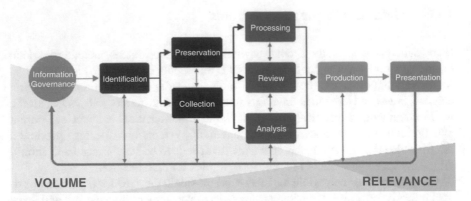

Metadata Repositories, and 47% are using Business Glossaries." Forty five percent
use homegrown solutions such as a Wiki or SharePoint. The four most important
tool functionalities cited in the survey results were metadata search, storage/reposi-
tory/database, interchange with other tools, which would include the metadata
ingestion and translation capabilities mentioned earlier, and a web-based portal.[19]

Emerging tools in the metadata space include those supporting eDiscovery and
automated tagging. See Fig. 16.2.

eDiscovery tools were originally used by legal teams to identify information that
might be relevant to a pending lawsuit or criminal investigation. The Identification
step in the conceptual process above locates potential sources of electronically
stored information (ESI) and determines its scope, breadth, and depth. The term ESI
refers to any information stored electronically, including electronic documents
such as spreadsheets and text documents, the contents of databases, and other less
structured content like phone messages and voicemails.[20]

This same approach is being applied to metadata management, for example,
to periodically scan data lakes, or evaluation sandboxes, to determine what new
datasets have been added, so that they can be evaluated to determine if they're
suitable for sharing and should therefore be added to the data asset inventory.

Emerging tools that use "some form of machine-enabled method and analytics" are
being used to understand content, "distilling semantic meaning from the datasets
themselves."[21] Increasingly, a first pass of the tagging process is being done through
automated means for both newly discovered data assets and, in many cases, for

---

[19] Burbank, R., & Row, C., "Emerging Trends in Metadata Management," Dataversity Education,
LLC, 2016.

[20] For more information on the phases of eDiscovery and the Electronic Discovery Reference
Model, see, www.edrm.net.

[21] Duncan, L., & De Simoni, G., "How Chief Data Officers Can Use an Information Catalog to
Maximize Business Value from Information Assets," Gartner, May 6, 2016.

subsets of existing data assets that are considered critical but either weren't tagged or done consistently. It is noteworthy that "most machine-learning systems reference an existing managed metadata vocabulary as a guide for automatic classification. The hierarchical structure and term equivalencies captured in a taxonomy or thesaurus can significantly improve the accuracy of a machine-learning-based system."[22]

---

[22] Stewart, D., "Automatic Classification and Tagging Make Metadata Manageable for ECM and Search," Gartner, August 5, 2015.

Chapter 17
Records Management

17.1 What Is Records Management

Records are "data or information in a fixed form that is created or received in the course of individual or institutional activity and set aside (preserved) as evidence of that activity."[1] What gives data its recordness—what allows us to sometimes think of data as records—is data's relationship to the activities that created it and in turn its evidence of those activities. How institutions conceive of "records" varies greatly. Some institutions understand records broadly, considering all documents to be records. Other institutions think of records more narrowly, considering only the documents that have been formally declared as a record in an authoritative record-keeping system as records. In this chapter, we take a relatively broad view of records to be any document with information fixed in any form that has a relationship with any business activity. Records can come in a variety of formats. Traditionally, we think of records as formal documents like an agenda or meeting minutes. The definition of records we use in this chapter is a broader notion of the term. Records can be a website, an instant message conversation, a voice mail, videos or surveillance tapes, an email, or a dataset. To properly manage records, it is important to understand the full information infrastructure and the variety of formats used within an organization.

In this chapter, we take data to mean "facts, ideas, or discrete pieces of information—information in its most atomized form."[2] The distinction between data and records has become increasingly complex as information technologies

---

[1] "Record" Pearce-Moses, R., Glossary of Archival and Records Terminology, http://www2.archivists.org/glossary/terms/r/record.

[2] "Data" Pearce-Moses, R., Glossary of Archival and Records Terminology, http://www2.archivists.org/glossary/terms/d/data.

© Springer International Publishing AG 2018
M. Fleckenstein, L. Fellows, *Modern Data Strategy*,
https://doi.org/10.1007/978-3-319-68993-7_17

have allowed institutions to handle data in remarkable complex and agile ways. With well-managed metadata, many pieces of data—discrete pieces of information—can be rendered in an instant to display as a record for a user. A doctor looking at an electronic health record, for example, uses an electronic health records system that renders a particular subset of data in a manner that he or she conceptually understands to be his or her patient's medical record—a record that provides evidence of the patient's medical care.

Because of this dynamic relationship between data and records, instead of categorizing some information as data and other information as records, "that is data over here, and those are records over there," it may be more profitable to distinguish between records and data in the context of their use. A researcher studying drunk driving, for example, would look at thousands of DUI arrest records as *data*—compiling, sorting, slicing, reconfiguring, and analyzing the information in countless ways to gain new knowledge about drunk driving. A judge, on the other hand, would look at a single DUI arrest record as a *record* that provides evidence of a particular action—a police officer arresting *a* person suspected of driving under the influence. Birth records can be used as *data* to draw conclusions about demographic trends or public health, but birth records can also be used as *records* to provide evidence of the birth of individual children.

Records management is the "systematic and administrative control of records throughout their life cycle to ensure efficiency and economy in their creation, use, handling, control, maintenance, and disposition."[3] This work is done to ensure the integrity of records—that records remain "whole and unaltered through loss, tampering, or corruption."[4] Records management is a rapidly evolving field. Within the past five years, information management and information technology professionals have begun to see records management as a component within the broader concept of information governance. Consultant George Parapadakis defines information governance as "a framework of people, principles, processes, and tools that defines why, when, and how information is managed within an organization, in order to maximize its value, fulfil obligations, reduce costs, and reduce risk."[5] This newly emergent area of practice has yet to coalesce around a singular definition.[6] Generally

---

[3] "Records Management" Pearce-Moses, R., Glossary of Archival and Records Terminology, http://archivists.org/glossary/terms/r/records-management.

[4] "Integrity" Pearce-Moses, R., Glossary of Archival and Records Terminology, http://archivists.org/glossary/terms/i/integrity.

[5] Parapadakis, G., "Nightmare definitions: What is Information Governance?" 2014, https://4most.wordpress.com/2014/06/26/what-is-ig.

[6] Another definition of information governance is offered by Gartner: "The specification of decision rights and an accountability framework to ensure appropriate behavior in the valuation, creation, storage, use, archiving and deletion of information. It includes processes, roles and policies, standards and metrics that ensure the effective and efficient use of information in enabling an organization to achieve its goals." Gartner, "IT Glossary" http://www.gartner.com/it-glossary/information-governance/. IBM defines information governance as "the activities and technologies that organizations employ to maximize the value of their information while minimizing associated risks and costs." IBM, "Information Governance Market Research Report." (2010) http://www.b-

speaking, however, there is a loose consensus that the notion of information governance raises the profile of information management—inclusive of records and data management—from an operational and compliance concerns to a core strategic concern of any organization. In other words, information governance is meant to garner the attention of senior executives and officers.

This new concept of information governance has also seen new articulations of other areas of work, described as either related to or a component of information governance. These areas include:

- *Data Governance*: A component of information governance. Whereas information governance addresses all types of unstructured and structured information, data governance has a more limited scope that is focused only on structured data.[7]
- *Document Management*: Focused on check-in/check-out, version control, security, and library services for business documents. Other aspects of document management include compound-document support, content replication, digital rights management, and version management.[8]
- *Web Content Management*: The process of controlling content for consumption over digital channels using specific management tools based on a core repository.[9]
- *Enterprise Content Management*: "A strategic framework and a technical architecture that supports all types of content (and format) throughout the content life cycle. As a strategic framework, ECM [Enterprise Content Management] can help enterprises take control of their content. It can contribute to initiatives around transactional processes, compliance, and records management as well as sharing and collaborating around content and documents. As a technical architecture, ECM can be delivered either as a suite of products integrated at the content or interface level or as a number of separate products that share a common architecture."[10]

Multiple articulations of these closely related areas of work are either part of, adjacent to, or encompassing of records management. This makes it challenging to navigate the records management and allied fields. You will come across different terminology to mean the same thing and the same terminology to mean different things. However, records management is at an exciting juncture where it is no longer seen as an isolated operational function but as a part of a larger information and data management framework that has strategic value for organizations.

A key, long-standing component of records management work also includes determining the legal, business, and historic value of a record, a process also undertaken by archivists performing archival appraisal. The value, description, and rules

---

eye-network.com/events/details/3966.

[7] See Chapter on "Data Governance" in this book for an in-depth discussion on data governance.

[8] Gartner, "2015 Magic Quadrant for Enterprise Content Management."

[9] *Ibid.*

[10] *Ibid.*

governing records within an institution are usually described in a records retention schedule. These are policy documents that list types of records belonging to an organization, what office(s) are responsible for managing these records, how long these records should be kept, and what should ultimately happen with these records (often referred to as their disposition). These instructions for how long to keep a record are sometimes dictated by local or federal law and should be reviewed by a lawyer who is familiar with the laws governing an organization's business. An institution's records management program, usually led by a records manager, typically administers records retention schedules. Records management is its own field with its own set of traditions and professional practices.

A records management program can fit within a data strategy by bringing expertise to bear on retention strategies for data, access rights, and compliance requirements. Records managers also provide a rich understanding of lifecycle management and the needs of data in each phase of the life cycle, from creation, to use, to storage, to reuse, to archives, and to destruction. Records managers, along with archivists, can also provide insights and solutions on how to preserve data so it is readable and understandable over time. Finally, the field of records management brings a framework of knowledge about data creation. In many cases, businesses, not-for-profit organizations, and government agencies do not generate data for the sake of generating data. Rather, they create records while conducting their business—think of the arrest records or birth records. From these records, an organization can generate data for analysis such as a retailer analyzing its sales records as data to understand strengths, weaknesses, and trends in its business. A core component of records managers' work is understanding the relationship between the activities and the records they generate. Thus records managers should be keenly aware of the *context* from which data is derived. This should provide insight into the *factors that influenced and shaped the creation* of the records and, in turn, the creation of the derived data.

17.2   Who Is Records Management

To effectively manage documents and content requires a dedicated team of records managers. Records management programs often consist of records managers, archivists, and electronic records management systems administrators. Successful records management teams are able to foster strategic alliances with departments such as IT, legal, risk management, internal audit, and compliance. This should be a collaborative partnership that collectively understands the business needs, technical infrastructure, and recordkeeping applications of the organization in detail.

In addition to understanding how to manage records, members of this team must also be familiar with the regulatory environment of the organization. They should have the authority to make, develop, implement, and manage the organization's records retention schedule. In addition to understanding how to manage records, members of this team must also be familiar with the regulatory environment of the organization, specifically, those laws and policies regarding retention and information protection. A records management team may also be responsible for implementing holds (or "freezes") to meet the legal discovery requirements.[11] Legal discovery of electronic records is also known as eDiscovery. They should also be familiar with the technologies associated with electronic records management, document management, content management, and data and information governance.

17.3 Benefits of Records Management

The benefits of an effective records management program are twofold. First, records management can improve the overall operational efficiency of data governance. A well-designed records management program can do this by facilitating accurate retrieval of the most relevant information. In this sense, they can support informed management decisions by bringing relevant information forward in a timely manner. Second, records management can be used to control the creation and carefully manage the growth of records and data. A records retention schedule can be used to identify the authoritative copy of a record, enabling people to safely destroy unofficial copies. Also, records that are no longer needed for active business purposes can be destroyed or archived to "reduce noise" or limit the growth of information that individuals face.

Records management has other business benefits. Through an understanding of the business functions, records managers can identify records that are essential to operating the institution and secure that vital information. This understanding can also help to ensure regulatory compliance through documentation and increase accountability. In addition, organizing and identifying which records are actively needed can improve the working environment by making records and data easier to find. Being able to find documents when they are needed can also enhance customer service and operational efficiency.

Thus an effective records management program enables institutions to identify the value of records and the ownership, responsibilities, and rights associated with those records. Records management programs can also facilitate the appropriate destruction of records that is legally defensible, compliant with relevant regulations, supportive of business needs, and ethically appropriate. By articulating the value and requirements associated with records, a records management program provides the foundation for making effective paper and electronic document and data management and storage decisions that are cost effective and supportive of core business operations. In short, the goal of a records management program is to enable records to be an asset rather than a liability.

---

[11] For an example of discovery requirements, see the Sarbanes-Oxley Act of 2002, which dictates that an organization undergoing possible litigation cannot destroy records related to the litigation, https://www.gpo.gov/fdsys/pkg/BILLS-107hr3763enr/pdf/BILLS-107hr3763enr.pdf.

17.4   Components of Records Management

Records management has three major components:

1. The production and acquisition of reliable records for legal and technical purposes
2. The assurance that records are created in an orderly and coherent manner and linked to the business functions they support
3. The transmission, retrieval, and preservation of authentic records.[12]

Records managers acquire reliable records by evaluating which office holds the authoritative copy of a document. For example, individuals may keep a copy of their travel records (receipt, tickets, etc.) but a records manager may determine that the authoritative copy of the travel records are held by the reimbursement office and that all other copies do not need to be kept. The authoritative copies are usually called the "official copy," "record copy," or "gold copy" of a record, depending on the institution.

Decisions about which copy is the authoritative copy should be documented in a records retention schedule. To know what records are being created and kept by individual offices, records managers should talk with offices about their business and the records they create to support their business functions and activity, the nature of their regulatory requirements, and how they store, retrieve, and use their records. These meetings are called records surveys and are very important in making a viable records retention schedule. Effectively enacting a records retention schedule and ensuring everyone at an organization complies with recordkeeping regulations may also require a large enterprise-wide outreach effort. In large organizations, a records management program may designate records liaisons within offices to help spearhead records outreach efforts and show their colleagues how to follow the retention schedule and effectively manage their records. Records liaison responsibilities are frequently part of someone's "other duties as assigned." Successful records liaisons need the support of their managers and the records management program.

Linking records creation with functions should also be documented in the records retention schedule. For example, even though the human resources department will hold records about hiring, hiring managers across an institution will also have a copy of job applications even though they are not a part of the human resources department. In this sense, the function of hiring people falls across all departments, and the way those records are handled should be performed on an enterprise-wide basis. It is important to educate everyone within an organization about their record-keeping responsibilities because the custody of the record may be distributed and there may be several copies of the same record in a variety of departments and

---

[12] Guercio, M., "Principles, Methods, and Instruments for the Creation, Preservation, and Use of Archival Records in the Digital Environment." *American Archivist* 64:2 (Fall/Winter 2001), pp. 238–269.

offices within an organization. These outreach efforts can be targeted and can focus on new employees or certain departments with critical or sensitive recordkeeping needs. Records management outreach efforts should be part of a persistent program—not one-offs—and should reach most of the organization.

Transmission and retrieval of authentic records concerns finding records that can be trusted, both formally in a court of law and informally by any user of records. "Authentic records" is a shorthand way of saying that a person judges a record to be what it purports to be. This judgment is based on the characteristics of the record itself and the recordkeeping systems and processes that created the record. The more robust, systematic, and well-documented recordkeeping processes and systems are, the more reasons they give a person to trust and presume the authenticity of a record.

In courts, the authenticity of records is normally presumed if they are created as part of a regular recordkeeping practice.[13] In some cases, this presumption may be challenged, requiring an organization to demonstrate the authenticity of their records. To do this, a records manager might have to explain the chain of custody for a document, articulating who made the document, what environment it was stored in, who had access to the document, and when changes were made to the document. Sometimes a records management program will take custody of records, especially those records that must be retained for long periods of time. In this case, the records management program should track where the document came from and when it came into its custody. There are some records or datasets that must be kept for decades, and this is when preservation tasks must be taken to ensure continued access to files despite obsolete hardware or software. Though it is not necessary for everyone to know what a records management team has in its custody, it is important to know to ask the team when an information need arises. The records management team is then responsible for finding and retrieving the most relevant documents for that information need.

17.4.1   Records Management and Data Management

Formal records management programs are usually the best situated mechanism to assess the importance of a document and its relationship to the business functions it supports. In this sense, a records management program can help an organization with its data management efforts by providing a map to the organization's data and the business functions that generated this data. Having this map and a records retention schedule can show data managers where to find data, what the governance of the data is, and the context of its creation.

Structured data only partially reflects how institutions manage information. Institutions manage unstructured data—electronic and paper documents and files—

---

[13] "Authenticity," "Records Management" Pearce-Moses, R., Glossary of Archival and Records Terminology, http://archivists.org/glossary/terms/a/authenticity.

by sorting and categorizing them by key indicators such as title, name, date, location, and subject. Information found in unstructured places—such as email, memoranda, presentations, call center logs, transcripts, video, text messages, and other documents—can be pertinent to data management and analysis needs.

Records, just like data, can be found in structured and unstructured places. A record becomes part of a dataset when the necessary content is transmitted to the data managers or is otherwise used as part of a data analysis. The third component of records management, managing authentic records, helps the data managers know that they have the correct and trustworthy set of content for analysis.

Leveraging both structured and unstructured data can provide enriched answers to questions institutions are seeking to answer. Understanding the distinction between structured and unstructured data is important to using both types of data. And, leveraging both can give clearer answers. For example, a grocery store chain may track demographics, time of year, and location data and correlate it to sales of a certain product. But say a certain product suddenly falls short in sales because it received bad press or because its freshness was consistently in question. External sources like social media or internal delivery or distribution logs may provide the answer. As Steve Andriole explained in a 2015 *Forbes* article, "Structured data analytics can describe and explain what's happening and unstructured data analytics can explain why it's happening. Together you get the whole picture."[14]

The integration of unstructured data with structured data is becoming increasingly relevant not only because it reflects the way people and institutions have stored information for a long time. Consider the following points:

- The amount of unstructured data is growing faster than structured data and is expected to account for up to 90% of all data in the next decade.[15]
- In the public sector, executive and legal policies on managing and retaining unstructured information in electronic form, such as digitized documents and email, have been stipulated.[16]
- The automated ability to tag media content is improving rapidly, allowing more and better integration of structured and unstructured content.[17]

These trends show the growing importance of managing documents and content. Technical solutions are quickly enabling the discovery of unstructured data. Through keyword searches and patterned searches (on nodes like names and zip codes),

---

[14] Andriole, S., "The other side of analytics," *Forbes*, http://www.forbes.com/sites/steveandriole/2015/03/05/the-other-side-of-analytics/#5e4f1e8f9a86.

[15] See Intel IT Center, "Big Data 101—Unstructured Data Analytics," http://www.intel.com/content/dam/www/public/us/en/documents/solution-briefs/big-data-101-brief.pdf.

[16] See, for example, Presidential Directive on Managing Government Records, issued August 24, 2012, which directs federal agencies to manage email as electronic records by the end of 2016 and to manage all permanent records electronically by the end of 2019. See also Amendment 34a in 2006 to the Federal Rules of Civil Procedure (FRCP), which incorporates "electronically stored information" into the legal discovery process.

[17] See, for example, Harris, D., "Google: Our new system for recognizing faces is the best one ever," *Fortune*, March 17, 2015.

systems can identify relevant information in emails and documents. These enterprise-wide search engine functionalities can deliver thousands of documents to a manager's desktop instantly. This, however, presents its own challenges. This kind of searching can provide too many results. The ability to find relevant information is outstripping the ability to evaluate the results and find value. Poor metadata can also contribute to this problem. It may cause the retrieval of irrelevant information or missing relevant information. Worst of all, bad metadata may provide people with bad information, causing them to make incorrect inferences about the data they are analyzing. Broadly speaking, information overload and poor metadata are key challenges of integrating structured and unstructured data.[18]

Systems are employing several strategies to combat the problem of information overload. One solution can be found in how the results are displayed. Results that are given visually can show the context of documents in relation to other documents or other vectors such as time. A visualization of the results can show relationships between documents, the documents with the most frequent use of a term, or the appearance of a search term over time. In other words, visualized results can give people the same search results, but instead of listing thousands of documents with the first ten on the screen, you get a picture of all the results. Another strategy that can help ameliorate information overload is having a robust records management program. Instead of trying to sort through an ever-expanding set of documents, a records management program can reduce the number of documents in results and, more important, provide a means of understanding the context and relationship of the documents returned in search results.

In many way, records managers and data managers can work together to complete the picture they are working on. Data managers can inform records managers about important datasets that fall into a records retention schedule. The data manager may know better than the records manager who created the data, where the data is stored, and the systems used for analysis. Records managers can help data managers, too, by helping to determine if the data storage system is trustworthy, providing a map that extends the data architecture to a wider information architecture, helping to destroy unneeded data based on the regulations outlined in the records retention schedule, and helping to ensure that unstructured datasets are authentic.

17.4.2   Records Management Frameworks

In this chapter, our description of records management reflects a predominately North American approach to records management. At the core of this tradition is conceptualizing the management of records in a life cycle. The life cyle in records

---

[18]Pfred, J. W., The Challenges of Integrating Structured and Unstructured Data, Accessed on February 23, 2016, https://www.landmark.solutions/Portals/0/LMSDocs/Whitepapers/2010-05-pnec-challenges-integrating-structured-and-unstructured-data-tech-paper.pdf.

management implies that a record's life has stages, much like the model used in the natural sciences to explain phases of life for any living creature. Creation, life, death. Records are created, they are actively used (records used frequently), they slide into semi-active use (records used infrequently), and they are ultimately disposed—either destruction or archives. The lifecycle approach has been widely adopted in knowledge management and records management in North America.

Another records management tradition to consider comes out of Australia. This tradition deemphasizes the records life cycle in favor of a theory and framework known as the records continuum. First articulated in the 1990s by archival scholar Frank Upward, the records continuum provides a framework for understanding the role of records from the acts they document out to their role in society.[19] Some of the records continuum's intellectual roots come out of a conceptual approach developed by the National Archives of Australia in the mid-twentieth century, and still used today, known as a series system.[20] This approach deemphasizes the distinction between the active and archival phases of a record's life. In this approach, records are closely tied to the business functions they support, and the ultimate disposition of a record is decided at creation—or even before. This mindset blurs the distinction between records managers and archivists, two fields that are remarkably bifurcated in North America. Even if you are in an organization that has a strong records life-cycle orientation, it is helpful to have an awareness of the intellectual heritage of the series system records continuum because they have had, if not adoption, influence across the globe. The two concepts influenced AS4390 Records Management: Australian Standard, which in turn served as an important basis for ISO15489 Information and Documentation—Records Management, the main standard for records management from the International Standards Organization.

17.4.3   Implementing Records Management Programs

A solid understanding of data management practices within the organization and principles in the field is particularly helpful. For structured and unstructured data to be properly related, the ontologies and tagging schemes that records managers develop must be in synch with the data architecture their institution's data management unit developed. The approach to governance of unstructured information is also very similar to that of structured information. A practical understanding

[19] Upward, F., "Structuring the Records Continuum Part One: Post-Custodial Principles and Properties," *Archives and Manuscripts* 24, No. 3 (1996) 268–85, available at http://www.infotech. monash.edu.au/research/groups/rcrg/publications/recordscontinuum-fupp1.html; "Structuring the Records Continuum Part Two: Structuration Theory and Recordkeeping," *Archives and Manuscripts*, 25, No. 1 (1997) 10–35, available at http://www.infotech.monash.edu.au/research/ groups/rcrg/publications/recordscontinuum-fupp2.html.

[20] Hurley, C, "The Australian ('Series') System: An Exposition," in The Records Continuum: Ian Maclean and Australian Archives—First Fifty Years (Canberra, Australia: Ancora Press, 1996), 150–172.

of data and records management concepts, such as minimizing duplicate information, identifying authoritative sources, quality of information, metadata management, and other data management topics can contribute greatly to effective records management.

Records management begins with documenting where in the organization information resides. The records and information management (RIM) industry refers to this as a "data map" or "data atlas." The term "data map" as it is used in this context refers to identifying systems, applications, and storage locations that house information relevant to the legal process, freedom of information (FOIA) requests, and more operational needs such as fiscal, administrative, and historical requirements for information.[21] Such an information data map also encompasses gathering metadata about stored information, such as the currency and age of information, the department responsible for the information, and its retention period.

Creating a data map has a remarkable similarity to documenting an organization's data architecture, which depicts systems, applications, and data stores in terms of where structured data resides and how it flows between those systems, applications, and data stores. The difference is that whereas a data architecture focuses on structured data such as tables and elements in a database, an information data map focuses on unstructured data such as policies, emails, procedures, lists, and diagrams. A good argument can be made, though, that both structured and unstructured data must adhere to many of the same data management and record-keeping principles to be useful to business, especially when the desire is to surface them jointly. Both data and records must have authoritative sources, be of high quality, and be easy to find, and their currency and accuracy not be in question. Both should also be governed by a retention policy. Both must continue to be well managed to be valuable.

Resource requirements for managing documents and content vary, depending on the organization's needs. Does the organization want to back-scan troves of paper documents? To what extent will resources be developed in-house versus leveraging the use of consultants? What information management policies is the organization trying to meet? What information and data governance structures already exist in the organization?

Consider the last question. If, for example, a data governance structure already exists, leveraging the existing data governance framework to incorporate records management will require relatively modest additional time commitments from executives and managers. The work of information stewards might also be reduced as they collaborate with data stewards. Aside from this overlap of functions and responsibilities, resource requirements for document and content management are similar to those of data governance and require some time commitment at all levels of the organization.

---

[21] The term "data map" used in the context of records management differs from that of the term used in data architecture, where a data map refers to the mapping of distinct data elements between different data models.

17.4.4   Records Management and Other Tools

As complex and confusing as the definitions of Information Governance (IG), Enterprise Content Management (ECM), Data Management (DM), and Records Management (RM) are, as discussed at the beginning of this chapter, the marketplace for these spaces is even more complex. In 2017, the hottest terminology in this marketplace was IG—every vendor in this space wants IG in their marketing literature, whether they provide traditional ECM/DM/RM tools, vertical specific tools, eDiscovery, or even hardware like desktop scanners. Analyst reports are a good resource to help wade through the hype to figure out the concrete capabilities of product solutions. Although industry analysts' opinions may have some bias toward vendors that purchase their services, they usually provide a good listing of the vendor landscape.

When evaluating these tools, an organization must understand the size and scope of what they are trying to achieve within their own environment. Larger enterprises (1000 people or more) may find it extremely hard to find a single records management application or even a suite of tools from a single vendor in which to build a complete lifecycle management solution for the entire enterprise. These organizations usually have multiple backend systems, information silos from disparate technologies, custom internal applications, departmental solutions that often serve specialized functions such as eDiscovery tools for legal offices, and data that resides in a hybrid environment on premises and in the cloud. These systems could include Enterprise Resource Planning (ERP) solutions to handle data that sustains organizations, such as HR and financial data. Other systems provide solutions for document management, records management, repository services, and business process workflows. Many vendors now offer solutions that can harness/integrate these various technologies into one interface for users. Be forewarned though, the most successful solution implementations are those that incorporate sacrifices. Consolidating data and records in as few manageable platforms as possible, as opposed to having a proliferation of optimized solutions for individual departments, creates the best opportunity for sustainable success.

Smaller organizations (under 250 people) usually have a little more luxury, although perhaps not the funding, to find solutions that can support their entire environment. If a small organization has a single technology infrastructure, a single records management solution may be sufficient for their recordkeeping needs. Several industry-specific solutions exist for niche markets that can provide outstanding solutions in specialized areas of work, such as aviation.

Potential new solutions are arising quickly. Most of them are built around cloud environments and Enterprise File Synchronization and Sharing solutions. Some are describing themselves as being a complete cloud data management and records management solution. For newer companies, those willing to completely shed the confines of traditional on-premises infrastructure or with a high percentage of mobile workforce, these solutions can offer many advantages. New technologies, business processes, and other enterprise applications are also important to consider when choosing the appropriate tool(s). Integration requirements with social media platforms, Business Process Management solutions, and enterprise resource planning (ERP) solutions are aggressively growing in the for-profit corporate sector.

Appendices

These appendices provide the reader with additional references for building out a data strategy. Many of the resources noted here are available for free. We tried to include only vendor-neutral resources. These resources include more detailed information on frameworks, industry bodies, and best practices. Whether you are an interested reader and learner, or you are helping your organization with a data strategy, we hope the information in the appendices adds to the value of this book and we encourage you to contact us at moderndatastrategy@gmail.com with any feedback you might have.

Appendix A: Frameworks

Data Management Frameworks

The Overview of Data Management Frameworks chapter in Part II looked at two common data management frameworks, the DMBOK and the CMMI DMM. In this section, we present additional highlights of these frameworks, as well as some other data and information management frameworks. We also present references to additional detail on these frameworks for readers who need or want to understand the landscape or one or more of these frameworks in more detail.

DAMA Data Management Body of Knowledge (DMBOK)

DAMA is a member-based organization whose goal is to "support an empowered global community of information professionals."

The DMBOK was originally published in 2009. An updated version is expected in 2017. DAMA has published its DMBOK2 Framework Outline, which this book references. The DMBOK2 terms the various data management domains as "knowledge areas."

© Springer International Publishing AG 2018
M. Fleckenstein, L. Fellows, *Modern Data Strategy*,
https://doi.org/10.1007/978-3-319-68993-7

The DMBOK segments data management into 11 knowledge areas. This framework is graphically depicted as a knowledge area wheel in which each knowledge area, except for data governance, is a segment of the wheel.[1] The exception is data governance, which it places at the center of the wheel and thus highlights it as central to all other data management. Otherwise, it makes no declarative statement about whether a particular knowledge area is more fundamental to data management than another.

For each knowledge area, the DMBOK discusses the types of activities performed, useful/required inputs, participant roles, typical deliverables, and more. The DMBOK is available at: https://www.dama.org/content/body-knowledge.

CMMI Data Management Maturity Model

In the late 1980s and 1990s, Carnegie Mellon University's (CMU) Software Engineering Institute (SEI) developed a Capability Maturity Model (CMM) for the Department of Defense that formalized the software development process. SEI subsequently worked with federal and commercial partners to expand the CMM into the Capability Maturity Model Integration (CMMI), a broad-based process improvement model that aimed to integrate many models into a single framework. Originally published in 2002, the third version of the CMMI was published in 2010. In 2013, the entire CMMI product suite was transferred to the CMMI Institute, a newly created organization at Carnegie Mellon. In 2016 the CMMI Institute was acquired by ISACA, the professional association for IT governance, assurance and cybersecurity professionals.

In 2014, the CMMI Institute released the Data Management Maturity (DMM) model. This model breaks down data management into five high-level categories and one supporting category. Table A.1 describes each CMMI category and breaks each category into three to five process areas.[2]

Table A.1 CMMI DMM categories

CMMI DMM category	Description
Data Management Strategy	Data Management Strategy encompasses process areas designed to focus on development, strengthening, and enhancement of the overall enterprise data management program. It provides an outline and specific best practices for achieving a broad and unified internal perspective about the importance of the organization's data assets and what is required to manage and improve them; gaining agreements through explicit and approved priorities; aligning the program with the organization's business strategy.
Data Governance	Data Governance encompasses process areas designed to help an organization achieve strong participation across the organization for implementing a data governance program and structure capable of functioning consistently across the broad scope of shared responsibilities; expanding and managing the organization-wide collection of approved business terms employed in the target data architecture, taxonomies, and ontologies; and the development and implementation of metadata to fully describe the organization's data assets.

(continued)

---

[1] See https://www.dama.org/content/body-knowledge.

[2] The process areas are diagrammed in Fig. 7.1 in the Chapter "Overview of Data Management Frameworks".

Table A.1 (continued)

CMMI DMM category	Description
Data Quality	Data Quality encompasses process areas designed to provide the means for an organization to fully understand the nature and quality of the data under management, as well as the mechanisms to evaluate, prevent, and remediate defects and to ensure that the quality of data meets business purposes and the organization's strategic objectives. In short, these process areas collectively describe a comprehensive data quality program, driven by a data quality strategy.
Data Operations	Data Operations encompasses process areas designed to help an organization ensure that data requirements are fully specified, data is traceable through all the business processes that produce or consume it, data changes and their processes are managed, and data sources are selected based on requirements, well controlled, and verified as authoritative.
Platform & Architecture	Platform and Architecture encompasses process areas designed to help an organization design an optimal data layer to meet present and future business objectives; establish and implement well-crafted, enforceable standards; select a platform and supporting technologies that meet scope and performance requirements; integrate disparate sources of data; and manage historical and aged data effectively.
Supporting Processes	Supporting Processes are foundational processes that supports adoption, execution, and improvement of data management practices, including measurement and analysis, process management, process quality assurance, risk management, and configuration management.

A key feature of the CMMI DMM framework is the application of maturity levels to certain data management areas, thus allowing an organization to assess its level of maturity in one or more independent data management domains. Table A.2 provides an overview of these maturity levels.

Table A.2 CMMI DMM capability and maturity levels[a]

Level	Description
1. Performed	Processes are performed ad hoc, primarily at the project level. They are typically not applied across business areas. Process discipline is primarily reactive, for example, data quality processes emphasize repair over prevention. Foundational improvements may exist, but improvements are not yet extended within the organization or maintained.
2. Managed	Processes are planned and executed in accordance with policy, employ skilled people with adequate resources to produce controlled outputs, involve relevant stakeholders, and are monitored, controlled, and evaluated for adherence to the defined process.
3. Defined	Set of standard processes is employed and consistently followed. Processes to meet specific needs are tailored from the set of standard processes according to the organization's guidelines.
4. Measured	Process metrics have been defined and are used for data management. These include management of variance, prediction, and analysis using statistical and other quantitative techniques. Process performance is managed across the life of the process.
5. Optimized	Process performance is optimized through applying Level 4 analysis for target identification of improvement opportunities. Best practices are shared with peers and industry.

[a]CMMI Institute, "Data Management Maturity (DMM) Model," Ver. 1.0, August 2014, Table 2, p. 7

The CMMI DMM framework does not cover some data management areas that are covered in other frameworks. For example, it states that its maturity framework is a useful front-end activity for areas such as large analytics implementations and master data management, both of which it does not cover as independent process areas. The model implies that the five included data management categories (and the one supporting process area) are fundamental to data management and serve as the basis for more advanced data management practices.[3]

The CMMI DMM framework is available at https://dmm-model-individual.dpdcart.com/

MITRE DMDF

MITRE's Data Management department has historically contributed to industry data management frameworks. We also leverage our own Data Management Domain Framework (DMDF), pictured in Fig. A.1, which we continue to evolve. The DMDF, at its highest level, is set of bubbles, each representing one or more data management domains. Larger bubbles represent broader data management areas and smaller

Fig. A.1 MITRE's data management model

---

[3] This line of thinking is further examined by Peter Aiken and summarized in the Data Strategy chapter, in the Determining the Scope of the Data Strategy Initiative section.

bubbles represent more narrowly focused areas. For example, although the Data Governance bubble is specific to one data management domain, the Data Technologies bubble touches on multiple other data domains, including policies, standards, and technologies. Each domain area is further detailed, including typical inputs, guideline, enablers, and outputs. Together, these domain sets represent frequent areas of data management engagement with our sponsors.

EDMC FIBO and DCAM

The Enterprise Data Management Council (EDMC), established in 2005, is a member association to create and implement standards for effective data management in the financial industry. EDMC's focus areas include the Financial Industry Business Ontology (FIBO) and the Data Management Assessment Model (DCAM). EDMC's contributors are primarily large commercial financial institutions.

FIBO is a business ontology standard that provides a business glossary (i.e., terms and relationships) for financial instruments, legal entities, market data and financial processes. Figure A.2 summarizes EDMC's FIBO Semantics Repository, which is publicly accessible at http://www.edmcouncil.org/semanticsrepository/index.html.

EDMC's Data Management Capability Assessment Model (DCAM) is a simple, self-assessment data management maturity model that covers maturity in component areas, including data strategy, data governance, data architecture, data quality, and technology architecture. In each of the component areas, the organization can

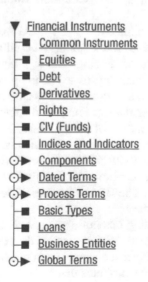

Fig. A.2 FIBO semantics repository

assess its maturity, ranging from "not initiated," through several "in-process" stages, to "capability achieved, and in some cases, "capability enhanced." The DCAM is available to EDMC members at http://www.edmcouncil.org/dcam.

Enterprise Architecture Frameworks

Enterprise architecture frameworks are significantly broader than data management frameworks and typically cover business process and various aspects of technology (e.g., applications, network).

FEAF-II Data Reference Model

In 1999, the Federal CIO published the Federal Enterprise Architecture Framework (FEAF), Version 1.1. This framework combined high-level business, data, applications, and technology architectures. In May 2012, OMB published a very high-level guide, the "Common Approach to Federal Enterprise Architecture," a discussion of governance, principles, and standards, among other things around the enterprise architecture (now segmented into strategic, business, data, system, and network architectures).[4] On January 29, 2013, the White House released Version 2 of the Federal Enterprise Architecture Framework (FEAF-II) to government agencies and it became available to the public about a year later. The FEAF-II leverages the same framework model put forth in the "Common Approach to Federal Enterprise Architecture."

The Federal Enterprise Architecture (FEA) Data Reference Model (DRM) constitutes one part of the FEAF-II. It documents a baseline taxonomy that can be leveraged when classifying and organizing data at a high level. The DRM outlines three levels of taxonomy, consisting of a hierarchy of four domains, 22 subject areas, and 144 topics. This structure is meant to aid organizations' high-level data definitions and ease of data exchange. Figure A.3 summarizes the DRM taxonomy. Details can be found in Appendix I of the FEAF-II.

Similarly, the other FEA reference models also have an associated taxonomy. The business reference model (BRM) breaks down 10 mission sectors, including defense, diplomacy, financial, environment, health, law, and transport, into 228 individual terms and definitions. The BRM's business-oriented terms may be useful in building out a business glossary.

In addition to the preceding taxonomies, the DRM presents an abstract model with three high-level data standardization areas: data description, data context, and data sharing. This is essentially a conceptual metamodel for the three standardization areas, detailing the metamodel attributes that make up each area. These standardization areas and attributes may be a useful baseline when building your own conceptual data model around the concepts of data description, context, and sharing.

---

[4] Federal Enterprise Architecture Framework v.2 (FEAF-II), Section C.2.3.3 "Information Sharing."

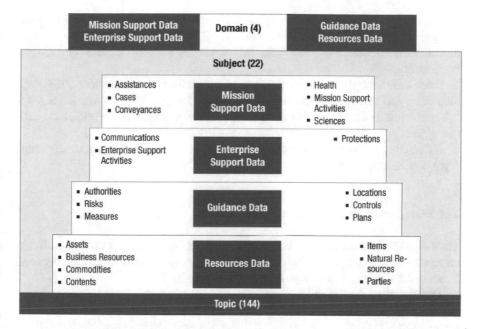

Fig. A.3 FEAF-II high-level DRM taxonomy

The Open Group Architecture Framework (TOGAF)

TOGAF began in the early 1990s and is managed by the Open Group, a vendor- and technology-neutral industry consortium. The framework focuses on four core architectures: business, applications, data, and technology. The TOGAF Architectural Development Method (ADM) is a process that breaks down the approach to the four architectures into phases A through H, beginning with a vision.

Phase A, the Architecture Vision, contains information on tying an architecture to business priorities. Although the TOGAF isn't limited to data, this type of information is useful for a data strategy in that it lists components necessary for tying an effort back to business priorities, including scope of impacted organizations, maturity assessments, budget requirements, and others.

Phase B, the Business Architecture, presents sections on business modeling and includes such models as the UML Business Class Diagram, very similar to a high-level conceptual data model. It also includes pointers to several industry-specific business models, such as telecommunications, accounting, and computer/electronics manufacturing. Such models can be useful when describing a business function in high-level data terms, for example, for when defining subject areas and categories as components of a conceptual data model.

Phase C, Chapter 10, focuses specifically on data architecture. This section, like the overall document, contains a generic description of such topics as the types of things needed, the steps to take, and sample outcome products, in this case, for data architecture. It does contain a pointer to sample data principals, located in Section

23.6.2, Data Principles. These principles specifically, and the approach generally for documenting principles contained in Chapter 23, Architecture Principles, can be useful when developing your own principles as part of a data governance framework.

Phases D through H cover topics such as additional architectures, delivery, migration, and change management. At almost 700 pages, TOGAF Version 9.1 is a behemoth that is challenging to navigate and contains limited information on data management.

A free copy of the TOGAF is available to members at https://www2.opengroup.org/ogsys/catalog/g116.

The DOD Architecture Framework (DODAF)

The DODAF developed by the U.S. Department of Defense is a publicly available enterprise architecture framework first developed in the 1990s. Its current version, Version. 2.02, stems from Version 2.0 published in 2009.

Traditionally, the DODAF documents three architectural viewpoints: operational, systems, and technical standards. With Version 2.0, these architectural viewpoints were expanded, including the addition of a data and information view (DIV). The DIV focuses on a conceptual, logical, and physical data model, providing successive generic descriptions of these data models.

Each view begins with a high-level component and then systematically drives toward more detailed views. When compiling a data strategy and tying it back to business needs, some of the other views are sometimes useful references. For example, the top operational views (OV) that show a high-level operational concept (OV1) and resource flows (OV-2 and OV-3) can help scope a data strategy initiative. Likewise, the top capability views (CV), that show a vision (CV-1) and capability taxonomy (CV-2) may be useful references, if available, when building a business glossary or data architecture.

A free copy of the DoDAF is available publicly at http://dodcio.defense.gov/Library/DoD-Architecture-Framework/.

Additional Frameworks, Models, and Standards Bodies

Table A.3 lists additional references to industry bodies that publish data management frameworks, enterprise architecture frameworks, data exchange models, and information management maturity models. Equally important, Table A.3 includes references to three industry standards bodies—ISO, ANSI, and NIST—that publish data standards, among other standards. Data standards become an important part of a data management framework when exchanging data.

Table A.3 Additional frameworks, models, and standards bodies

Framework	Description
MIKE2.0	This is an open source information management best practices framework with core focus on business intelligence, enterprise data management, search, enterprise content management, information asset management, and information strategy/architecture/governance. Membership is free and provides access to a wide variety of industry contributions on data management. MIKE2.0 espouses the Scaled Agile Framework Architecture (SAFe), an evolutionary approach to business needs. More information can be found at: http://mike2.openmethodology.org/wiki/What_is_MIKE2.0 A companion book, "Information Development Using MIKE2.0," is also available.
National Information Exchange Model (NIEM)	The NIEM framework promotes enterprise-wide information exchange standards across disparate agencies and their partners. This data exchange framework is an XML-based framework used in the United States. Its contributors and users include federal, state, and local agencies, as well as private industry. NIEM maintains a core set of reference schemas and allows participants to publish compliant extensions and variations. Existing extensions include the areas of biometrics, emergency management, intelligence, immigration, international trade, and other areas. More information can be found at https://niem.gov
Zachman Framework	This two-dimensional enterprise architecture framework uses the y-axis to classify a product from contextual to detailed and the x-axis to segment products into process, data, event, organizational, geographical, and goal/rule quadrants. The data quadrants focus on products such as an entity relationship model and additional data details. More information can be found at https://www.zachman.com/about-the-zachman-framework
NARA Records and Information Management (RIM) Maturity Model	In 2012, the White House authored a directive that all agencies will manage email as electronic records by the end of 2016 and manage all records electronically by the end of 2019. In response, NARA developed a spreadsheet-based maturity scoring model that assesses organizational maturity in management and organizational structure, policy/standards/governance, and program operations. Many areas parallel data management maturity. More information can be found at https://www.archives.gov/records-mgmt/prmd.html
American National Standards Institute (ANSI)	ANSI provides a forum for over 200 ANSI-accredited standards developers representing organizations in the private and public sectors. These groups work to develop voluntary consensus national standards. For example, Health Level Seven (HL7), which is responsible for the HL7 electronic health record data exchange standards,[a] is one of several American National Standards Institute (ANSI)-accredited Standards Developing Organizations (SDOs) operating in the healthcare arena. ANSI data exchange standards extend to numerous other areas, including business transactions, emergency management, biometric data, and industrial data exchange. More information can be found at https://www.ansi.org/
International Organization for Standardization (ISO)	ISO is the world's largest standards developing organization. Between 1947 and 2008, ISO published more than 17,000 international standards. ISO currently publishes 84 data management and interchange related to data management.[b] Other data standards include ISO 8000, a multipart strategy on data quality, ISO/IEC 11179 for metadata driven exchange, and industry vertical data exchange models. More information can be found at http://www.iso.org/iso/home.html

(continued)

Table A.3 (continued)

Framework	Description
National Institute of Standards (NIST)	For over 50 years, NIST has developed and distributed standard reference data. NIST's development of scientific reference data standards is driven by the Standard Reference Data Act of 1968, declaring standardized scientific and reference data of vital importance and authorizing the Secretary of Commerce to seek copyright for standardized reference data.[c] NIST maintains dozens of standards databases, most for free, in diverse areas, including biometrics, identity, law enforcement, international trade, and many technical areas. More information can be found at http://www.nist.gov/srd/

[a]See "Health Level Seven International," HL7 provides a framework for the exchange, integration, sharing, and retrieval of electronic health information. These standards set the language, structure and data types required for seamless integration between systems. http://www.hl7.org/implement/standards/index.cfm?ref=common
[b]See "ISO/IEC JTC 1/SC 32 Data management and interchange," http://www.iso.org/iso/home/standards_development/list_of_iso_technical_committees/iso_technical_committee.htm?commid=45342
[c]See "Standard Reference Data Act," http://www.nist.gov/srd/upload/publiclaw90-396.pdf

Appendix B: Examples of Industry Drivers

Examples of Public Sector Data Strategy Drivers

Several mandates and industry drivers are spurring the federal government's effort toward improved data management. In the following partial list and brief description of sample mandates and drivers, successful execution, in each case, relies significantly on an effective data strategy:

Open Data Policy: Managing Information as an Asset[5]

This White House Memorandum from 2013, mandates that federal agencies information resources accessible, discoverable, and usable. It states that agencies collect and create information in a way that supports downstream processing and dissemination. In addition, this Executive Order cites a number of related guidelines and mandates, all significantly addressing how data and information must be managed. Thus, managing data is a de facto part of federal strategic plans.

---

[5]See Presidential Memorandum "Open Data Policy – Managing Data as an Asset," May 9, 2013, https://obamawhitehouse.archives.gov/sites/default/files/omb/memoranda/2013/m-13-13.pdf.

The DATA Act[6]: Government-Wide Financial Data Standards

In 2014, the President signed the Digital Accountability and Transparency Act (DATA Act), which requires the Department of the Treasury and the White House Office of Management and Budget to transform U.S. federal spending from disconnected documents into open, standardized data, and to publish that data online. It requires government-wide financial data standards for any federal funds and mandates the common data elements for financial and payment information reported.

National Strategy for Information Sharing and Safeguarding[7]

The Intelligence Reform and Terrorism Prevention Act of 2004 establishes a Program Manager for an Information Sharing Environment (PM-ISE). Housed within the Office of the Director of National Intelligence (ODNI), the PM-ISE coordinates intelligence integration and information sharing needs. It facilitates automated sharing of terrorism information, promoting standards, architecture, security, access, and associated privacy protections.

National Mandate for Data Center Consolidation[8]

The Federal Data Center Consolidation Initiative (FDCCI) is a Federal CIO mandate that requires government agencies to reduce the overall energy and real estate footprint of their data centers, with the targeted goals of reduced costs, increased security, and improved efficiency. As data volume and data types increase exponentially (e.g., video, social media), this requires prudent attention to data quality, such as eliminating unnecessarily duplicate data, and storing poor or outdated data.

Electronic Health Records (EHR) and Interoperability[9]

Interoperability is the ability of different information systems and applications to communicate, exchange data, and use the information that has been exchanged. EHR interoperability focuses on data an exchange schema and exchange standards to permit data to be shared across clinicians, lab, hospital, pharmacy, and patient regardless of the application or application vendor.

---

[6] See "Digital Accountability and Transparency Act of 2014" or the "DATA Act," https://www.congress.gov/113/bills/s994/BILLS-113s994es.xml.

[7] See "Information Sharing Environment—The Role of the PM-ISE," https://www.ise.gov/about-ise/what-ise.

[8] See "The Federal Data Center Consolidation Initiative," https://cio.gov/drivingvalue/data-center-consolidation/.

[9] See "What is EHR and Why Is It Important?" https://www.healthit.gov/providers-professionals/faqs/what-ehr-interoperability-and-why-it-important.

Federal CIO Roadmap[10]

The Federal CIO Roadmap specifies areas of responsibilities for Federal CIOs. Prudent use and reporting of data spans many of these responsibilities, including Strategy/Planning (aligning agency business strategy and IT investments), Enterprise Architecture (architecting performance improvement), Budget Formulation (evaluating capital performance), and Program Management and Performance (how the agency uses data and analysis to make decisions).

Federal Data Protection

Data protection covers both data security and privacy. This is a highly dynamic field with many contributors and constantly changing drivers and mandates, which go beyond this document. These are often spurred by major data breaches and require detailed attention to the management of data privacy and security.

One fundamental data security mandate is the Federal Information Security Management Act of 2002 (FISMA),[11] which requires each federal agency to develop, document, and implement an agency-wide program to provide information security for the information and information systems that support the operations and assets of the agency.

White House Digital Service Playbook[12]

This guide by the Federal CIO outlines the government's approach to digital services best practices making information accessible, seamless, comprehensive for the public. It outlines key "plays" drawn from the private and public-sector that will help Federal agencies deliver services that work well for users and require less time and money to develop and operate. Several of these "plays" have a data management component, including:

- Contract specifications that software and data generated by third parties remains under government control, and can be reused
- Preparing for the impact of a catastrophic data loss
- Ensuring personal data is properly managed
- Publishing open data and enable reuse
- Cataloging data in each agency's enterprise data inventory
- Ensuring rights to data developed by third parties is releasable and reusable at no cost to the public

---

[10] See "Federal CIO Roadmap," http://ocio.os.doc.gov/s/groups/public/@doc/@os/@ocio/@oitpp/documents/content/prod01_002082.pdf.

[11] See "Federal Information Management Security Act of 2002," http://csrc.nist.gov/drivers/documents/FISMA-final.pdf.

[12] See "U.S. Digital Service Playbook," https://playbook.cio.gov/.

President's Memorandum on Transparency and Open Government[13]

This memorandum calls for creating openness in Government. It aims to openly disclose information for citizens about what government is doing and refers to information maintained by the federal government a national asset. It calls on Executive departments and agencies to harness new technologies to put information about their operations and decisions online and readily available to the public, and solicit public feedback to identify information of greatest use to the public. Although this memorandum contains no language on data interoperability, quality or standards, it is clear that if such standards are not in place, open data will be difficult to interpret.

Executive Order: Making Open and Machine Readable the New Default for Government Information[14]

This order from 2009 mandates that government information be "managed as an asset throughout its life cycle to promote interoperability and openness, and, wherever possible and legally permissible, to ensure that data are released to the public in ways that make the data easy to find, accessible, and usable." In parallel the order mandates that privacy and security be part of each stage in the information life cycle. The order calls out Data.gov as a governmental website with this kind of information, all of which is machine readable.

Executive Order: Improving Public Access to and Dissemination of Government Information and Using the Federal Enterprise Architecture Data Reference Model[15]

This memorandum urges federal agencies to organize and categorize information to make it searchable across agencies, in order to improve public access and dissemination (section I), and reference the Federal Enterprise Architecture Data Reference Model (DRM) as a guideline for concepts, terms, and approaches in fulfilling data management responsibilities. It highlights the importance of data management concepts, such as identifying how information and data are created, maintained, accessed, and used; describing relationships between an agency's information systems data elements and information systems of other agencies; and using formal information models to efficiently categorize, disseminate, and share information.

[13] See "President's Memorandum on Transparency and Open Government—Interagency Collaboration," https://obamawhitehouse.archives.gov/sites/default/files/omb/assets/memoranda_fy2009/m09-12.pdf.

[14] See "Executive Order—Making Open and Machine Readable the New Default for Government Information," https://obamawhitehouse.archives.gov/the-press-office/2013/05/09/executive-order-making-open-and-machine-readable-new-default-government.

[15] See "Improving Public Access to and Dissemination of Government Information and Using the Federal Enterprise Architecture Data Reference Model," https://obamawhitehouse.archives.gov/sites/default/files/omb/memoranda/fy2006/m06-02.pdf.

Additional Examples

Many other public guidelines and laws exist to help the government manage information, make it available to the public, and protect it from abuse, including:

- Freedom of Information Act
- Privacy Act of 1974
- Government in the Sunshine Act
- Paperwork Reduction Act
- OMB Circular A-130

Examples of Private Sector Data Strategy Drivers

As mentioned in the beginning of this book, the primary drivers for a data strategy are increased revenue, reduced cost, risk mitigation, and compliance. Whereas the public sector is more focused on risk reduction and compliance, the private sector focuses more on revenue generation and cost reduction. However, both risk reduction and compliance may come into play in the private sector as well. For example, most commercial enterprises strive to mitigate risk by providing correct information to their customers for good service and to assuage potential lawsuits.

Many industries are also subject to compliance requirements. For example, mandatory and voluntary compliance standards, such as the Dodd-Frank Wall Street Reform and Consumer Protection Act, and the Basel Accords, respectively, ensure capital adequacy in financial institutions. Many other industries have compliance requirements guidelines and mandates, including drug testing, healthcare privacy, state insurance reporting, telecommunications licensing, hourly wage compliance, and many others. All these compliance requirements require correct data.

Appendix C: Additional References

Data Governance References

Questions Data Management Helps to Answer

The following questions often go unanswered without data governance.
Authority and Accountability for Data

- Who do I ask when I need data or have an issue with data?
- What rules and regulations impact my data?
- How do we get business components to consider enterprise needs and risks?

Clear Escalation Path for Issues

- I can't get authority to access the data I need; how do I escalate this issue?
- How do we prevent the creation of yet another data warehouse?

Transparency

- How do I determine the right place to get my data?
- How current is my data?
- There are multiple versions of final action; how do I know which I should use?
- Why wasn't I informed about the changes to my data?

Data Quality and Risk

- Is the quality of my data fit for my need?
- Why isn't my beneficiary data consistent with other reports?
- How do I get my data quality issues fixed?

Collaboration

- How do I know who uses the data I create?
- Why does it take so long to get access to the data I need to do my job?
- How do we achieve a balance between business need and enterprise risk?

Data Management Principle Examples

Data management principles are foundational statements of organizational values. They are a means to help institute a data management mindset at an enterprise level and drive policy, standards, and guidelines. Table C.1 lists examples of data management principles.

Table C.1 Data management principle examples

Principle	Description
Transparency	Knowledge about data should be made transparent to stakeholders. This includes data definitions; decisions about the data such as the intent behind its collection, its value, who uses it, and for what purpose; and initiatives relating to the data.
Data Quality	For data to be trusted and useful, the processes used to ensure the data's quality must be standardized and transparent.
Security and Privacy	Data must be collected, used, and shared in ways that ensure individuals' privacy rights, and it must be protected from unauthorized use, disclosure, disruption, modification, or destruction.
Data Sharing and Reuse	The enterprise invests in managing its data effectively and efficiently, which requires maximizing reuse and minimizing unnecessary redundancy.
Accessibility	The enterprise must value and trust staff, contracted resources, and authorized users, providing them with meaningful access and the appropriate tools to leverage data in a timely manner.
Training	All new and existing staff should have training on data and its importance to the organization's mission, and in-depth training should be available to users of data.
Data as an Asset	Given that data has intrinsic value to the organization, data and metadata should be treated as assets in which the organization invests, providing adequate resources to manage and support the data for its stakeholders.
Accountability and Stewardship	Every type of data must have designated stewards who collaborate with users of the data.
Data Standardization	The enterprise must develop, manage, and update data standards that promote and facilitate data reuse, reduce risks, and improve overall cost efficiency.

Additional Topics for Data Policies, Standards, or Guidelines

The Data Governance chapter discussed how principles can evolve to policies and then more specific standards. One example, treating data as an asset, is detailed in the body of the chapter. Here are additional examples of topics for which policies, standards, or guidelines might be defined:

- Roles and corresponding data responsibilities such as for a data steward, system owner, system maintainer, project manager, or data user.
- Classification of data across a spectrum from public to confidential to various levels of sensitivity. This might also address the classification of different types of personal and private data.
- Authoritative sources (which all users—systems or individuals—should use, types of authoritative sources, and the criteria. Criteria might cover what constitutes "authoritative," as well as responsibilities relating to the creation and maintenance of the list of authoritative sources, even the approach and timeframes for compliance as new sources are added.
- Data modeling, which could include multiple levels of detail.

  - A high-level policy or standard might require:

    Data architecture or a data modeling group must maintain conceptual and enterprise logical data models.
    Projects must create a logical data model from the enterprise logical model, note any differences, and discuss them with the maintainers of the enterprise model.
    Projects storing data must create a physical data model based on the project logical model and note any differences, e.g., denormalizations, made for performance and how data quality will be ensured.

  - At a more detailed level, data modeling naming standards, content standards, and processes for model management could be developed.

- Review of data sharing or dissemination to external parties by the data steward.
- Inclusion of sufficient metadata, when sharing data, included to provide users with necessary context to understand the data.
- Data movement/data redundancy—requiring data movement control and documentation/publication of lineage where redundancy is justified by either performance or differences in usage patterns.
- Data quality might include:

  - Requiring stewards to collaborate with users on data quality requirements and expectations.
  - Requiring that data be edited at the point it is imported or created and that the same edits be enforced if the data is changed after setup.
  - Requiring that updates to an attribute must conform completely to the definition of the attribute (i.e., no overloading/reusing of attributes).
  - Specifying that stewards, users and system owners/maintainers are all responsible for reporting and tracking data quality issues through standard tools.

- Data integration might include requirements that systems owners/maintainers sharing data internally translate the data first into a standard format such as the enterprise logical model and translate proprietary identifiers to master identifiers. If data is integrated in a master or data warehouse, the data steward should be included in the requirements and user acceptance testing, as well as in the resolution of data quality issues.
- Data retention (archive and purge) should be event-based and based on a business unit of work, that archived data should be stored in a way that is technology neutral and the schema should be preserved as well.

Data Governance Charter Examples

The first example is a charter for the executive level as depicted in the data governance framework in the Data Governance chapter. The second is an example of a charter for the management level. Note that these charters can differ based on the formality and maturity of the organization. Their purpose is to solidify data governance adoption.

Executive Data Governance Charter

Mission: Provides executive leadership for developing data management principles and policies that support and improve the operation of the organization's programs.

Core Responsibilities:

- Provides a forum for executive oversight of the enterprise's data management practices, including data quality, integration, administration, architecture, warehousing, and risk management.
- Ensures that the organization's business needs and data management practices are aligned with the its mission and in compliance with privacy and security protections. Approves data-related strategies and roadmap priorities.

Clarifies and resolves common data governance challenges, for example, exploring solutions as they relate to privacy, security, trust, and agency compliance issues, including precedent-setting data requests. As needed, reviews escalated issues of data quality, risk, resource, and budget allocations. Acts as the ultimate decision point in the escalation process.

- Identifies and oversees priorities that drive the use and disclosure of data in support of organizational initiatives.
- Promotes partnership between program stakeholders and the organization's data managers to ensure compatibility with its target enterprise data architecture.
- Oversees the development and implementation of data management and privacy principles that seek a consistent, consolidated, and coordinated approach for the management, use, and dissemination of the organization's data.

- Appoints management-level data governance members to represent each business area/organization, and coordinates with them on a regular basis.
- Ensures that data stewards are identified and accountable, including for administering data use and disclosure policies, procedures, and agreements.
- Ensures data-related policies and procedures, including the process for how the enterprise responds to data requests, are documented and made available to agency employees and outside requestors.
- Periodically assesses the health and progress of data governance, data management, and the data ecosystem as a whole.

Reporting: Operates under the auspices of <insert executive sponsor or sponsoring organization>.

Membership: Led by a Chair and comprising the executive leadership of the business units that have a direct and substantial programmatic stake in the creation or use of data, including privacy and confidentiality. The specific member organizations and individual members are documented separately in a data governance participation matrix.

Chair and Staff: The Chair is responsible for chairing and directing meetings unless they designate a separate facilitator.

Data Governance Operations is responsible to the Chair for identifying critical issues; establishing meeting agendas; preparing policy option memoranda and position papers; disseminating minutes, decisions, and other documents to appropriate business and IT units for necessary action; and performing other duties as required by the Chair and other data governance executives.

Meetings: Meets monthly or as needed, depending on issues that arise.

Decision Model: Is a decision-making body that strives for consensus when making decisions. If consensus cannot be achieved, a paper representing each divergent viewpoint is prepared and presented to the organizational leadership.

Coordination: Copies of meeting minutes are routinely shared with other executives. When required, decision memoranda are forwarded to other executives for approval.

Transparency: Information about activities (e.g., meeting agendas, minutes) and policies on data and privacy are posted on a data governance portal or website.

Management Level Data Governance Charter

Mission: Business-driven body that facilitates communication between business units; makes recommendations to the executive level on data-related policies, standards, budget priorities, data quality, and escalated issues; and ensures that the business needs are captured, considered and appropriately balanced with enterprise risk. Supported in its work by Data Governance Operations.

Governance Principles

- Business units are the primary owners, drivers, and stakeholders.
- Members will act with integrity and treat each other civilly.
- Members will actively participate, including:

  - Regularly attend meetings or ensure a backup attends.
  - Make every effort to vote on recommendations and decisions when a vote is scheduled.
  - Provide updates from other areas on current and future projects and issues.
  - Coordinate with their component's data stewardship personnel and their data governance specified executive regularly and continually.

- Members will represent their organizations and strive to maintain an enterprise perspective because key data assets should be managed on an enterprise level that encompasses the broad range of enterprise strategic business and data objectives.
- Data standards and policies will be clearly defined, documented, and communicated so they can be enforced at the enterprise level.
- Clearly define data management roles and responsibilities at the data manager and data stewardship levels.
- Prioritize data initiatives and activities based on the combined input of IT projects and business-driven strategic data goals.

Roles and Responsibilities

The overarching role of the management level is to make decisions regarding data management to facilitate data stewards' and data users' ability to do their jobs. When applicable, make recommendations to the executive level on data and interfacing systems and applications.

The responsibilities of the members collectively and individually include, but are not limited to:

- Defining data management principles, policies, and standards for executive approval.
- Collaborating with projects on data-related strategies and roadmap priorities.
- Defining data stewardship and how it should be implemented agencywide.
- Defining and executing an escalation process for data issues that have crossorganization impact.
- Reviewing data risks that have cross-organization impact; collaborating on mitigations and contingencies.
- Making recommendations on spending priorities related to data capabilities and infrastructure.
- Promoting standardization of data by identifying and prioritizing types of data where a lack of standardization is creating business issues or risks. Creating working groups as needed to collaborate on resolutions.
- Working with data stewards to educate users on data best practices.
- Promoting the use of enterprise data assets.
- Ensuring that decisions and standards are documented and communicated to them and that their issues are escalated to the applicable data governance level, when appropriate.

- Continually updating and coordinating with the executive level.
- Establishing and participating in smaller working groups of members, if needed, to make progress on specific topics and tasks.

Responsibilities of the Chair include:

- Schedule and lead regular committee meetings.
- Request agenda items from members and ensure that an agenda is sent out in advance of each meeting.
- Ensure meeting minutes are documented and published in a timely manner, including parking lot items beyond the scope of the scheduled meeting, action items, recommendations or decisions made, and the associated voting information.
- Follow up on assignments and action items assigned to committee members.
- Formally represent the manager level when communicating with the executive level.

Membership

The management-level members will be appointed by their business unit's corresponding executive member. Each member must have the authority to speak for and otherwise make commitments on behalf of their business unit. Members must also understand the data needs and/or implications of the projects sponsored by their business unit. Nonvoting technical advisors to individual business unit representatives are welcome to participate in the meetings.

Voting members should be senior-level representatives from the various business units and IT and include:

- Substantial consumers of enterprise data
- Significant producers/suppliers/sources of enterprise data

More than one member may be requested from large or critical business units. For each organization, determine and document the targeted number of members.

Decision Making

In making its decisions, management-level members will consider recommendations, analyses, and evaluations from designated business or technical experts. Decisions will be made by majority vote. Each business unit will have a set number of votes, as defined in this charter. A voting member and alternate voting member will be defined by the corresponding member. Votes should be cast in person, when possible, but can be provided by proxy or email prior to the meeting for which the vote is scheduled. When at an impasse, items will be escalated to the executive level to make the final decision.

Votes will be recorded in meeting minutes, which will be published. Where appropriate, the results of votes on a recommendation/decision will be shared.

Change in Membership

Members will notify the Chair of any needed change in representatives whether due to employee turnovers or reorganizations. The Chair will contact the corresponding executive to identify a new representative.

Data Architecture References

Data architecture can extend beyond the organization. Often organizations share their data and receive data from other organizations. Corporations clearly benefit from the plethora of available data to them. Perhaps they are collaborating with supply chain partners to optimize inventory or services, or they may be using social media data freely available to them to drive business performance. Government agencies are increasingly on the hook to share data as well. Open data and data transparency acts, executive orders, memoranda, directives, policies, and guidelines abound, driving government to share data. In addition, different parts of government are increasingly having to share data digitally. For example, states must share data for Medicaid, a $415 billon program in FY2012,[16] with the federal government to get reimbursed. When sharing data beyond the organization, standards in how data is exchanged to preserve its intended meaning become especially significant.

Many of these standards are industry-specific. Some of these standards are published by international and national bodies like ISO and ANSI, respectively (see the Data Management Frameworks section for a description of these standards bodies). Data exchange, associated standards, and the industry organizations that produce them are areas that continue to evolve rapidly.

Exchange Standards

There are many exchange standards and most include metadata requirements. Table C.2 lists a few examples.

Table C.2 Examples of exchange standards

Organization	Location	Description
National Information Exchange Model (NIEM)	https://www.niem.gov	NIEM promotes enterprise-wide information exchange standards across disparate agencies and their partners. It is an XML-based framework used in the United States. Its contributors and users include federal, state, and local agencies, as well as private industry. NIEM maintains a core set of reference schemas and allows participants to publish compliant extensions and variations. Existing extensions include biometrics, emergency management, intelligence, immigration, international trade, and other areas.
Health Level Seven International (HL7)	http://www.hl7.org/	HL7 is a standards body but the term HL7 is used generically to refer to the electronic health information exchange standards they create.

(continued)

---

[16] See The Henry J. Kaiser Family Foundation, "Total Medicaid Spending," http://kff.org/medicaid/state-indicator/total-medicaid-spending/, accessed February 2, 2015.

Table C.2 (continued)

Organization	Location	Description
Mortgage Industry Standards Maintenance Organization (MISMO)	http://www.mismo.org/	MISMO is a standards development body but is used to refer to the mortgage industry standards they create to exchange data between stakeholders, such as a bank selling a loan to a governmentsponsored entity.
Society for Worldwide Interbank Financial Telecommunication (SWIFT)	https://www.swift.com/	SWIFT is a financial messaging standard.
National Data Exchange (N-Dex)	https://www.fbi.gov/services/cjis/ndex	N-DEx provides criminal justice agencies with an online tool for sharing, searching, linking, and analyzing information across jurisdictional boundaries. N-Dex is NIEM conformant.
Federal Enterprise Architecture Framework v.2 (FEAF-II), Section C.2.3.3 "Information Sharing"		This section of the FEAF-II points to several sources that promote data sharing. They include the previously mentioned NIEM exchange model, as well as the following other references: • Data.gov, which publishes machine readable datasets published by the Executive Branch of the federal government: www.data.gov • Information Sharing Environment, which promotes responsible data sharing: https://www.ise.gov/about-ise/what-ise • Linked Open Data, which promotes best practices for publishing and connecting data on the web: http://linkeddata.org/home

Data Quality References

The industry bodies listed in Table C.3 provide additional resources, including free reports and white papers.

Table C.3 Additional data quality references

Organization	Description	Source
MIT Information Quality	Available research on information quality from one of the nation's top institutions.	http://mitiq.mit.edu
International Association for Information and Data Quality (iaidq)	A not-for-profit, vendor-neutral professional society promoting and defining information and data quality.	http://www.iaidq.org

Data Warehousing and Business Intelligence References

The industry bodies listed in Table C.4 provide additional resources, including free reports and white papers.

Table C.4 Additional data warehousing and business intelligence references

Organization	Description	Source
The Data Warehousing Institute	Non-profit membership community specializing in data warehousing.	www.tdwi.org
The Kimball Group	These data warehousing experts closed their doors on 12/31/2015 but maintain a large collection of articles on their website.	http://www.kimballgroup.com/

Data Security References

Data Security Frameworks

Various standards and frameworks have emerged over the years. Some of these standards and frameworks are intended for wide usage, whereas others focus on specific industries or data processing activities. For example, International Standards Organization (ISO) is an independent, non-governmental international organization that publishes standards for many industries.[17] A suite of ISO standards addresses "data security management," including the widely used ISO/IEC 27001:2013, *Information technology—Security techniques—Information security management systems—Requirements*, and ISO/IEC 27002:2013, *Information technology – Security techniques – Code of practice for information security controls*.[18]

Another example of an international standards-producing body is the Payment Card Industry (PCI) Security Standards Council, founded by the five payment brands: American Express, Discover Financial Services, JCB International, MasterCard, and Visa Inc. The PCI Security Standards Council "maintains, evolves, and promotes the Payment Card Industry Security Standards," including the PCI Data Security Standard (PCI DSS), and conducts other activities in support of that purpose.[19] Though ISO standards are intended to support a variety of business environments, the PCI DSS focuses on the protection of account data (e.g., credit card accounts) for all organizations that play a role in payment card processing.

---

[17] http://www.iso.org/iso/home/about.htm (accessed February 21, 2017).

[18] See more about ISO/IEC 27001 at: http://www.iso.org/iso/home/standards/management-standards/iso27001.htm. See more about ISO/IEC 27002 at http://www.iso.org/iso/catalogue_detail?csnumber=54533 (accessed February 21, 2017).

[19] https://www.pcisecuritystandards.org/about_us/.

The Framework for Improving Critical Infrastructure Cybersecurity[20] (known as the "Cybersecurity Framework") developed by NIST is an example of a framework that is developed for a subset of industries, in this case, those that own and operate "critical infrastructure" that support the vitality of the United States[21] NIST developed the Cybersecurity Framework in collaboration with the government and the private sector. Though the impetus for creating the Cybersecurity Framework was critical infrastructure protection, the framework can be widely used regardless of industry and focus on the critical infrastructure and is also being adopted by other countries.[22]

NIST SP 800-37, *Guide for Applying the Risk Management Framework (RMF) to Federal Information Systems, A Security Life Cycle Approach*, provides RMF guidance. The intent of the RMF is to improve data security, strengthen risk management processes, and encourage reciprocity among federal agencies.[23] The RMF emphasizes (1) building data security capabilities into federal information systems through the application of state-of-the-practice management, operational, and technical security controls; (2) maintaining awareness of the security state of information systems on an ongoing basis though enhanced monitoring processes; and (3) providing essential information to senior leaders to facilitate decisions regarding the acceptance of risk to organizational operations and assets, individuals, other organizations, and the nation arising from the operation and use of information systems.[24] In addition to the RMF guidance provided in NIST SP 800-37, NIST provides supplementary guidance for each RMF step in one or more Federal Information Process Standards (FIPS) and Special Publications (SP), all of which are freely available on their website.[25] For example, NIST SP 800-53, Rev. 4, *Security and Privacy Controls for Federal Information Systems and Organizations*, organizes information security activities into security control families and provides over 850 controls as a resource for identifying appropriate security measures to meet requirements.[26]

These frameworks and standards have some topics in common with each other. Table C.5 lists the main topics of three widely used frameworks and standards. The topics are listed in alphabetical order rather than in the order in which they appear in the original documentation.

Beginning in May 2017, U.S. federal agencies are required by Executive Order to use the Cybersecurity Framework.[27] The Cybersecurity Framework and the RMF

---

[20] https://www.nist.gov/cyberframework.

[21] The Department of Homeland Security identifies 16 critical infrastructure sectors on their website: https://www.dhs.gov/critical-infrastructure-sectors.

[22] Italy is an example of another country that is openly using the Cybersecurity Framework to develop its own version. http://www.cybersecurityframework.it/en.

[23] NIST SP 800-37, Rev1, Section 1.1.

[24] NIST SP 800-37, Rev1, Section 1.1.

[25] http://csrc.nist.gov/publications/index.html.

[26] https://doi.org/10.6028/NIST.SP.800-53r4.

[27] https://www.federalregister.gov/documents/2017/05/16/2017-10004/strengthening-the-cybersecurity-of-federal-networks-and-critical-infrastructure.

Table C.5 Examples of security topics addressed in common frameworks and standards

NIST SP 800-53, Rev 4, security control families[a]	ISO domains[b]	Cybersecurity framework categories[c]
• Access Control	• Access Control	• Access Control
• Audit and Accountability	• Asset Management	• Analysis
• Awareness and Training	• Business Continuity	• Anomalies and Events
• Configuration Management	• Communication	• Asset Management
• Contingency Planning	• Compliance	• Awareness and Training
• Identification and Authentication	• Cryptography	• Business Environment
	• Human Resources	• Communications (Recover)
• Incident Response	• Incident	• Communications (Respond)
• Information Security Program Management Maintenance	Management Organization	• Data Security
		• Detection Processes
• Media Protection	• Operations	• Governance
• Personnel Security	• Physical Security	• Improvements (Recover)
• Physical and Environmental Protection	• Policy	• Improvements (Respond)
	• Supplier Relationships	• Information Protection Processes and Procedures
• Planning		
• Risk Assessment	• System Acquisition	• Maintenance
• Security Assessment and Authorization		• Mitigation
		• Protective Technology
• System and Communications Protection		• Recovery Planning
		• Response Planning
• System and Information Integrity		• Risk Assessment
		• Risk Management Strategy
• System and Services Acquisition		• Security Continuous Monitoring

[a]At the time of this publication, plans to review NIST SP 800-53 were under way. Rev. 5 may include adjustments to these categories, including incorporating one or more privacy control families to accommodate the controls in Rev 4, Appendix J, Privacy Control Catalog
[b]ISO/IEC 27002:2013, Information technology—Security techniques—Code of practice for information security controls, https://www.iso.org/obp/ui/#iso:std:iso-iec:27002:ed-2:v1:en
[c]Framework for Improving Critical Infrastructure Cybersecurity, v 1.0, February 2014, https://www.nist.gov/cyberframework

complement each other and as of the time of publication, work is beginning to determine how the two frameworks can most effectively be used together. NIST Interagency Report (NISTIR) 8170, "The Cybersecurity Framework, Implementation Guidance for Federal Agencies"[28] provides a starting point for the dialogue among federal agencies to determine the path forward. The diagram in Fig. C.1 offers a view of how they align from a strategic point of view (as opposed to the operational system-level point of view discussed in the Data Security chapter). The alignment is based one eight cybersecurity use cases from the critical infrastructures users that also apply to federal agencies (middle column) and how they align with the organization, mission/

---

[28] http://csrc.nist.gov/publications/drafts/nistir-8170/nistir8170-draft.pdf.

Level 1 Organization	Integrate enterprise and cybersecurity risk management by communicating with universally understood risk terms.	Core	
Level 2 Mission/ Business Processes	Manage cybersecurity requirements using a construct that enables integration and prioritization of *all* requirements.	Profile(s)	
	Integrate and align cybersecurity and acquisition processes by relaying cybersecurity requirements and priorities in a common and concise language	Profile(s)	
	Evaluate organizational cybersecurity using a standardized and straightforward measurement scale and set of self-assessment criteria.	Implementation Tiers	
	Manage the cybersecurity program by determining which cybersecurity outcomes necessitate common controls, and apportioning work and responsibility for those cybersecurity outcomes (supports RMF Implement & Monitor).	Profile(s)	
	Maintain a comprehensive understanding of cybersecurity risk using a standardized organizing structure (supports RMF Authorize).	Core	
	Report cybersecurity risks using a universal and understandable reporting structure.	Core	
Level 3 System	Inform the tailoring process using a comprehensive reconciliation of *all* cybersecurity requirements (supports RMF Implement).	Profile(s)	

Special Publication 800-39 (left axis label) — *Cybersecurity Framework Components* (right axis label)

Fig. C.1 Federal cybersecurity uses (NISITR 8170, Figure.)

business process, and system perspectives discussed in the RMF (left column) as well as the components of the Cybersecurity Framework (right column).

When designing or updating systems, Cybersecurity Framework Profiles may influence the specific standards and controls organizations implement and, in terms of the RMF, how they are implemented as well as the rigor with which they are assessed and monitored. For example, when a Mission Objective in a Cybersecurity Framework Profile requires more focus on Data Security Subcategories, the corresponding NIST SP 800-53 controls that support those Subcategories may be:

- implemented with automated tools instead of relying solely on policy and procedures,
- assessed more thoroughly before they system is authorized than other controls, and
- monitored at a greater frequency and intensity than controls that support lower priority Mission Objectives.

Data Security Operations

The need for data security practices continues to grow as we become more dependent on technology, particularly networked technology. As the field of data security matures, practitioners are moving from a compliance mindset, where data security was considered achieved when a checklist of certain activities were complete, to an ongoing risk management mindset, where risk posture is actively managed. In general, organizations rely on a combination of administrative (i.e., policy and procedure), technical, and physical controls to implement their data security programs and practices and they rely heavily on training and awareness activities so that their workforce has the foundational knowledge necessary to support the organization's security objectives.

Organizations typically subscribe to some form of enterprise risk management. Most U.S. government agencies use the RMF developed by NIST as well as its many companion documents that are focused on security practices that support RMF implementation. According to NIST SP 800-37, the RMF:

- Promotes the concept of near-real-time risk management and ongoing information system authorization through the implementation of robust continuous monitoring processes;
- Encourages the use of automation to provide senior leaders with the necessary information to make cost-effective, risk-based decisions with regard to the organizational information systems supporting their core missions and business functions;
- Integrates data security into the enterprise architecture and system development life cycle;
- Provides emphasis on the selection, implementation, assessment, and monitoring of security controls, and the authorization of information systems;
- Links risk management processes at the information system level to risk management processes at the organization level through a risk executive (function); and
- Establishes responsibility and accountability for security controls deployed within organizational information systems and inherited by those systems (i.e., common controls).[29]

Managing risks to information and information systems depends on activities at the organizational level, within mission or business processes, and at the information system level. All three levels play a critical role in how information is protected. RMF tasks are completed prior to placing an information system into operation or continuing its operation to ensure that (1) information system-related security risks are being adequately addressed on an ongoing basis; and (2) the authorizing official explicitly understands and accepts the risk to organizational operations and assets, individuals, other organizations, and the nation based on the implementation of a defined set of security controls and the current security state of the information system.[30]

The Cybersecurity Framework provides a structured way to incorporate cybersecurity into an organization's risk management program and introduces a taxonomy that provides an easily consumable way of understanding cybersecurity. The Cybersecurity Framework is "composed of three parts: the Framework Core, the Framework Implementation Tiers, and the Framework Profiles. Each Framework component reinforces the connection between business drivers and cybersecurity activities."[31] Figure C.2 describes the three parts.

---

[29] NIST SP 800-37, Rev 1, Section 1.2.

[30] NIST SP 800-37, Rev 1, Section 2.1.

[31] Cybersecurity Framework, v1.0, Section 1.1.

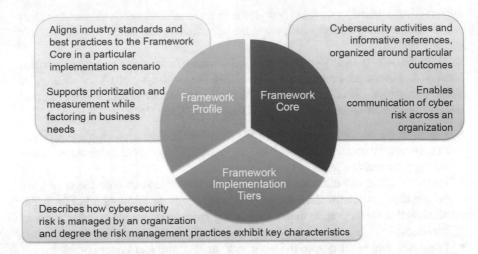

Fig. C.2 Cybersecurity framework components (https://www.nist.gov/cyberframework/upload/cybersecurity_framework_coast_guard_maritime_public_meeting_2015-01-15.pdf.)

When NIST released version 1.0 of the Cybersecurity Framework in February 2014, it also released a roadmap of additional planned activities. For the foreseeable future, NIST will continue to maintain the framework and may make periodic updates as needed.[32] More information regarding the Cybersecurity Framework is discussed in the Implementing Data Security chapter.

Metadata References

Catalog Standards and Metamodels

Table C.6 lists common examples of standards for cataloging digital artifacts such as documents, pictures, and videos.

Vocabulary Standards

Web Ontology Language (Owl) is standard for documenting ontologies and taxonomies. A tree is an analogy used to describe what a taxonomy is. The most frequent example cited is taught in high school biology: Kingdom–Phylum–Class–Order–Family–Genes–Species. Ontologies usually include multiple taxonomies,

---

[32] At the time this chapter was written, a draft version 1.1 of the framework was available for public comment.

Table C.6 Catalog standards & metamodels

Organization	Location	Description

Dublin Core	http://dublincore.org/ documents/dcmi-terms/	Dublin Core is a foundational standard used by other standards. It defines a small set of attributes that cover three categories: instantiation, content, and intellectual property rights:
		• Instantiation
		  – Date
		  – Format
		  – Identifier
		  – Language
		• Content
		  – Title
		  – Description
		  – Coverage
		  – Relation
		  – Source
		  – Subject
		  – Type
		• Intellectual property rights
		  – Creator
		  – Contributor
		  – Publisher
		  – Rights

Metadata Object Description Schema (MODS)	http://www.loc.gov/ standards/mods/	MODS was created by the Library of Congress and is similar in purpose to Dublin Core but it adds several attributes from MARC 21, a library standard that predates the metadata standards. It's sometimes used with METS (Metadata Encoding and Transmission Standards), an xml schema for metadata.
Metadata Encoding and Transmission Standard (METS)	http://www.loc.gov/ standards/mets/ METSOverview. v2.html#descMD	The METS schema is a standard for encoding descriptive, administrative, and structural metadata regarding objects within a digital library.
The Getty Museum	http://www.getty.edu/ research/publications/ electronic_publications/ intrometadata/ crosswalks.html	The Getty Museum developed a metadata crosswalk that maps metadata across several different standards, including Dublin Core, MODS, and MARC.
Data Catalog Vocabulary (DCAT)	http://www.w3.org/TR/ vocab-dcat/	DCAT is a standard vocabulary used to describe datasets in data catalogs. It borrows from other vocabularies such as Dublin Core.
The Common Warehouse Metamodel (CWM)	http://www.omg.org/ spec/CWM/1.1/PDF/	CWM is an Object Management Group (OMG) specification for metadata typically captured for a warehouse and for other relational databases. The stated purpose in the specification is "to enable easy interchange of warehouse and business intelligence metadata between warehouse tools, warehouse platforms, and warehouse metadata repositories in distributed heterogeneous environments."

sometimes with overlapping topics, and use more rigor in defining the relationships between the layers of hierarchies to facilitate use by computer processes.

Table C.7 lists examples of specific vocabulary standards.

Table C.7 Examples of vocabulary standards

Organization	Location	Description
FOAF (Friend of a Friend)	http://xmlns.com/foaf/spec/	FOAF is a vocabulary used to describe people and organizations.
Simple Knowledge Organization System (SKOS)	http://www.w3.org/TR/skos-reference/	SKOS is "a common data model for sharing and linking knowledge organization systems via the Web."
Asset Description Metadata Schema (ADMS)	http://www.w3.org/TR/vocab-adms/	ADMS is a schema and vocabulary to describe assets.
Schema.org	http://Schema.org	Schema.org is a shared vocabulary for webpage and email markup, aka tagging. This shared vocabulary is sponsored by industry search engines (Google, Microsoft, Yahoo, and Yandex) to improve searches of webpages so that engines can provide better responses to user requests.

ISO Standards

Numerous ISO standards relate to metadata, some of which are free, but others must be purchased. Generally, they are granular standards, for example, defining fundamental terms and concepts. Most are building blocks and will not be of direct use to an enterprise metadata program. See http://www.iso.org/iso/home/search.htm?qt=metadata&sort=rel&type=simple&published=on for examples.

Data Analytics References

Central to a scalable analytic environment is the ability to cost-effectively store a large amount of data and then to efficiently analyze it. The most prominent example of an environment that accommodates both cost-effective data storage scalability as well as processing efficiency is the Hadoop ecosystem. The Hadoop ecosystem leverages commodity servers that are linked together into an information network as its physical infrastructure. It then uses the Hadoop Distributed File System (HDFS), a Java-based file system that was designed to span large clusters of commodity servers. To store huge data, the files are stored across many machines. These files are stored this way because scalability in this environment is very cost effective, and to prevent possible data losses in case of a machine failure. HDFS has demonstrated production scalability of up to 200 PB of storage and a single cluster of 4500 servers, supporting close to a billion files and blocks. By distributing storage and computation across many servers, the combined storage resource can grow (or shrink) linearly with demand while remaining economical at every amount of storage.[33]

The base Hadoop software framework is composed of the following modules[34]:

- Hadoop Common: The common utilities that support the other Hadoop modules
- Hadoop Distributed File System (HDFS): A distributed file-system that stores data on commodity machines, providing high-throughput access to application data
- Hadoop YARN: A framework for job scheduling and cluster resource management
- Hadoop MapReduce: A YARN-based system for parallel processing of large datasets

The number of software components in the Hadoop environment used to analyze data continues to evolve. The term Hadoop has come to refer not just to the preceding base modules, but also to the ecosystem, or collection of additional software packages that can be installed on top of or alongside Hadoop, such as Apache Pig, Apache Hive, Apache HBase, Apache Phoenix, Apache Spark, Apache ZooKeeper, Apache Flume, Apache Sqoop, Apache Oozie, Apache Storm.[35] Such extensions to the Hadoop environment allow for things such as a SQL-like programming language (Pig), a data warehouse infrastructure on top of Hadoop (Hive), an interface for exchanging data between Hadoop and relational databases (Sqoop), and more. In addition to tools from the open source Apache Software Foundation many private and public companies are developing packages and platforms around the Hadoop ecosystem.

Besides Hadoop, variations in database technologies are being increasingly added to the mix of data stores. Though traditional, row-based relational data stores remain the most common form of housing cleansed and trusted data, analytics takes advantage of data in native form, which comes in many formats. Other types of data stores include columnar databases, graph databases, document databases, and keyvalue databases. These types of data stores are typically more cost effective, more scalable, and faster to query than traditional, relational databases. They do come with some trade-offs, though, in that this increase in performance and flexibility in the underlying data structure does not necessarily provide the same level of data integrity as relational databases.

Relational: Relational databases are organized around tables that contain columns and rows of data with a unique key identifying each row. The most common way of storing data is row-oriented. The underlying file structure that stores the data stores the key value, followed by the value of each column. So, for example, for the following data[36]

---

[33] See "What HDFS Does," http://hortonworks.com/apache/hdfs/.

[34] See "What is Apache Hadoop," http://hadoop.apache.org/.

[35] See "Apache Hadoop," https://en.wikipedia.org/wiki/Apache_Hadoop#cite_ref-openlibrary1_65-1.

[36] This example makes use of the Wikipedia explanation of row-oriented vs. column-oriented databases. For additional details, see https://en.wikipedia.org/wiki/Column-oriented_DBMS.

RowId	EmpId	Lastname	Firstname	Salary
001	10	Smith	Joe	40,000
002	12	Jones	Mary	50,000
003	11	Johnson	Cathy	44,000
004	22	Jones	Bob	55,000

the underlying file structure looks like this:

001:10,Smith,Joe,40000;
002:12,Jones,Mary,50000;
003:11,Johnson,Cathy,44000;
004:22,Jones,Bob,55000;

This is useful if an entire record or most of a record is queried each time, for example, listing out an employee's profile.

Columnar: A columnar database stores data as columns rather than rows. The resulting file structure, rather than storing the value of each *row* sequentially, as shown above, stores values for a given *column* sequentially, as shown here:

10:001,12:002,11:003,22:004;
Smith:001,Jones:002,Johnson:003,Jones:004;
Joe:001,Mary:002,Cathy:003,Bob:004;
40000:001,50000:002,44000:003,55000:004;

This is ideal when querying all or most of the values of a given column, for example determining the range of salaries.

Graph: A graph database is a NoSQL database and uses nodes (relational equivalent are entities), edges (relational equivalent are relationships), and properties (information about a node—entity attributes in relational equivalent, or information about a relationship). Graph database designs explicitly define information about a relationship, including the type of relationship as well as properties about a relationship. Such properties might include when the relationship was first established, for example. This type of relationship information goes above and beyond relational designs, which can only imply details about relationships. The data models in Figs. C.3 and C.4 depict similar data modeled in relational and graph form, respectively.[37]

Document: A document database, another NoSQL data store, stores data more like objects. In other words, each "document" can store the same data that might be represented across multiple, related tables in a relational database. Thus a relational database might normalize information about a person, department, project, and organization across multiple, normalized tables (as shown earlier), whereas a document database might store all data for a given person—person data, department data, project data, and organization data—in a single document.

---

[37] See "From Relational to Neo4j," https://neo4j.com/developer/graph-db-vs-rdbms/.

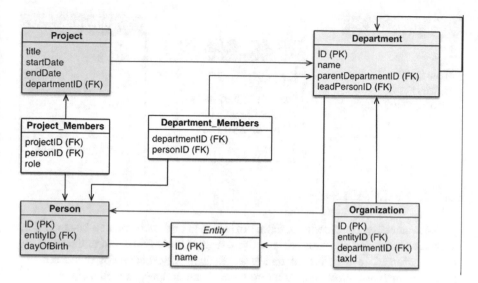

Fig. C.3 Relational data model

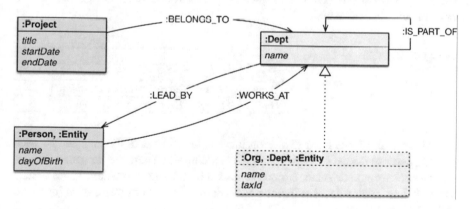

Fig. C.4 Equivalent graph data model

In addition, the structure of each document may vary, as shown in Fig. C.5.[38] In this example, the label and/or structure of how name is stored varies between documents. The author notes that this is simply an example, and that any schema variations between documents' structures must be well thought out because they require the query coder to account for the variations when matching content.

---

[38] For additional detail, see Lobel, L., "Relational Databases vs. NoSQL Document Databases," June 1, 2015, https://lennilobel.wordpress.com/2015/06/01/relational-databases-vs-nosql-document-databases/.

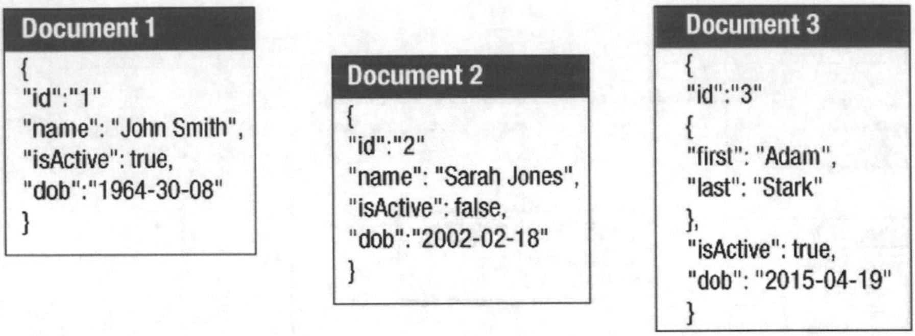

Document 1

```
{
"id":"1"
"name": "John Smith",
"isActive": true,
"dob":"1964-30-08"
}
```

Document 2

```
{
"id":"2"
"name": "Sarah Jones",
"isActive": false,
"dob":"2002-02-18"
}
```

Document 3

```
{
"id":"3"
{
"first": "Adam",
"last": "Stark"
},
"isActive": true,
"dob": "2015-04-19"
}
```

Fig. C.5 'Schema-less' documents

Fundamentally, document databases offer scale and performance because they allow for changes of all kinds without the stringent underlying referential integrity that is enforced in a relational database. Realistically, document databases use groupings such as collections, structure such as hierarchies, as well as tags to lend some degree of organization and structure.

Key Value: A key value database stores a key and associated values. Therefore, tables in a key value database are typically wide and flat. Table C.8 gives a simple example of a key value table.

Table C.8 Key value examples

Key	Value
BMW	{"1-Series", "3-Series", "5-Series", "7-Series"}
Toyota	{"Prius", "Camry", "Tundra", "Avalon"}
Ford	{"Focus", "Explorer", "F100", "Fusion"}

This structure lends itself to storing large amounts of data that can be accessed quickly because the list of values can grow indefinitely. There are no constraints on what values are stored. Values stored are thus subject to interpretation. Types of data stored in key value databases include analytic results, system transaction logs, and individual profile data.

Records Management References

Table C.9 lists useful references for records management.

In the public, federal sector, numerous guidelines and mandates exist to facilitate records management. They are authored by a variety of sources, including the National Archives (NARA), the Office of Management and Budget (OMB) and others. Table C.10 is an overview of some of them.[39]

---

[39] ISO also authors standards on records management, including ISO 15489 and ISO 30301.

Table C.9 Records management industry bodies

Organization	Location	Description
ARMA International	www.arma.org	<ul><li>Professional organization.</li><li>Provides publications and training in records and information management.</li><li>Offers several certificate programs, including Certified Records Manager (CRM) certification.</li><li>Publishes Information Governance Maturity Model.</li><li>Hosts conferences and lists several relevant publications.</li></ul>
AIIM (Association for Information and Image Management)	www.aiim.org	<ul><li>Professional organization.</li><li>Community for information professionals.</li><li>Offers Certified Information Professional (CIP) certification.</li></ul>
NARA (National Archives and Records Administration)	www.archives.gov	<ul><li>Federal agency that serves as the archives of the U.S. federal government and issues regulations, guidance, and assistance to federal agencies concerning the management and disposition of federal records.</li><li>Leads federal standard for records and information management and archiving.</li><li>Publishes self-scoring Records and Information Management (RIM) Maturity Model.</li><li>Offers much records and information management guidance.</li></ul>

Table C.10 Federal records management guidelines and mandates

Guideline	Description	Source
M-12-18 Managing Government Records Directive	Presidential memorandum requiring agencies to manage all email as electronic records by the end of 2016 and all records electronically by the end of 2019.	https://obamawhitehouse.archives.gov/sites/default/files/omb/memoranda/2012/m-12-18.pdf
M-14-16 Guidance on Managing Email	Follow-Up Presidential memorandum requiring agencies to manage email as electronic records.	https://obamawhitehouse.archives.gov/sites/default/files/omb/memoranda/2014/m-14-16.pdf
NARA Bulletin 2010-05 Guidance on Managing Records in Cloud Computing Environments	Addresses records management considerations in cloud computing environments.	https://www.archives.gov/records-mgmt/bulletins/2010/2010-05.html
NARA Bulletin 2014-04 Format Guidance for Transfer of Permanent Records	Specifies which file formats are acceptable when transferring permanent electronic records to NARA.	https://www.archives.gov/records-mgmt/bulletins/2014/2014-04.html
NARA Bulletin 2014-06 Guidance on Managing Email	Reminds federal agencies about their records management responsibilities regarding email.	https://www.archives.gov/records-mgmt/bulletins/2014/2014-06.html

(continued)

Table C.10 (continued)

Guideline	Description	Source
NARA Bulletin 2015-02 Guidance on Managing Electronic Messages	Provides records management guidance for electronic messages. Specifically, this bulletin applies to text messaging, chat/instant messaging, messaging functionality in social media tools or applications, voice messaging, and similar forms of electronic messaging systems.	https://www.archives.gov/records-mgmt/bulletins/2015/2015-02.html
NARA Bulletin 2015-04 Metadata Guidance for the Transfer of Permanent Electronic Records	Defines the minimum set of metadata elements that must accompany transfers of permanent electronic records to the National Archives.	https://www.archives.gov/records-mgmt/bulletins/2015/2015-04.html
Electronic Code of Federal Regulations (eCFR) §1236—Electronic Records Management	Specifies high-level records management controls that should be in place for federal agencies. Other, related eCFR regulation include: • Electronic Code of Federal Regulations (eCFR) §1223—Managing Vital Records • Electronic Code of Federal Regulations (eCFR) §1224—Records Disposition Programs • Electronic Code of Federal Regulations (eCFR) §1227—General Record Schedules • Electronic Code of Federal Regulations (eCFR) §1229—Emergency Authorization to Destroy Records	http://www.ecfr.gov/cgi-bin/text-idx?rgn=div5&node=36:3.0.10.2.25
Federal Records Act of 1950	Provides the legal framework for federal records management, including record creation, maintenance, and disposition.	https://www.gpo.gov/fdsys/granule/USCODE-2011-title44/USCODE-2011-title44-chap31
Presidential and Federal Records Act Amendments of 2014	Modernizes records management by focusing more directly on electronic records.	https://www.congress.gov/bill/113th-congress/house-bill/1233

Appendix D: Acronyms and Glossary of Terms

Acronym List

Acronym	Title
ADM	(TOGAF) Architectural Development Method
ADMS	Asset Description Metadata Schema
AIIM	Association for Information and Image Management
ANSI	American National Standards Institute
API	Application Program Interface
BI	Business Intelligence
BRM	Business Reference Model
CDO	Chief Data Officer
CEO	Chief Executive Officer
CFO	Chief Financial Officer
CIO	Chief Information Officer
CIPSEA	Confidential Information Protection and Statistical Efficiency Act
CISO	Chief Information Security Officer
CMM	Capability Maturity Model
CMMI	Capability Maturity Model Institute
DMM Model	Data Management Maturity Model
CNSS	Committee on National Security Systems
COBIT	Control Objectives for Information and Related Technologies
COO	Chief Operating Officer
COPPA	Children's Online Privacy Protection Act
COTS	Commercial Off-the-Shelf
CRM	Customer Relationship Management
CRO	Chief Risk Officer
CSC	Critical Security Controls
CTO	Chief Technology Officer
CV	Capability Viewpoint
CWM	Common Warehouse Metamodel
DAMA	Data Management Association
DBA	Database Administrator
DBMS	Database Management System
DCAM	Data Management Capability Assessment Model
DCAT	Data Catalog Vocabulary
DG Charter	Data Governance Charter
DGO	Data Governance Operations
DHS	Department of Homeland Security
DIV	Data and Information Viewpoint
DLD	Data Lifecycle Diagram
DLP	Data Loss Prevention

(continued)

DM	Data Management
DMBOK	Data Management Body of Knowledge
DMDF	Data Management Domain Framework
DMM	Data Management Maturity
DoDAF	Department of Defense Architecture Framework
DQ	Data Quality
DRM	Data Reference Model
DW	Data Warehouse
DWaaS	Data Warehousing as a Service
EA	Enterprise Architecture
eCFR	Electronic Code of Federal Regulations
ECM	Enterprise Content Management
EDM	Enterprise Data Management
EDMC	Enterprise Data Management Council
EDRM	Electronic Discovery Reference Model
EDW	Enterprise Data Warehouse
EHR	Electronic Health Record
EIM	Enterprise Information Management
ELC	Engineering Life Cycle
ELT	Extract, Load, Transfer
EMM	Enterprise Metadata Management
ERP	Enterprise Resource Planning
ESI	Electronically Stored Information
ETL	Extract, Transform, and Load
FDCCI	Federal Data Center Consolidation Initiative
FEA	Federal Enterprise Architecture
FEAF	Federal Enterprise Architecture Framework
FIBO	Financial Industry Business Ontology
FIPPs	Fair Information Practice Principles
FISMA	Federal Information Security Management Act of 2002
FOAF	Friend of a Friend
FOIA	Freedom of Information Act
FTC	Federal Trade Commission
FY	Fiscal Year/Financial Year
GPS	Global Positioning System
HDFS	Hadoop Distributed File System
HEW	U.S. Department of Health, Education, and Welfare
HIPAA	Health Information Portability and Accountability Act
HL7	Health Seven International
IAM	Institute of Asset Management
IG	Information Governance
IoT	Internet of Things
IP	Internet Protocol
IRB	Internal Review Board
IRS	Internal Revenue Service
ISO	International Standards Organization

(continued)

ISSM	Information System Security Manager
ISSO	Information System Security Officer
MDM	Master Data Management
METS	Metadata Encoding and Transmission Standard
MIKE2.0	Method for Integrated Knowledge Environment
MISMO	Mortgage Industry Standards Maintenance Organization
MODS	Metadata Object Description Schema
NARA	National Archives and Records Administration
N-Dex	National Data Exchange
NIEM	National Information Exchange Network
NIST	National Institute of Standards and Technology
NoSQL	Not Only SQL
NSS	National Security Systems
OCM	Organizational Change Management
ODNI	Office of the Director of National Intelligence
ODS	Operational Data Store
OECD	Organization for Economic Cooperation and Development
OMB	Office of Management and Budget
OV	Operational Viewpoint
OWL	Web Ontology Language
PB	Petabyte
PCI-DSS	Payment Card Industry Data Security Standards
PHI	Protected Health Information
PIA	Privacy Impact Assessment
PII	Personally Identifiable Information
PM-ISE	Program Manager for an Information Sharing Environment
POC	Point of Contact
PPM	Privacy Program Manager
RM	Records Management
RMF	(NIST) Risk Management Framework
ROI	Return on Investment
ROT	Redundant, outdated, or trivial
SaaS	Software as a Service
SAFe	Scaled Agile Framework Architecture
SAOP	Senior Agency Official for Privacy
SDLC	Systems Development Life Cycle
SDO	Standards Developing Organization
SEC	Securities Exchange Commission
SEI	Software Engineering Institute
SES	Senior Executive Service
SKOS	Simple Knowledge Organization System
SKU	Stock Keeping Unit
SLA	Service Level Agreement
SME	Subject Matter Expert
SOR	System of Record

(continued)

SORN	System of Records Notice
SOX	Sarbanes-Oxley Act
SQL	Structured Query Language
SSD	Solid State Drive
SWIFT	Society for Worldwide Interbank Financial Telecommunication
TDWI	The Data Warehouse Institute
TOGAF	The Open Group Architecture Framework
UML	Unified Modeling Language
VP	Vice President
XML	Extensible Markup Language
ZB	Zettabyte

Glossary of Terms

Term	Definition
Agile Development	Evolutionary development by cross-functional teams focused on rapid delivery, continuous improvement, and a flexible approach to change. Agile is a response to the waterfall approach to development, which is sometimes perceived as having cycle times that are too long and not quick enough to incorporate changes in organizational direction.
Analytic Environment	A "data highway"[a] with multiple caches of increasing latency and data quality, beginning with an environment of raw data that is available in near real time and ending with a data warehouse of trusted data with high data quality, available at higher latency. These data stores are loosely coupled, each accommodating business needs in an appropriately timely fashion.
Analytics	Analytics combines the use of mathematics and statistics with computer software to derive business knowledge from data. Analytics can be segmented into four types: descriptive, diagnostic, predictive, and prescriptive.[b] Descriptive analytics focuses on describing something that has already happened and suggesting its root causes. Diagnostic analytics answers the question of "why" did an event occur. More complex predictive and prescriptive analytics can help companies anticipate business opportunities and public institutions better serve society.
Architectural Development Method	A TOGAF a process that breaks down the approach to four architectures (business, applications, data, and technology) into phases A through H, beginning with a vision.
ARMA International	A professional organization focused on records management.
Association for Information and Image Management (AIIM)	A professional organization focused on information management.
Authoritative Source	Any data source that is trusted by the organization. This may be the system of record (SOR) where data first originates within the organization or a trusted secondary source such as a data warehouse or another downstream data store.

(continued)

Big Data	Big data describes data so large and so complex that it cannot be managed by conventional means.
Business Glossary	A registry of consistently applied terms for data representations of products and services.
Business Intelligence (BI)	Business intelligence is a reporting and analysis layer implemented on top of a data warehouse for historical reporting and trend analysis.
Business Reference Model (BRM)	One part of the Federal Enterprise Architecture Framework (FEAF). The BRM breaks down 10 mission sectors, including defense, diplomacy, financial, environment, health, law, and transport, into 228 individual terms and definitions. Terms in the BRM are business-oriented terms that may be particularly useful in building out a business glossary.
Capability Viewpoint (CV)	Part of the Department of Defense Architecture Framework (DoDAF). OV-1 is the most general of these models. OV-2 through OV-6 are successively more detailed. Other DoDAF views include All Views (AV), Capability Views (CV), Data and Information View (DIV), Project Views (PV), Services View (SvcV), Standards View (StdV), and Systems View (SV).
CMMI's Data Management Maturity (DMM) Model	A framework for assessing the maturity of various data management areas.
Confidential Information Protection and Statistical Efficiency Act (CIPSEA)	Title V of the E-Government Act, establishes confidentiality protections on data collected by or on behalf of U.S. government agencies for statistical purposes.
Customer Relationship Management (CRM)	An approach for managing and analyzing customer interactions and data throughout the customer life cycle.
Data Accessibility	A data management domain focused on the ability to find and retrieve necessary, relevant data easily and in a timely manner.
DATA Act	Digital Accountability and Transparency Act, which requires the Department of the Treasury and the White House Office of Management and Budget to transform U.S. federal spending from disconnected documents into open, standardized data and to publish that data online.
Data Analysis	A data management domain, focused on collecting, cleansing, and evaluating data using one or more data analysis techniques in order to gain a broader insight on the business or process the data is describing.
Data Analytics	See *Analytics*.
Data and Information Viewpoint (DIV)	Part of the Department of Defense Architecture Framework (DoDAF). DIV-1 is the most general of the DIV models, the conceptual data model. DIV-2 through DIV-3 reflect the logical and physical data models, respectively. Other DoDAF views include All Views (AV), Operational Views (OV), Operational View (OV), Project Views (PV), Services View (SvcV), Standards View (StdV), and Systems View (SV).
Data Architecture	A data management domain focused on the definition, design, location, dissemination, delivery, and development of data in the enterprise.
Data Asset	A data store, such as a database, file, or data extract, and its contents. A data asset and a system may not have a one-to-one relationship. A system can encompass multiple data assets. Similarly, a data asset may serve multiple systems.

(continued)

Data Asset Inventory	A list—and subsequent detailing—of production databases and other data stores.
Data Broker	Data brokers collect information, such as consumer information, from a wide variety of sources to yield marketing, risk-mitigation, and people search results. They often sell this data.
Data Cleansing	Detecting and correcting (or removing) corrupt or inaccurate data from a dataset.
Data Engineering and Administration	A data management domain focused on designing and developing data solutions, including collecting data from source systems, applying data transformation and quality control, storing data, making data available, and using database programming and database administration.
Data Exchange Framework	A framework, such as NIEM, focused on exchanging data through the use of a data exchange standard.
Data Governance	A data management domain focused on the exercise of authority and control (planning, monitoring, and enforcement) over the management of data assets. The data governance function guides how all other data management functions are performed.
Data Governance Charter	A formal document that identifies roles and responsibilities for data governance, usually implemented at the executive and managerial levels.
Data Governance Operations (DGO)	A small team of (usually) full-time data governance experts who facilitate data governance across all levels: executive, managerial, and operations.
Data Integration	A data management domain focused on the process of providing standardized access, aligning fragmented data and information assets that reside in multiple autonomous, heterogeneous, and distributed platforms.
Data Lake	A storage repository that holds a very large amount of data, from various sources and formats, in native format.
Data Lifecycle Diagram	The Data Lifecycle Diagram (DLD) focuses on how specific data is imported/created, integrated, stored, and flows across the entire enterprise. A variation of the DLD focuses on a specific business use case; in this variation, the term "data lifecycle" refers to the life cycle of data across a business use case, rather than the life cycle of data from conception to purging/destruction.
Data Lineage	Tracing data movement from its origin throughout the enterprise.
Data Management	The people, processes, and technology necessary to manage an organization's data from inception to purging. DAMA defines data management as "an overarching term that describes the processes used to plan, specify, enable, create, acquire, maintain, use, archive, retrieve, control, and purge data."[c]
Data Management Body of Knowledge (DMBOK)	A data management framework, published by the Data Management Association (DAMA), that segments data management into 11 knowledge areas, similar to data management domains.
Data Management Capability Assessment Model (DCAM)	EDMC's Data Management Capability Assessment Model (DCAM) is a simple, self-assessment data management maturity model that covers maturity in component areas, including data strategy, data governance, data architecture, data quality, and technology architecture.
Data Management Domain	Refers to a particular area of data management, such as data governance, data architecture, or master data management. Data management domains are inconsistently termed. For example, DAMA refers to domains as "knowledge areas," SEI CMMI refers to them as "categories" and sub-categories, which it terms "process areas," and EDMC terms domains as "component areas." This book uses the term "data management domains."

(continued)

Data Management Domain Framework (DMDF)	MITRE's framework of data management areas.
Data Management Framework	A framework (such as the DMBOK, the CMMI DMM, or the DMDF) that breaks down different areas of data management.
Data Management Principles	Foundational statements of organizational values meant to help institute a data management mindset at an enterprise level and drive policy, standards, and guidelines.
Data Mart	A subset of the data warehouse, often specific to a business unit. The data mart may contain additional, local data that is not found in the data warehouse.
Data Model	A representation of how data is stored. Data models may be at a very high, conceptual level, depicting subject areas or data categories, or they can be at the granular level, depicting entities (tables) and attributes (fields). Depending on the type of data store (e.g., relational, graph, document) the nature of the data model will differ. Data models can span the enterprise or be specific to a system or data store. They can be logical, reflecting business entities and attributes, or physical, reflecting how data is actually stored.
Data Preparation	Encompasses activities required to transform raw data into a usable dataset for training, testing, and validating the analysis.
Data Preparation Tool	These tools allow business users to analyze data with minimal involvement from IT. They complement existing enterprise data integration tools. Data preparation tools can be used for rapid prototyping and for projects that need quick turnaround. They are business-user friendly and place responsibility for understanding the underlying data infrastructure on the tool user.
Data Profiling	A technique applied to a data source (database, file, etc.) to discover the characteristics of its datasets. Profiling examines data sources using statistical methods to establish snapshots of data structure, content, rules, and relationships.
Data Provenance	See *Data Lineage*.
Data Quality	A data management domain focused on ensuring that the data being monitored is "fit for use" with a focus on mission-critical data.
Data Reference Model (DRM)	One part of the FEAF outlining three levels of taxonomy, consisting of a hierarchy of four domains, 22 subject areas, and 144 topics. The DRM is meant to aid organizations' high-level data definitions and ease of data exchange.
Data Requirements	A data management domain focused on defining and using data requirements across all levels of the enterprise in the development and maintenance of data applications.
Data Scientists	Highly specialized individuals who understand statistics, software development, and ideally, business context. This may also be accomplished by a team combining individual skills.
Data Standards	Data standards promote and facilitate data reuse, reduce risks, and improve overall cost efficiency. Data standards may specify not only a definition, but also how a given data item is represented, a list of valid values, a field format, and so on. Detailed (or low level) data standards might include standard terms and definitions, standard code sets (e.g., country codes), or data exchange standards. Higher level data standards may be reflected as a policy or guidelines, for example, projects should have a logical data model based on the enterprise model, if one exists.

(continued)

Data Steward	Data stewards have specific accountabilities for managing data. These responsibilities may be formally outlined as part of data standards or a charter. Ideally, a data steward is responsible for a sphere of specific data across the enterprise, rather than just a system. Data stewards coordinate data management with their peers and communicate and escalate issues, when needed. They engage people from all parts of the organization—from the business side and IT, and from executives to operational staff—with clearly stated roles and responsibilities. Formal data stewards have explicit accountability and support, whereas informal data stewards lack a formal network to coordinate their efforts.
Data Strategy and Planning	A data management domain focused on the goals, objectives, and associated strategic actions required to align the vision of the organization with the data-related activities and priorities of the enterprise.
Data Technologies	A data management domain focused on enabling technologies as key components for improving mission effectiveness by developing an enterprise-wide data architecture that supports the management of information and data assets across the data life cycle.
Data Transformation	A data management domain focused on converting f data from its current form to a new form.
Data Visualization	A data management domain focused on placing data in a visual context to help people understanding its significance.
Data Warehousing	A data management domain, a data warehouse (sometimes referred to as an enterprise data warehouse) facilitates the management of data used for reporting and analysis. It reflects "snapshots" of the enterprise-level operational environment over time. It is populated with data from multiple source systems that are typically operational systems within in the enterprise (e.g., Case Management, HR, Payroll, Accounts Payable).
Database Administration	A data management domain focused on activities that a database administrator performs to ensure the database is available to support business operations and processing. Tasks include performance monitoring and tuning, backup and recovery, database queries, and database access and security.
Database Programming	A data management domain focused on developing and executing programmatic interfaces into data, providing technical access to data in databases, flat files, nontraditional data systems, and any other electronic form.
Department of Defense Architecture Framework (DoDAF)	A publicly available enterprise architecture framework developed by the U.S. Department of Defense.
Document Management	Document Management focuses on check-in/check-out, version control, security, and library services for business documents. Other aspects of document management include compound-document support, content replication, digital rights management, and version management.[d]
eDiscovery	An iterative, nonlinear process focused on the electronic discovery of information to satisfy processes such as litigation and FOIA. This process includes information governance, identification, preservation, collection, processing, review, analysis, production, and presentation.
Electronic Code of Federal Regulations (eCFR)	Regulations that specify high-level records management controls that should be in place for federal agencies.

(continued)

Electronically Stored Information (ESI)	Any information stored electronically, including structured data, documents, and other unstructured content like phone messages and voicemails.
Enterprise Architecture	A framework that combines business, data, applications, and technology architectures. A conceptual blueprint that defines the structure and operation of an organization, an enterprise architecture is significantly broader than a data management framework, and typically covers business process and various aspects of technology (e.g., applications, network).
Enterprise Resource Planning (ERP)	A process by which a company manages and integrates the important parts of its business. It also refers to ERP applications, which integrate areas such as planning, purchasing, inventory, sales, marketing, finance, and human resources.
Extensible Markup Language (XML)	Coding that defines a set of rules for data in both human-readable and machine-readable formats.
Extract, Load, Transfer (ELT)	Refers to extracting data from the source, loading it into the target in raw form, and transforming it later, if and when needed, by applying analytics. See also *ELT*.
Extract, Transform, and Load (ETL)	Refers to how tools, used with structured data, first extract data from a source, then transform it to match the target environment and then load data to the target environment. See also *ELT*.
Fair Information Practice Principles (FIPPs)	Principles that establish process-based requirements for the treatment of personal information.
Federal Data Center Consolidation Initiative (FDCCI)	A federal CIO mandate requiring government agencies to reduce the overall energy and real estate footprint of their data centers.
Federal Enterprise Architecture Framework(FEAF)	Also referred to as FEA, it includes the Data Reference Model (DRM), among other enterprise architecture models.
Federal Information Security Management Act (FISMA)	Passed in 2002, FISMA requires each federal agency to develop, document, and implement an agency-wide program to provide information security for the information and information systems.
Foundational Data Management Domains	These are data management domains that touch many or most other data management domains. For example, data quality, data governance, and data architecture underlie just about all other domains. Different frameworks differ somewhat in how they view foundational data management domains. For example, the CMMI DMM incorporates metadata management into data governance, one of its foundational data management practices, whereas others may explicitly define metadata management as a foundational data management domain.
Freedom of Information Act (FOIA)	A law that gives individuals the right to request information from the federal government.
Hadoop Distributed File System (HDFS)	A distributed file system that stores data on commodity machines, providing high-throughput access to application data.
Health Information Portability and Accountability Act (HIPAA)	A privacy law specifying protection of protected health information (PHI) handled by any "covered entity"—healthcare provider, healthcare clearinghouse, or healthcare plan.

(continued)

Health Seven International (HL7)	A standards body, but the term "HL7" is used generically to refer to the electronic health information exchange standards this body creates.
Information	This book uses data and information somewhat interchangeably. Information is sometimes distinguished from data in that data becomes information when placed in context. Another differentiation often mentioned is that data is structured (e.g., relational database), whereas information includes unstructured content, such as images. However, this line is becoming increasingly blurred.
Information and Data Sharing	A data management domain focused on the mechanisms that enable and support the exchange of information within and between organizations, programs, initiatives, and systems.
Information Management	The acquisition of data or information, and its management to address organizational business needs, until it is no longer needed.
International Standards Organization (ISO)	An independent, nongovernmental international organization that publishes standards for many industries.
Internet Protocol (IP)	A set of rules governing the format of data sent over the Internet and networks.
Master Data Management (MDM)	A data management domain focused on the synchronization of one or more key data domains, such as person, customer or product, across the enterprise to ensure authoritative and consistent information.
Metadata Management	A data management domain focused on management of data that describes various facets of an information asset to improve its usability throughout its life cycle.
Metadata Repository	A repository of standardized metadata for the organization. This might include additional information, such as relationships to other metadata.
MIT Information Quality	Data quality research from Massachusetts Institute of Technology, one of the top U.S. educational institutions.
Mortgage Industry Standards Maintenance Organization (MISMO)	A standards development body, but it is used to refer to the mortgage industry standards they create to exchange data between stakeholders, such as a bank selling a loan to a government-sponsored entity.
National Data Exchange (N-Dex)	N-Dex provides criminal justice agencies with an online tool for sharing, searching, linking, and analyzing information across jurisdictional boundaries. N-Dex is NIEM conformant.
National Information Exchange Network. (NIEM)	NIEM is a framework and set of standards that promote enterprisewide information exchange across disparate agencies and their partners.
Not Only SQL (NoSQL)	Refers to an environment of data stores that includes those that use a mechanism for data storage and retrieval that is other than the tabular structure used in relational databases.
Open Data Policy	This White House Memorandum from 2013 mandates that federal agencies information resources accessible, discoverable, and usable.
Operational Data Store (ODS)	A data store used to store operational data for querying, to reduce the overhead on operational systems. Data is typically stored at the same level as in operational systems. Querying the ODS provides almost the same low latency as querying operational system. The ODS often contains data integrated from multiple sources. The ODS differs from the data warehouse in that the amount of historical information in an ODS is not much.

(continued)

Operational Viewpoint (OV)	Part of the Department of Defense Architecture Framework (DoDAF). CV-1 is the most general of these models. CV-2 through CV-7 are successively more detailed. Other DoDAF views include All Views (AV), Operational Views (OV), Data and Information View (DIV), Project Views (PV), Services View (SvcV), Standards View (StdV), and Systems View (SV).
Personally Identifiable Information (PII)	Any information about an individual maintained by an agency, including (1) any information that can be used to distinguish or trace an individual's identity, such as name, social security number, date and place of birth, mother's maiden name, or biometric records; and (2) any other information that is linked or linkable to an individual, such as medical, educational, financial, and employment information.[e]
Petabyte (PB)	A measure of storage, equivalent to 2^{50} bytes
Privacy and Security	Data Security (also known as Information Security and Cybersecurity) is a data management domain that, in the context of data management, focuses on ensuring that the organization's data assets are protected and secured. The principles of data security fall into three main categories or qualities: confidentiality, availability, and integrity. Data Privacy is the ability of an individual to exercise control over the collection, use, and dissemination of his or her Personally Identifiable Information (PII).
Privacy Impact Assessment (PIA)	An analysis of how PII is handled within a system to ensure handling conforms to applicable legal, regulatory, and policy requirements regarding privacy.
Program Manager for an Information Sharing Environment (PM-ISE)	Established by the Intelligence Reform and Terrorism Prevention Act of 2004 and housed within the Office of the Director of National Intelligence (ODNI), the PM-ISE coordinates intelligence integration and information sharing needs. It facilitates automated sharing of terrorism information, promoting standards, architecture, security, access, and associated privacy protections.
Records Management	Records management is the "systematic and administrative control of records throughout their life cycle to ensure efficiency and economy in their creation, use, handling, control, maintenance, and disposition."[f] Records are "data or information in a fixed form that is created or received in the course of individual or institutional activity and set aside (preserved) as evidence of that activity."[g]
Redundant, outdated, or trivial (ROT)	Refers to the fact that not all data is valuable. Some content is redundant, outdated, or trivial (ROT) and need not be stringently managed.
Sandbox	Refers to an experimental environment in which new approaches can be tested to query and manipulate data.
Semantic Layer	A data translation layer, often used in business intelligence tools that translates data terms as they are stored in a database to terms that make sense to the business user.
Society for Worldwide Interbank Financial Telecommunication (SWIFT)	A financial messaging standard.
Stock Keeping Unit (SKU)	A product and service identification code for a product, often portrayed as a machine-readable bar code.

Structured Data	Data stored with a high degree of organization, where the same data is stored the same way and is related to other data in a predictable manner. For example, a person's name may be stored as: first name, middle name, and last name. Each part is defined in length and format. It may be related to one or more addresses, which are equally structured.
Structured Query Language (SQL)	A query language used to query relational databases.
System of Record or SOR (Architectural)	This specifies the authoritative source of data within an organization. This is the authoritative system where data is first entered or received. This differs from the System of Record Notice (SORN), which is a requirement for federal agencies to publish personal information managed by personal identifier.
System of Records Notice (SORN)	A federally required disclosure in the Federal Register, of personal information collected by federal agencies and used by personal identifier. Note that this differs from an architectural system of record (SOR), which specifies the authoritative source of data in an organization.
The Data Warehouse Institute (TDWI)	A data management membership organization focused on data warehousing.
The Open Group Architecture Framework (TOGAF)	A vendor- and technology-neutral industry consortium. The TOGAF focuses on four core architectures: business, applications, data, and technology.
Unified Modeling Language (UML)	A general-purpose, developmental, modeling language in the field of software engineering that is intended to provide a standard way to visualize the design of a system.
Unstructured Data	Data stored in a nonorganized manner. Traditionally, content such as documents, images, and other media have been termed unstructured. However, with the introduction of NoSQL databases, all types of data may be stored in an unstructured way. Conversely, the lines between structured and unstructured data are becoming more blurry. For example, with face recognition software, it is now possible to identify an image of a person in a structured way.
Web Ontology Language (OWL)	A semantic web language designed to represent rich and complex knowledge about things, groups of things, and relations between things.
Zettabyte (ZB)	A measure of storage, equivalent to 2^{70} bytes

[a]Kimball, R., "Newly Emerging Best Practices for Big Data," The Kimball Group, September 30, 2012
[b]Gartner Business Intelligence Summit, "Back to Basics" Relevance, Resources, and Renovation, April 2012. These categories vary somewhat, depending on the source. For example, not all sources encompass the "diagnostic analytics" category
[c]See DAMA DMBOK2 Framework at https://www.dama.org/sites/default/files/download/DAMA-DMBOK2-Framework-V2-20140317-FINAL.pdf
[d]Gartner, "2015 Magic Quadrant for Enterprise Content Management"
[e]NIST SP 800-122, April 2010, p. 2-1
[f]"Records Management" Pearce-Moses, R. Glossary of Archival and Records Terminology. http://archivists.org/glossary/terms/r/records-management
[g]"Record" Pearce-Moses, R. Glossary of Archival and Records Terminology. http://www2.archivists.org/glossary/terms/r/record

References

Adelman, S., Moss, L., & Abai, M., *Data Strategy*, Addison-Wesley Professional, June 15, 2005.

Aggarwal, S., and Manual, N., "Big data analytics should be driven by business needs, not technology," McKinsey Global Institute, June 2016, http://www.mckinsey.com/business-functions/mckinsey-analytics/our-insights/big-data-analytics-should-be-driven-by-business-needs-not-technology

Aiken, P., & Billings, J., *Monetizing Data Management: Finding the Value in Your Organization's Most Important Asset,* Technics Publications, 2013.

Aiken, P., "Succeeding at data management—BigCo attempts to leverage data," *Journal of Data and Information Quality (JDIQ),* Vol. 7, Is. 1-2, May 2016, http://dl.acm.org/citation.cfm?id=2893482

Almquist, E., Senior, J., & Springer, T., "Three promises and perils of big data," Bain & Company, 2015. http://www.bain.com/Images/BAIN_BRIEF_Three_promises_and_perils_of_Big_Data.pdf

Andriole, S., "Unstructured data: The other side of analytics," *Forbes*, March 5, 2015, http://www.forbes.com/sites/steveandriole/2015/03/05/the-other-side-of-analytics/#5e4f1e8f9a86

Anglin, A., "UPS: Optimizing delivery routes," Harvard Business School Digital Initiative, April 12, 2015. https://openforum.hbs.org/challenge/understand-digital-transformation-of-business/data/ups-optimizing-delivery-routes/comments

Banker, R. D., Hu, N., Pavlou, & P. A., Luftman, J., "CIO reporting structure, strategic positioning and firm performance," *MIS Quarterly*, Vol. 35, Is. 2, June 2011.

Belissent, J., "Better Your Business Performance with a Chief Data Officer," Forrester Research, Inc., September 2015.

Beyer, M., Lapkin, A., & De Simoni, G., "Gartner clarifies the definition of metadata," Gartner, August 13, 2014.

Bidel, S., Joyce, R., "The Forrester Wave: Data Management Platforms, Q4 2015," Forrester Research Inc., November 10, 2015

Big Data: The Organizational Challenge. Bain & Company. Web. September 2013. http://www.bain.com/publications/articles/big_data_the_organizational_challenge.aspx

Blair, M. M., "Unseen Wealth," Brookings Institution, 2001.

Botega, J., "Chief data officer role shifts to offense," *Wall Street Journal*, April 7, 2015.

Bowen, R., & Smith, A. R., "Developing an enterprise-wide data strategy," *Healthcare Financial Management,*" April 2014.

Brunson, D., "Certified data and the certification process for financial institutions," TechTarget, December 6, 2005. http://searchdatamanagement.techtarget.com/news/2240111233/Certified-Data-and-the-Certification-Process-for-Financial-Institutions

© Springer International Publishing AG 2018
M. Fleckenstein, L. Fellows, *Modern Data Strategy*,
https://doi.org/10.1007/978-3-319-68993-7

Burbank, R., & Row, C., "Emerging Trends in Metadata Management," Dataversity Education, LLC, 2016.

Bureau of the Fiscal Service, Department of Treasury, https://www.transparency.treasury.gov/dataset/data-registry

CEB, "CEB Digital Enterprise 2020," https://www.cebglobal.com/information-technology/digital-enterprise-2020/trend-spotter.html

Center for Judicial Studies, Duke Law, "Enterprise Discovery Reference Model," http://www.edrm.net/frameworks-and-standards/edrm-model/

Cisco Systems, "Cisco Visual Networking Index (VNI)," Cisco Systems, June 2016, http://www.cisco.com/c/en/us/solutions/collateral/service-provider/visual-networking-index-vni/vni-hyperconnectivity-wp.html

Cisco Systems, "The Zettabyte Era — Trends and Analysis," http://www.cisco.com/c/en/us/solutions/collateral/service-provider/visual-networking-index-vni/vni-hyperconnectivity-wp.html

City and County of San Francisco http://sfgov.org/sfc/sanfranciscowifi

City of New York & CityBridge, https://www.link.nyc/

CMMI Institute, "Building Enterprise Data Management Capabilities Elearning Course Companion Guide, http://cmmiinstitute.com/sites/default/files/resource_asset/DMM%20Elearning%20Course%20Companion%20Guide.pdf

CMMI Institute, "Data Management Maturity (DMD) Model," Ver. 1.0, CMMI Institute, August 2014, https://dmm-model-individual.dpdcart.com/

Committee on National Security Systems, http://www.cnss.gov

Dalle Mule, L., & Davenport, T., "What's your data strategy?" *Harvard Business Review*, MayJune 2017.

DAMA International, "The DAMA Guide to the Data Management Body of Knowledge," Technics Publications, 2009, https://www.dama.org/content/body-knowledge

DAMA International, DAMA-DMBOK2 Framework, March 6, 2014, https://www.dama.org/sites/default/files/download/DAMA-DMBOK2-Framework-V2-20140317-FINAL.pdf

"Data Growth, Business Opportunities, and the IT Imperatives," EMC and IDC, April 2014, http://www.emc.com/leadership/digital-universe/2014iview/executive-summary.htm

Davenport, T., & Patil, D.J., "Datascientist: The sexiest job of the 21st century," *Harvard Business Review*, October 2012, https://hbr.org/2012/10/data-scientist-the-sexiest-job-of-the-21st-century/

Davenport, T., "Analytics 3.0," *Harvard Business Review*, December 2013.

De Simoni, G., "How Metadata Improves Business Opportunities and Threats," Gartner, August 13, 2014.

De Simoni, G., "Metadata Is the Fish Finder in Data Lakes," Gartner, October 5, 2015.

De Simoni, G., "Overcoming the Challenges to Implementing Enterprise Metadata Management Across the Organization," Gartner, published August 14, 2012, refreshed August 27, 2014.

De Simoni, G., "The Growth of the Metadata Management Tool Market Is a Reality," Gartner, March 24, 2016.

Department of Commerce, Office of the Chief Information Officer, "Federal CIO Roadmap," http://ocio.os.doc.gov/s/groups/public/@doc/@os/@ocio/@oitpp/documents/content/prod01_002082.pdf

Dublin Core Metadata Initiative, http://dublincore.org/documents/dcmi-terms/

Duhigg, C., "How companies learn your secrets," *New York Times*, February 16, 2012.

Duncan, L., & De Simoni, G., "How Chief Data Officers Can Use an Information Catalog to Maximize Business Value from Information Assets," Gartner, May 6, 2016.

Electronic Discovery Reference Model, Duke University Law Center for Judicial Studies, https://www.edrm.net

"Executive Order—Making Open and Machine Readable the New Default for Government Information," https://obamawhitehouse.archives.gov/the-press-office/2013/05/09/executive-order-making-open-and-machine-readable-new-default-government

Federal Bureau of Investigation, "Intellectual Property Theft/Piracy," https://www.fbi.gov/investigate/white-collar-crime/piracy-ip-theft

Federal Enterprise Architecture Framework v.2 (FEAF-II), Section C.2.3.3 "Information Sharing."

"Federal Information Management Security Act of 2002," http://csrc.nist.gov/drivers/documents/FISMA-final.pdf

Federal Records Act of 1950, https://www.gpo.gov/fdsys/granule/USCODE-2011-title44/USCODE-2011-title44-chap31

Federal Trade Commission, "Data Brokers—A Call for Transparency and Accountability," May 2014.

Federal Trade Commission, "FTC Issues Follow-Up Study on Credit Report Accuracy," January 21, 2015 https://www.ftc.gov/news-events/press-releases/2015/01/ftc-issues-follow-study-credit-report-accuracy

Ferguson, Mike, "Master Data Management – The Impact of Big Data," presented at Enterprise Data World, March 30, 2015

Fleckenstein, Mike, "Managing Master Data – Parts 1- 4," Inside Knowledge Magazine, 2007

Fleckenstein, Mike, "Valuing Data as an Asset to Aid Data Governance" Information Management, June, 2016

Fisher, T., *The Data Asset—How Smart Companies Govern Their Data for Business Success*, John Wiley & Sons, 2009.

Forrester Wave—Enterprise Data Warehouse, Q4 2015, December 7, 2015.

Framework for Improving Critical Infrastructure Cybersecurity, v 1.0, February 2014, https://www.nist.gov/cyberframework

"From Relational to Neo4j," https://neo4j.com/developer/graph-db-vs-rdbms/

Fryman, L., "What Is a Business Glossary," BeyeNETWORK, September 13, 2012, http://www.b-eye-network.com/view/16371

Gartner Business Intelligence Summit, "Back to Basics" Relevance, Resources, and Renovation, Gartner, April 2012.

Gartner, "2015 Magic Quadrant for Enterprise Content Management."

Gartner, "Gartner Says Advanced Analytics Is a Top Business Priority," October 21, 2014 http://www.gartner.com/newsroom/id/2881218

Gartner, "IT Glossary" http://www.gartner.com/it-glossary/data information-governance/

Goetz M., Leganza G., & Evelson B., "Vendor Landscape–Data Preparation Tools, Forrester Research, Inc., February 2016.

Goetz, M., & Peyert, H., "Consider New Data Governance Software to Support Business-Led Efforts," Forrester Research, Inc., March 2014

Goetz, M., Owens, L., & Jedinak, E., "Build Trusted Data with Data Quality," Forrester Research, Inc., February 26, 2015, https://www.forrester.com/report/Build+Trusted+Data+With+Data+Quality/-/E-RES83344

Google, "Google Flu Trends Data," https://www.google.org/flutrends/about/

"GPRA Modernization Act of 2010," https://www.gpo.gov/fdsys/pkg/BILLS-111hr2142enr/pdf/BILLS-111hr2142enr.pdf

Guercio, M., "Principles, methods, and instruments for the creation, preservation, and use of archival records in the digital environment." *American Archivist* 64:2 (Fall/Winter 2001), pp. 238–269.

Harris, D., "Google: Our new system for recognizing faces is the best one ever," *Fortune*, March 17, 2015.

Harrison, S. S., & Sullivan, H. P., *Edison in the Boardroom: How New Leading Companies Realize Value from Their Intellectual Property*, John Wiley & Sons, December 2006, "A Brief History" section.

"Health Level Seven International," http://www.hl7.org/implement/standards/index.cfm?ref=common

Heudecker, N., Beyer, M., & Edjlali, R., "The Demise of Big Data, Its Lessons and the State of Things to Come." Gartner Research, August 19, 2015.

Hurley, C., "The Australian ('Series') System: An Exposition," in The Records Continuum: Ian Maclean and Australian Archives—First Fifty Years (Canberra, Australia: Ancora Press, 1996), 150–172.

"Improving Public Access to and Dissemination of Government Information and Using the Federal Enterprise Architecture Data Reference Model," https://obamawhitehouse.archives.gov/sites/default/files/omb/memoranda/fy2006/m06-02.pdf

Inmon, W. H, Strauss, D., & Neushloss, N., *DW 2.0: The Architecture for the Next Generation of Data Warehousing,* Morgan Kaufmann, July 28, 2010.

Intel IT Center, "Big Data 101 – Unstructured Data Analytics," http://www.intel.com/content/dam/www/public/us/en/documents/solution-briefs/big-data-101-brief.pdf

Internal Revenue Manual – 4.48.5 Intangible Property Valuation Guidelines, Web, Autumn 2014. http://www.irs.gov/irm/part4/irm_04-048-005.html

"Information Sharing Environment—The Role of the PM-ISE," https://www.ise.gov/about-ise/what-ise

ISO/IEC 27001: http://www.iso.org/iso/home/standards/management-standards/iso27001.htm

ISO/IEC 27002, https://www.pcisecuritystandards.org/about_us/

ISO/IEC 27002:2013, Information technology—Security techniques—Code of practice for information security controls, https://www.iso.org/obp/ui/#iso:std:iso-iec:27002:ed-2:v1:en

"ISO/IEC JTC 1/SC 32 Data management and interchange," http://www.iso.org/iso/home/standards_development/list_of_iso_technical_committees/iso_technical_committee.htm?commid=45342

"ISO/IEC JTC 1/SC 32 Data management and interchange," http://www.iso.org/iso/home/standards_development/list_of_iso_technical_committees/iso_technical_committee.htm?commid=45342

Kimball, R., "Newly Emerging Best Practices for Big Data," The Kimball Group, September 30, 2012.

Ladley, J., *Data Governance—How to Effectively Design, Deploy, and Sustain an Effective Data Governance Program,* Morgan Kaufmann, 2012.

Ladley, J., *Making EIM Work for Business*, Elsevier Inc., 2010.

Lakshmi, R., et al. "Market Guide for Self-Service Data Preparation for Analytics," Gartner Research, March 5, 2015.

Laney, D., "Introducing Infonomics: Valuing Information as a Corporate Asset," Gartner Research, March 21, 2012.

Lee, Y. W., Madnick, S. E., Wang, R. Y., Wang, F. L., & Zhang, H., "A cubic framework for the chief data officer: Succeeding in a world of big data." *MIS Quarterly Executive*, Composite Information Systems Laboratory (CISL), MIT Sloan School of Management, March 2014, http://web.mit.edu/smadnick/www/wp/2014-01.pdf

Leganza, G., 'Information Strategies Move Center Stage," Forrester Research, Inc., May 20, 2013.

Leganza, G., "Changing Your Approach to Information Strategy? You're Not Alone," Forrester Research, Inc., October 2, 2014.

Leganza, G., "Drive Information Strategy Performance Management with Capability Models," Forrester Research, Inc., October 2, 2014.

Leganza, G., "Information Strategies Move Center Stage," Forrester Research, Inc., May 20, 2013.

Lobel, L., "Relational Databases vs. NoSQL Document Databases," June 1, 2015, https://lennilobel.wordpress.com/2015/06/01/relational-databases-vs-nosql-document-databases/

Logan, D., Popkin, J., & Faria, M., "First Gartner CDO Survey: Governance and Analytics Will Be Top Priorities in 2016," Gartner Research, January 6, 2016.

Logan, D., & Raskino, M., "CIO Advisory, The Chief Data Officer Trend Gains Momentum," Gartner Research, January 13, 2014.

Logan, D., Raskino, M., & Bugajski, J., "Business Case for the Chief Data Officer," Gartner Research, February 29, 2016.

Lohr, S., "For Big Data Scientists, 'Janitor Work' Is Key Hurdle to Insight," *New York Times*, August 17, 2014.

Manyika, J., Chui, M., Brown, B., Bughin, J., Dobbs, R., Roxburgh, C., & Byers, A. H., "Big data: The next frontier for innovation, competition, and productivity," McKinsey Global Institute, June 2011.

Mearian, L., "As police move to adopt body cams, storage costs set to skyrocket," *Computerworld*, September 3, 2015, http://www.computerworld.com/article/2979627/cloud-storage/as-police-move-to-adopt-body-cams-storage-costs-set-to-skyrocket.html

Methany, M. *Federal Cloud Computing: The Definitive Guide for Cloud Service Providers.* Syngress Publishing, 2012. See "A Historical View of Federal IT."

Moody, D., & Walsh, P., "Measuring the Value of Information: An Asset Valuation Approach," ECIS, 1999.

Muller, M., "The Essentials of Inventory Management," 2nd Ed., AMACOM, a division of The American Management Association, 2011.

National Cyber Security Framework (Italy), http://www.cybersecurityframework.it/en

NCTA, "Growth in the Internet of Things," August 13, 2015 https://www.ncta.com/platform/broadband-internet/behind-the-numbers-growth-in-the-internet-of-things-2/

NIST, "Cybersecurity Framework," https://www.nist.gov/cyberframework

NIST, "cybersecurity_framework_coast_guard_maritime_public_meeting_2015-01-15," https://www.nist.gov/cyberframework/upload/cybersecurity_framework_coast_guard_maritime_public_meeting_2015-01-15.pdf

NIST Publications http://csrc.nist.gov/publications/index.html

NIST SP 800-37, Rev 1, *Guide for Applying the Risk Management Framework to Federal Information Systems, A Security Life Cycle Approach*, February 2010.

NIST SP 800-39, *Managing Information Security Risk*, Section 3.1.

NIST SP 800-39, March 2011, Footnote 1, pg. IV.

NIST SP 800-53, Rev 4, Appendix J, page J-1.

NIST SP 800-53, Rev. 4, Section 1.1.

NIST SP 800-122, Guide to Protecting the Confidentiality of Personally Identifiable Information (PII).

NIST SP 800-137, Information Security Continuous Monitoring (ISCM) for Federal Information Systems and Organizations.

NIST Special Publications (SP) http://csrc.nist.gov/publications/PubsSPs.html

O'Kane, B., Palance, T., & Moran, P. M., "Magic Quadrant for Master Data Management Solutions," Gartner, January 19, 2017.

OMB Circular A-108, Federal Agency Responsibilities for Review, Reporting, and Publication under the Privacy Act, 2016.

OMB Circular A-11 (2015), https://obamawhitehouse.archives.gov/omb/circulars_a11_current_year_a11_toc

OMB Circular A-130 (2016), Appendix II, 5.a.

OMB Circular A-130, 10.a.

OMB Circular NO. A-130, Appendix II, 5.i.

Organization for Economic Cooperation and Development (OECD), The OECD Privacy Framework, 2013.

Orr, J., *Data Governance for the Executive,* Senna Publishing, LLC, 2011.

Parapadakis, G., "Nightmare definitions: What is Information Governance?" 2014, https://4most.wordpress.com/2014/06/26/what-is-ig

Pearce-Moses, R., A Glossary of Archival and Records Terminology, http://archivists.org/glossary/terms

Peyert, H., & Goetz, M., "The Forrester Wave: Data Governance Tools, Q2 2014," Forrester Research, Inc., June 2014.

Pfred, J. W., The Challenges of Integrating Structured and Unstructured Data, 2016, https://www.landmark.solutions/Portals/0/LMSDocs/Whitepapers/2010-05-pnec-challenges-integrating-structured-and-unstructured-data-tech-paper.pdf

"Porter's Five Forces Analysis," https://en.wikipedia.org/wiki/Porter%27s_five_forces_analysis

"Presidential and Federal Records Act Amendments of 2014," https://www.congress.gov/bill/113th-congress/house-bill/1233

Presidential Memorandum "Open Data Policy—Managing Information as an Asset," May 9, 2013, https://obamawhitehouse.archives.gov/sites/default/files/omb/memoranda/2013/m-13-13.pdf

Presidential Memorandum on Open Government Directive, December 8, 2009, https://obamawhitehouse.archives.gov/open/documents/open-government-directive

"President's Memorandum on Transparency and Open Government—Interagency Collaboration," https://obamawhitehouse.archives.gov/sites/default/files/omb/assets/memoranda_fy2009/m09-12.pdf

R. Bean (NewVantage Partners) interviewed by D. Kiron. "Organizational alignment is key to big data success." *Sloan Management Review*, MIT, January 2013.

Redman, T. C., "Manage Data with Organizational Structure," HBR Blog Network, November 26, 2012.https://hbr.org/2012/11/manage-data-with-organizationa/

Redman, T. C., *Data Driven: Profiting from Your Most Important Business Asset,* Harvard Business Press, 2008, p. 56.

Redman, T., "Data's Credibility Problem," *Harvard Business Review*, December 2013, https://hbr.org/2013/12/datas-credibility-problem

Reference Open Data, Data Act, Records Retention, m 13 13, m 12 18.

Ross, J. W., & Feeny, D. F., "The Evolving Role of the CIO," Center for Information Systems Research, Sloan School of Management, MIT, August 1999.

Ross, J. W., Beath, C. M., & Quadgraas, A., "You May Not Need Big Data After All Learn—How lots of little data can inform everyday decision making," *Harvard Business Review*, December 2013.

Sarbanes-Oxley Act of 2002, https://www.gpo.gov/fdsys/pkg/BILLS-107hr3763enr/pdf/BILLS-107hr3763enr.pdf

Sebastian-Coleman,L.,"Identifyingdataqualityissuesviadataprofiling,reasonability,"http://search-datamanagement.techtarget.com/feature/Identifying-data-quality-issues-via-data-profiling-reasonability

Seiner, R. S., "Non-Invasive Data Governance—The Path of Least Resistance and Greatest Success," Technics Publications, 2014.

"Seizing the information advantage How organizations can unlock value and insight from the information they hold," PwC, September 2015. http://www.ironmountain.com/Knowledge-Center/Reference-Library/View-by-Document-Type/White-Papers-Briefs/S/~/media/Files/Iron%20Mountain/Knowledge%20Center/Reference%20Library/White%20Paper/S/Seizing%20The%20Information%20Advantage.pdf

Shaw, T., Ladley, J., & Roe, C., "Status of the Chief Data Officer: An Update on the CDO Role in Organizations Today," Dataversity Education, Fall 2014.

Soares, S., "IBM Data Governance Unified Process," IBM Corporation, 2010.

"Standard Reference Data Act," http://www.nist.gov/srd/upload/publiclaw90-396.pdf

Stay on Top of New BI Technologies to Lead Your Enterprise into the Not-Too-Distant Future," Forrester Research, Inc., March 1, 2016.

Stewart, D., "Automatic Classification and Tagging Make Metadata Manageable for ECM and Search," Gartner, August 5, 2015.

"Structuring the Records Continuum Part Two: Structuration Theory and Recordkeeping," *Archives and Manuscripts*, 25, No. 1 (1997) 10–35, http://www.infotech.monash.edu.au/research/groups/rcrg/publications/recordscontinuum-fupp2.html

Symantec, Inc., "Underground black market: Thriving trade in stolen data, malware, and attack services," November 15, 2015 http://www.symantec.com/connect/blogs/underground-black-market-thriving-trade-stolen-data-malware-and-attack-services

Technopedia, "Data Classification," https://www.techopedia.com/definition/13779/data-classification

Tech Target, Inc., "The Certification Process" http://www.b-eye-network.com/images/content/4Big.jpg

The Department of Homeland Security, https://www.dhs.gov/critical-infrastructure-sectors

The Henry J. Kaiser Family Foundation, "Total Medicaid Spending," http://kff.org/medicaid/state-indicator/total-medicaid-spending/Accessed February 2, 2015.

The Institute of Asset Management, "Asset Management—An anatomy," ver. 2.0, Institute of Asset Management, 2014, https://www.theIAM.org

The Institute of Asset Management, "Work & Organization," https://theiam.org/about-us/work-organisation

Tracey, B., "Business Strategy (The Brian Tracey Success Library)," AMACOM, April 22, 2015.

Truck, M., Hao, J., & First Mark Capital, "Big Data Landscape," http://mattturck.com/wp-content/uploads/2016/03/Big-Data-Landscape-2016-v18-FINAL.png

U.S. Congress, "Digital Accountability and Transparency Act of 2014" or the "DATA Act," https://www.congress.gov/113/bills/s994/BILLS-113s994es.xml

U.S. Congress, Office of Technology Assessment, Federal Government Information Technology: Management, Security, and Congressional Oversight, OTA-CIT-297 (Washington, D.C.: U.S. Government Printing Office, February 1986).

U.S. Department of Homeland Security, Privacy Policy Guidance Memorandum, Memorandum 2008-01, 2008.

"U.S. Digital Service Playbook," https://playbook.cio.gov/

U.S. National Institute of Standards and Technology (NIST), Cybersecurity Framework, Ver. 1.0, 2014.

U.S. Office of the White House, "The White House Names Dr. DJ Patil as the First U.S. Chief Data Scientist," https://obamawhitehouse.archives.gov/blog/2015/02/18/white-house-names-dr-dj-patil-first-us-chief-data-scientist

U.S. Office of Management and Budget (OMB), Circular A-130, Managing Information as a Strategic Resource, 2016.

U.S. Office of Management and Budget (OMB), OMB Guidance for Implementing the Privacy Provisions of the E-Government Act of 2002, Memorandum M-03-22, 2003.

U.S. Office of Management and Budget (OMB), Role and Designation of Senior Agency Officials for Privacy, Memorandum M-16-24, 2016.

Upward, F., "Structuring the Records Continuum Part One: Post-Custodial Principles and Properties," *Archives and Manuscripts* 24, No. 3 (1996) 268–85, http://www.infotech.monash.edu.au/research/groups/rcrg/publications/recordscontinuum-fupp1.html;

Van der Muelen, R. "Managing the Data Chaos of Self-Service Analytics," Gartner Research, December 17, 2015, http://www.gartner.com/smarterwithgartner/managing-the-data-chaos-of-self-service-analytics/

W3C Web Ontology Language (OWL), https://www.w3.org/2001/sw/wiki/OWL

Wang, R. Y., and Strong, D. M., "Beyond Accuracy: What Data Quality Means to Data Consumers," M. E. Sharpe, Spring 1996, http://mitiq.mit.edu/Documents/Publications/TDQMpub/14_Beyond_Accuracy.pdf

"What HDFS Does," http://hortonworks.com/apache/hdfs/

"What Is Apache Hadoop," http://hadoop.apache.org/

"What Is EHR and Why Is It Important?" https://www.healthit.gov/providers-professionals/faqs/what-ehr-interoperability-and-why-it-important

Wikipedia, "Column-oriented DBMS," https://en.wikipedia.org/wiki/Column-oriented_DBMS